Praise for
CARDIAC ARREST

"The Howard Root story is a harbinger of a newly aggressive
government prosecution strategy – one that is troubling.
Simply an urge to have bodies swinging from lamp posts isn't
a very edifying way for the Justice Department to proceed."
– MICHAEL MUKASEY, former U.S. Attorney General

"A gripping case study in the perils of big government.
Read it before you're next."
– PETE HEGSETH, author of *In the Arena*
and *FOX News* contributor

"Howard Root's account of the government's ruthless
prosecution of him and his company reads like a nightmare tale.
It must be read by everyone in the med-tech industry as a
wake-up call about one of the biggest threats to growth and
innovation for one of America's most important industries."
– DAVID CASSAK, editor-in-chief, *The MedTech Strategist*

"A call to arms for business that shocks as it entertains."
– MARK DUVAL, president of DuVal & Associates
and former general counsel of 3M Pharmaceuticals

CARDIAC ARREST

Five Heart-Stopping Years as a CEO on the Feds' Hit-List

By Howard Root

with Stephen Saltarelli

AUTHOR's NOTE

This is a true story, subject to the limitations of my notes and memory. All quotes from court transcripts and written documents are verbatim, edited only for length. All dialog from conversations and phone calls are my best recollection of what was said or reported to me. I am sure I have misheard what others have said in at least some situations, and for that I apologize. I also freely admit that this book is written from my perspective, recording the events as I experienced them.

Cover design and photography by Thomas Ashby.

www.cardiacarrestbook.com

ISBN 978-1-48358-838-4

To Daphne, Valentin, Christine, Stephen, Rebecca,
Maria, Debra, Yvonne, Randall, Dan, Deeana,
Steven, Lisa, Edwin, Kimberly and Cheryl

The 12 jurors and 4 alternates – the only people standing
between the federal prosecutors, their desired destruction of
Vascular Solutions, and my imprisonment

CONTENTS

STEP 3 – TREATMENT

Step 1

SYMPTOMS

CHAPTER 1

ICE CREAM SUBPOENA

June 28, 2011

I t all began with ice cream.

Town car to fancy building; hour-long meeting with investors; back to town car. That's how the rest of my week was looking. When you run a public company that's mostly owned by mutual funds, you can see a big chunk of your shareholders in a couple days if you plan it right. Hence the trip to Boston to sleep-walk through the same presentation on my company – Vascular Solutions, Inc. ("VSI") – that I'd given hundreds of times. The trip promised to be busy, sure, but predictable.

That's fine. Because I, Howard Root, am a creature of routine. I would get on this flight, take the meetings, and be back for Fourth of July weekend on the lake, like always. If you miss the Fourth in Minnesota, they say, you've missed half the summer. Not me this year. And since I'd arrived at the Minneapolis airport a full two hours early, I wasn't missing my flight, either. I targeted an hour-and-a-half, but traffic from our office in the western suburbs was light. Great. That meant I had time for my favorite pre-flight ritual: a cone at

Ben & Jerry's, free from my wife Beth's reminders of my recent weight gain.

My phone buzzed midway through my triple caramel chunk. I used my free hand to wrestle it from my pocket and saw that the call was from our main office line. Probably my assistant, Molly. I've never been coordinated enough to eat and hold a business conversation at the same time, and I wasn't interested in trying now. Nor was I about to toss a perfectly good cone. I'd call her back after the last bite.

As I crunched away at the bottom of my pre-flight treat, I checked the voicemail. It wasn't Molly who called. No – it was our general counsel, Michael Blum, and he sounded nervous. "Howard, I need you to call me before you get on the flight." Blum wasn't one to fluster easily, and a mysterious voicemail from our in-house lawyer will earn a call back from me every time.

I called Blum, and he was indeed flustered. "I just took a call from a lawyer in Texas, Kimberly Johnson," he began. "She says we're going to be served a subpoena tomorrow."

That didn't sound like an emergency to me – I was glad I finished the cone. Over the 14 years since I started the company, we'd been party to an array of lawsuits – from patent claims to vendor disputes to trademark issues. I could count at least 10 of those suits, and a bunch more where someone in a medical malpractice case needed our manufacturing records. Each one of those matters began with a subpoena or complaint, and my lawyers were always the ones who broke the news to me. Nothing unusual.

"Did she say who she's representing?" I asked.

The tone of Blum's response was gloomy. "The U.S. Attorney's Office for the Western District of Texas."

Hmm. That *was* unusual. This definitely wasn't a patent infringement case. Still, I doubted the government was suing us. Maybe some hospital got caught up in something and the government needed our sales invoices for its case. But then I heard Blum say the word "whistleblower."

To me, "Western Texas" and "whistleblower" could only mean one man, Eddie Pedregon. A former pharma sales rep with no experience in medical devices, we hired Eddie to cover our El Paso territory in 2007. He had some conduct issues, but if we fired every sales rep who drank too much at a sales meeting and did something inappropriate, there wouldn't be many left. So when Eddie told me in 2009 that he was leaving to join a company that sold urology products, it was a loss, but not a major one. He gave his two weeks' notice and moved on, just as we did.

But a month after he left, it became clear that Eddie hadn't joined some small urology shop. Instead, he'd taken a job at Spectranetics, one of our competitors in our biggest business – coronary interventions (tools for treating heart disease). Armed with our confidential customer information and price sheets, Eddie could convert all our El Paso catheter business to his new employer. That was the reason we had a non-compete clause in every employee's contract, and after Eddie's flagrant violation of it, I'd considered naming the thing after him.

I say "flagrant" because Eddie started working for Spectranetics two weeks *before* he quit working for VSI. Nice work, if you can get it – two paychecks for the same trip to the same hospital. During his double-agent period, Eddie's new manager sent an email to the entire Spectranetics salesforce praising Eddie's visits to tell doctors about his new job. Eddie sold "over 5K today based on those calls," his manager said, on a day when VSI was still paying his salary.

To stop the bleeding, I went to court and got a restraining order against his Spectranetics employment, and later a check from the same company for the damage Eddie did to our El Paso business. Last I heard, Eddie was divorced, back to working as a high school softball coach, and hurting for cash. If there ever was a prototype for a West-Texas whistleblower, it was "Fast" Eddie Pedregon.

When I arrived at Boston's Logan airport, riled up after thinking about Eddie for three hours, the subpoena was waiting for me in my inbox. It came with a message from Blum:

> **I wanted to see if the prosecutor would tell me whether the target of the investigation is a Vascular Solutions' employee or a health care provider. She mentioned that Vascular Solutions is the direct target of the investigation, and that the investigation is criminal in nature.**

Whoa. My little Minnesota medical device company was the target of a federal criminal investigation in Texas? Seriously?

My throat tightened as I read the subpoena. It called for us to turn over 15 categories of documents, all related to our Vari-Lase line of products, which use laser energy to treat varicose veins. The breadth of the U.S. Attorney's requests made reading the tea leaves difficult, but they kept coming back to our Short Kit – one of the lowest-selling options in the Vari-Lase product line, and its use to treat perforator veins – one of the least-frequently treated varicose veins. This was a criminal investigation? It made no sense to me.

I emailed Blum: "Call Tom Vitt and schedule a meeting at Dorsey & Whitney for as soon as I get back. We need a litigator to look at this and tell us what's going on here."

CHAPTER 2

THE BRIEFING

JULY 5, 2011

We met in a well-windowed conference room at the Minneapolis office of Dorsey & Whitney – the law firm I'd worked at 20 years prior as a young lawyer. Back then, I gave legal advice. Now, I needed legal advice. Joining Blum and me were Tom Vitt, Dorsey's genial courtroom giant who handled all our litigation matters, and a colleague he said was "the guy" to manage a federal criminal investigation.

"The guy" was Bill Michael, the co-head of Dorsey's white-collar crime practice, who arrived at the meeting looking like a less-rugged Harrison Ford. His heavily-starched dress shirt and steely eyes hinted at his military past, and as Bill Michael spoke, it was hard not to be impressed by the Green Beret turned federal prosecutor. With 100 jury trials to his name, Bill Michael was just the guide I needed in this unfamiliar land.

But right now, he didn't know anything – about my company, about varicose veins, or about me. Luckily for him, I'd spent my Fourth of July weekend prepping a 90-slide briefing instead of floating on my boat around the lake. But before I fired up the PowerPoint, I gave a few opening remarks.

"I already know this is a serious matter, for both the company and me. We all know that last year another medical device company went through a criminal investigation and even had its CEO indicted. Nobody wants that here – especially me."

The joke landed flat. This Bill Michael guy was all business. Good – I liked that.

"But we can't kill the company trying to save it. If we over-react and panic our shareholders and employees, the company will be dead before we even begin." I looked around at the silver-plated water pitchers and bus-sized cherrywood conference table and felt the need to add one more thing. "Legal costs alone are a significant issue, so we need to manage and plan those, okay?"

Nods all around, including from my expensive new lawyer. *To the projector!*

After briefly explaining the causes of varicose veins, I corrected the most common misperception of the disease. "We all know varicose veins look ugly, but they aren't just a cosmetic problem. Left untreated, the crushing pressure of all that pooling blood in the vein can cause skin ulcers and, eventually, amputation of the leg." I scrolled through a few unpleasant photos to drive the point home, before moving to the treatments.

"Years ago, doctors treated varicose veins using a barbaric procedure called vein stripping. In it, the leg is fileted open and the entire vein is literally ripped out. Once the diseased vein is gone, the blood finds its way back to the heart through the remaining healthy veins.

"But around 10 years ago, two doctors developed a new way to permanently shut down varicose veins using laser energy to heat them from the inside. Through just a needle prick, a doctor inserts a thin glass rod called a laser fiber into the patient's vein, turns it on, and pulls it through the diseased portion of the vein. This procedure is called endovenous laser ablation, and unlike with vein stripping, the patient walks in and walks out an hour later with their varicose veins fixed and only a Band-Aid over the needle puncture.

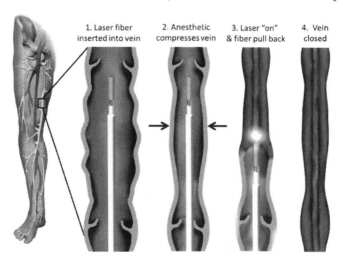

1. Laser fiber inserted into vein　2. Anesthetic compresses vein　3. Laser "on" & fiber pull back　4. Vein closed

"At least seven other companies make laser systems for the treatment of varicose veins. Ours is called Vari-Lase and has two parts: a console that generates the laser energy, and a disposable kit with everything else the doctor needs – the needle, the glass fiber, and a plastic tube called an introducer sheath that acts as a tunnel for the physician to push the fiber into the vein.

Vari-Lase laser console   Vari-Lase procedure kit

"Because there are so many different lengths of varicose veins, and because doctors love to buy customized products, we sell over 80 different versions of our procedure kit. This subpoena looks like it's all about one version we started selling in 2007, called the Short Kit. The only difference between the Short Kit and our other kits is the length of that introducer sheath – the tunnel. The Short Kit's sheath [circled below] is 10 centimeters long, which you can compare to the Flex, our longest, at 100 centimeters. We even sell a version that's shorter than the Short Kit, called the 5 centimeter kit. So that's like the 'Shorter Kit.'"

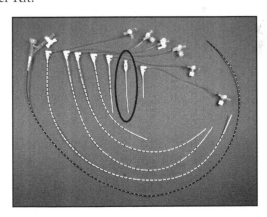

Next, I gave a brief anatomy lesson. "There are two parallel tracks of veins in the leg: deep veins, which are closer to the bones, and superficial veins, which are closer to the skin. The short veins that connect these two tracks are called perforator veins. Although perforator veins are only rarely treated, as far as I can tell, they're the entire focus of the subpoena."

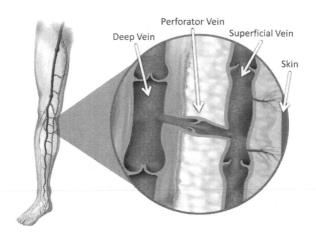

I knew everyone was familiar with the U.S. Food & Drug Administration ("FDA"), but its role here was a bit nuanced. "As I'm sure you know, we need FDA's permission to sell a medical device in the U.S. But the FDA doesn't approve the medical device itself. Instead, it approves the use of the medical device to treat a particular medical condition. It's like saying 'you can sell this hammer only if the label says it's to be used exclusively for hitting these nails.' That use, slapped on every device we sell, is called the device's *indications*. And Vari-Lase has a fairly long and technical indications, as you can see on this slide:

> Vari-Lase is indicated for the treatment of varicose veins and varicosities associated with superficial reflux of the great saphenous vein and for the treatment of incompetence and reflux of superficial veins in the lower extremity.

"Now here's the thing. In general, all types of varicose veins, including perforators, are part of a common condition. You see, when one vein fails, it puts extra pressure on the vein next to it, which often fails in turn. There's a domino effect. And because perforator veins are connected to the great saphenous vein, a diseased perforator is 'associated with' superficial reflux of the great saphenous. It's also important to know that a diseased perforator is usually treated above the muscle fascia, in the superficial portion of the vein. So even though the *word* 'perforator' isn't specifically listed in the indications, the *treatment* of perforators is still generally covered by these indications."

Forty slides in now, and I figured I was losing them … just when I needed to sprinkle some legal issues into the confusion.

"It seems from the subpoena that the government thinks Vari-Lase is being illegally promoted 'off-label' to treat perforator veins. That is, they believe our indications don't cover the treatment of perforator veins, but that we are selling the Short Kit for perforators anyway.

"And here's where the law is weird. It's 100% legal for doctors to use a medical device however they want to treat a patient, even if that treatment is off-label. FDA itself has recognized that off-label use is essential to the practice of medicine. Many cancer treatments, for example, are off-label, as is virtually every device used in children, like miniaturized guidewires for heart interventions.

"But there's a big catch: While the off-label *use* of the product is completely legal, the government takes the position that it's *criminal* for a company sales rep to talk with a doctor about that use."

Bill Michael got up from the table. I thought he'd heard enough of my lecture on law he already knew, but he assured me he had a bad back and just needed to stretch out for a bit. I continued as he paced.

"In May 2007, while we were developing a kit that would allow doctors to easily treat perforator and other short veins, which we'd later call the 'Short Kit,' we asked FDA for permission to add the word 'perforator' to our indications.

"Since we thought our indications already covered perforators generally, we simply asked FDA to 'clarify' that this was the case before we added the word 'perforator' to the label. We had added specific wording to our indications twice before – both cleared by the FDA – but this third time FDA wanted something they had never required before. They wanted to see a study, in either humans or sheep. We didn't understand why, but we had already started a study of perforator treatment in humans, so we said 'okay.' Unfortunately, we didn't complete that study in time, and six months later, our application to add the word 'perforator' was automatically withdrawn for inaction.

"So then we did exactly what FDA asked us to do; we told all our sales reps not to promote the newly-launched Short Kit for perforators, period. Until the word 'perforator' was specifically on the label, we said, our reps could only promote it for short veins, not for perforators. It was extra-cautious, but we've taken that approach with all our products, and it's why we have yet to have any issues with FDA in over 14 years of business."

> **2007 Instructions to U.S. Sales Reps**
>
> "Do not indicate that the Short Kit is approved to treat perforator veins until we have the cleared indication."
>
> "The Short Kit is not specifically approved for treating perforators, but VSI does have a study on this indication which is nearing completion."

At this point, I sensed Bill Michael thought I was sugarcoating it. As a former Army JAG and federal prosecutor, he'd surely seen plenty of defendants contrive stories of their own innocence. He didn't call me out, but I could tell he wouldn't believe me until he'd talked to the witnesses himself and seen the documents. Fine – that's what he was here for. Who needs a gullible lawyer, anyway?

"The sales numbers show that our reps aren't out there promoting perforators. The Short Kit makes up just 0.1% of our total sales, and over two-thirds of our sales reps have never sold a single one. Trust me, if I told our sales reps to go out and promote the Short Kit for perforators, those numbers would be a lot higher."

I had saved the most important fact for the final slide. "I had my people scour our records, and I did my own search, too. There hasn't been a single report of a patient suffering a serious complication with the Short Kit, ever."

While that was technically irrelevant to the legal analysis, I knew it was critical to how the investigation would be perceived. It was the first thing I looked at, and I figured the prosecutors would do the same.

Given how insignificant the Short Kit was, I figured this should go away quickly if we played it right. As I powered down the projector, I realized 90 slides was probably overkill, but it set the tone. I was ready to get Bill Michael up and running on this, and he didn't need to spin his wheels at $650 an hour piecing together the background I already knew.

Before leaving, I told the team our timing was good. The government's subpoena asked for us to turn over a PowerPoint presentation called "TREAT-ING PERFORATOR VEINS!!!" We didn't know what it was or who created it. But luckily, our annual summer sales meeting in Minneapolis was coming up the next week. We could collect a few sales reps' laptops, do some sniffing, and hopefully find it. I'd let Bill Michael – the top white-collar lawyer in the best law firm in the Twin Cities – handle that. I walked out of the meeting with a cautious smile, confident I was in good hands.

CHAPTER 3

THE 20 MILLION DOLLAR LIE

JULY 2011

It turned out Danny McIff had the PowerPoint. That was the report from our forensics firm the morning after examining the laptop of our buzz-cut Utah sales rep. Unfortunately, it was in his trash folder. Actually, the hidden backup to his trash folder. Digital fingerprints showed that McIff had created the PowerPoint years ago and deleted it just days after he received the company-wide order not to delete any documents related to Vari-Lase or perforators.

"TREATING PERFORATOR VEINS!!!" was 18 slides, poorly written, horribly formatted, and painfully off-message. It was mostly filled with anatomy lessons, tips on doing the procedure, and a hodge-podge of other clinical information. There was only one reference to Vascular Solutions, a boast that "we have the best perf tech." Not the sort of thing you would hand out to a doctor, and certainly not something that went through the legal and compliance review we require for marketing literature. What was this thing? And why did he delete it?

I pulled McIff out of a training session the next day to meet Bill Michael and find out. Whether Danny knew it or not, deleting documents in a legal investigation is a big deal. The "don't delete" email we sent to everyone hadn't disclosed that this was a *federal criminal* legal investigation, so it wasn't criminal obstruction of justice, but it still was insubordinate and dishonest.

At first, Danny lied about it. He told Bill Michael he hadn't deleted anything. Later, that became, "If I *accidentally* deleted them, what would my exposure be?" Then Danny continued denying it, saying, "I don't know anything about that" when confronted with the forensic deletion report during a follow-up phone call with Bill Michael. Less than an hour after that call ended, though, Danny called back and said he had accidentally deleted a few documents while trying to load some vacation photos onto his laptop. When Bill Michael called B.S. on Danny's vacation-photo-*oopsie* story, the charade ended. McIff admitted, finally, that he'd created the PowerPoint and then intentionally deleted it.

But why? I knew that Danny had worked at his doctor father's vein clinic in Salt Lake City before he came to Vascular Solutions. That clinic, it just so happened, was the national expert in laser perforator vein treatment. During his time there as a medical assistant, Danny saw hundreds of perforators treated using other companies' laser products and had seen nothing but good results.

So, in early 2008, when we were still working with the FDA to add the word "perforator" to our indications, Danny got a request from his ultra-confident and rule-bending boss, Kip Theno, our Western regional manager. "Give a 'best practices' training at our upcoming regional meeting," he instructed Danny. "People are covering all sorts of topics, and I'd like you to talk about perforators."

Theno ignored my rule against sales reps creating "rogue" marketing materials, and Danny did as he was asked. He delivered the presentation to 12 VSI salespeople at a Holiday Inn in Burbank. And now, three years later, he was going to be fired for deleting it. I had no choice. He'd put the company at risk by disobeying a clear and simple order to retain his documents, and then he lied about it … a lot. On August 6, 2011, he handed in his sales bag and left the company. But that wouldn't be the last I'd see of Danny McIff.

We turned everything that we recovered from Danny over to the government, along with the million-plus pages of other documents they requested. Six years of sales meetings, tens of thousands of sales rep weekly reports, design specifications, meeting minutes, and every email that mentioned the word "Vari-Lase" – a lot of paper.

I know, because I spent more than one Sunday in the office that summer copying and organizing documents myself. As a former lawyer, I wanted it done right, so it'd only have to be done once. By giving the government everything they'd asked for, we would demonstrate cooperation. More important, I thought, the documents themselves would clear us. Once the prosecutors in San Antonio saw what this was all about – how we were extra-cautious in instructing our sales reps not to promote for perforators, how we barely sold any Short Kits, and how the device didn't harm a single patient – this whole thing would go away. About this, I was severely wrong.

After we turned over our million-plus pages of documents, the government went radio silent. The type of long, uneasy silence you can't help but hear.

The optimistic side of me thought the prosecutors looked at the documents, saw we'd done nothing wrong, and forgot about us. But months passed without the arrival of an official declination letter confirming as much. Then, in July 2012, a full year after we'd received the subpoena, a phone call from Bill Michael. "They want to interview Shane Carlson in Minneapolis next month."

They hadn't gone away. Worse yet, their investigation was expanding.

But why would the government kick off their interviews with Shane, a regional manager for a small region that hardly sold any Short Kits? There's no way he knew much about this, so I was sure he wouldn't have anything bad to say. But my real worry was that the government would go too far down a road with a dead end. Just as I wanted them to get the right documents in response to their subpoena, I wanted them to talk to the right people. We had nothing to hide, but that didn't mean we had nothing to show.

I told Bill Michael to get me a sit-down meeting with the government attorneys. It probably isn't every day that prosecutors get asked by the CEO of their corporate target for an interview, but it's not every day I get investigated by the Feds, either. They accepted my offer, and we scheduled a two-day interview for August 6 and 8, 2012. And then, on August 2, they canceled it and wouldn't reschedule.

I never got an explanation why they canceled, but the events of August 1 were probably as good an indicator as any. That day, Shane was interviewed by four prosecutors, led by the Civil Frauds Section of the U.S. Department of Justice ("DOJ"). Shane's role, like that of all regional managers, was to supervise about 10 sales reps. At the time, we had 70 sales reps spread across the country, and I obviously couldn't be watching each one at all times. Managers like Shane handled the day-to-day stuff, checking in with our reps about their visits to doctors and reporting back on any problems.

During the interview, Shane told the prosecutors that he didn't think there was some plot to market the Short Kit for perforators and that the device was mostly used to treat short vein segments. Shane also said he never had any conversations with Danny McIff about marketing for perforators. It was only the first employee interview, but Lauren Hash Bell, a criminal prosecutor from the DOJ headquarters in D.C., had apparently heard enough. She wasn't even the one leading the questioning, but she reportedly rose from her seat, stood over Carlson, and exclaimed, "If you don't start telling the truth, I'm going to bring you in front of the grand jury and then you'll tell the truth." Bill Michael, at the interview on behalf of the company, stepped in and asked Hash Bell why she was threatening Carlson. She reportedly answered, coldly, "Why do you think I'm threatening him?"

The interview ended shortly after that, and with it, the prosecutors' trip to Minneapolis. Suddenly, this seemed less like an investigation and more like an inquisition. Were they really threatening to convene a grand jury? Over this? The only reason you need a grand jury, Bill Michael told me, is to bring a felony charge. A felony? Was that even possible?

I was getting ahead of myself, Bill Michael told me. He assured me that Hash Bell was all bark, and that this had all the hallmarks of a prosecution team deciding whether to "intervene" in (read: take over) a whistleblower civil lawsuit from a disgruntled former employee.[1] A DOJ civil attorney was leading the interviews, after all.

Four months later, in December 2012, Bill Michael's assessment was confirmed when the government delivered the worst Christmas present I've ever gotten – the "United States Complaint In Intervention."

They were in it now. The Complaint In Intervention made the govern-

---

[1] Under the Federal False Claims Act, a whistleblower may bring a suit in the government's shoes and receive up to 20% of its recovery. Passed in 1863, "Lincoln's Law" was designed to crack down on shady contractors who sold the Union Army sick mules, lame horses, and fetid rations. In a time when federal resources were paper-thin, the enforcement mechanism (described on the Senate floor as "setting a rogue to catch a rogue") was clever. Today, the False Claims Act is big business, routinely netting the government billion-dollar settlements and returning $6.10 for every dollar spent on its enforcement. In 2009, for instance, six whistleblowers who filed suit against Pfizer divvied up $102 million of a $2.3 billion settlement.

ment's intentions, along with the identity of their whistleblowers, clear. After a background section that claimed "VSI's devices are not now, and have never been, cleared or approved for treating perforator veins" came the big reveal.

> **DeSalle Bui formerly worked for Vascular Solutions as a sales representative, selling the "Short Kit." [He] commenced an action on November 19, 2010, under the *qui tam* provisions of the False Claims Act, which enable a private person to bring an action in the name of the government.**

DeSalle Bui. *Of course.* The memory rushed back to me, and I raced to check my files. Since DeSalle covered the Phoenix territory, and the complaint was out of Texas, I had completely forgotten about him. *Oh god.*

Way back in 2009, amateur bodybuilder DeSalle Bui left VSI after Shane Carlson beat him out for a promotion to regional manager. Just like with Eddie Pedregon, I received reports that DeSalle immediately began working for a competitor in violation of his non-compete agreement. DeSalle's case played out a little differently, though. When I sent a letter reminding him of his non-compete and asking for an explanation, DeSalle lashed out.

DeSalle sent a letter back to me alleging that he was racially discriminated against by not receiving the promotion, coerced into signing his non-compete agreement, and had been witness to a grab bag of legal violations – from kickbacks, to Medicare fraud, to off-label promotion.

I went back to his letter. There it was – the Short Kit allegation – a single paragraph toward the end of a lengthy, emotional missive. Attached to the letter had been that PowerPoint, "TREATING PERFORATOR VEINS!!!," which he said was presented at a sales meeting. When we investigated that claim, we found that it hadn't been presented at any of our national sales meetings or created by anyone in marketing. We looked into DeSalle's other wild allegations, too, but found no basis for those either. So I wrote back to DeSalle and asked him for any additional information he had to substantiate his allegations. He didn't write back, but he did sue.

DeSalle's original lawsuit, filed in secret in 2010, was now public. Reading it was like unlocking a Rosetta Stone as to what had happened over the last 18 months of this investigation. At its heart, a whistleblower complaint is a sales document. Whistleblower attorneys know that each suit they file automatically gets reviewed by government attorneys, and if the government chooses to intervene, that means a lot less work for them and a much better chance of recovering money.

So DeSalle's complaint, which alleged violations of federal laws and the laws of 23 states, lead with the sexy. In the first paragraph, he said that not only had we marketed off-label, but that we had done so by paying kickbacks and teaching doctors how to scam Medicare. In the second paragraph, he noted that VSI was a public company with 2009 sales of $66 million. Pervasive wrongdoing, deep pockets … that was his message.

DeSalle continued by talking up his own credibility and exaggerating the scope of the alleged scheme. As the complaint stated in grammatical and factual error, "Mr. Bui was a top ranking sales representatives [sic] for Vascular Solutions." In reality, he was never ranked in the top half of our sales force during his brief two years at the company.

DeSalle, and more likely his attorneys, estimated "upon information and belief" that 60% of Vari-Lase patients were beneficiaries of Medicare, while another 20% were on Medicaid. If true, that would make the case more attractive to prosecutors, because there'd be more "false claims" that the government could recover – in triplicate – under the False Claims Act. DeSalle's estimate was, however, grossly inaccurate. The vast majority of patients who have varicose vein treatments are women in their late thirties to fifties, in part due to the high correlation of the disease to pregnancy. Upon my own "information and belief," I'd estimate that the Medicare/Medicaid numbers are closer to 25% and 5%, respectively.

And although DeSalle claimed that "at least 25% of Vari-Lase laser ablation procedures involve off-label use for the treatment of perforator veins," I would later learn that he'd never once seen a doctor treat a perforator with Vari-Lase. Not once. That lack of personal knowledge was a problem, because under the False Claims Act, a whistleblower needs to have some sort of inside or non-public information. But DeSalle had a solution. This, from his whistleblower complaint:

"[Bui's] allegations … are corroborated by a former Vascular Solutions representative for parts of Texas and New Mexico with the initials E.P."

There he was – "Fast" Eddie Pedregon. The man I initially suspected … and still knew had to be involved somehow. "E.P." alleged that a doctor in Amarillo, Texas, was illegally pitched on perforators, the jurisdictional hook that allowed DeSalle to bring his case in Western Texas. DeSalle couldn't have known it at the time, but the doors his claim opened at the U.S. Attorney's Office for the Western District of Texas turned out to be the perfect ones. For him, at least …

I squinted at the whistleblower lawsuit. Then back at the government's intervention suit. It was incredible how much DeSalle the government had adopted. The legalese had been rewritten, sure, but the sloppy foundation was singularly DeSalle Bui's. The idea that VSI wasn't approved for perforators. The claim that Medicare didn't pay for perforator treatment. The notion that Danny McIff's PowerPoint was some case-making, smoking-gun bombshell. It was all in there, lifted wholesale. The middling sales rep had sold the government prosecutors a fable – hook, line, and sinker.

DeSalle's story also explained why Lauren Hash Bell had gotten so mad at Shane Carlson. The prosecutor was trying to make the case she'd been handed. DeSalle was saying he'd promoted the Short Kit for perforators (apparently unsuccessfully, as he never sold any or even saw one used) because his manager Shane told him to. But Shane, the first VSI employee the government talked to, flatly denied it. He was stonewalling them, Hash Bell must have thought.

DeSalle's bill of goods probably also explained why this whole thing hadn't gone away quietly. Before the government read those million pages of documents I organized for them, before they ever saw that we told our reps *not* to promote for perforators, or that there was no patient harm and almost no sales, they'd heard Bui's loudest allegation, Paragraph #118.

"Upon information and belief, Vascular Solution's [sic] off-label and otherwise deceptive marketing of its [Vari-Lase] products has resulted in damages to the government of approximately 20 million dollars."

Incredible. Here's what the government was chasing – the desperate machinations of an ex-employee out for money. DeSalle's share of the hypothetical $20 million would be $4 million, a life-changing payday. But to have any chance at shaking millions from our pockets, he'd need to tell a story big enough to entice the federal government into intervening. If he could just lure them in, he'd suddenly have the credibility and resources of the Department of Justice behind his vengeful grift.

It wasn't until much later, when I read DeSalle's public divorce file, that I understood just how wrong things were in DeSalle Bui's world and how badly he needed that payday. In her divorce petition citing irreconcilable differences, DeSalle's estranged wife wrote that he had a hairpin temper, a penchant for driving 100 mph in his Porsche with the kids in the car, and a nasty habit of "paddling" his teenage son to tears. The Bui family had five vehicles – two Lexuses, a Porsche, a Mercedes, and DeSalle's beloved Harley, but the divorce ordered the sale of most and stuck DeSalle with almost $80,000 in yearly alimony and child support obligations. According to his ex-wife, DeSalle went derelict in his payments, was having an affair with a married woman, and had a dark history of self-harm. In one incident she recounted, DeSalle took some pills and sent her a single text: "Have my body cremated." She rushed over in time to get DeSalle to the hospital and saved his life.

I felt bad for the guy's family, and even him to some degree. But with that came a sense of disbelieving awe at the system. We've deputized the personally desperate, the professionally disgruntled, the financially destitute, and made their enterprising lawyers line cooks for the Department of Justice's next meal of lucrative fast-food "justice."

I'd been served up.

CHAPTER 4

DOJ BLIND DATE

FEBRUARY 5, 2013

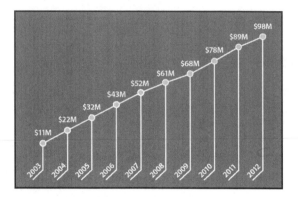

While I was being served up by DeSalle and Eddie, Vascular Solutions was serving up another banner year. That was the conclusion of our glossy 2012 annual report, which showed double-digit sales growth for the ninth straight year, a feat none of our competitors could match. This year's success owed largely to a breakout year for what was becoming our first true blockbuster product – the GuideLiner catheter.

Three years since its launch, the GuideLiner had become the premier tool for interventional cardiologists working in hard-to-reach areas in the heart. It rose to prominence in September 2010, when a top cardiologist went before a packed crowd at the world's biggest cardiology conference and gushed, unprompted, that "the GuideLiner makes impossible cases possible and difficult cases easier."

He was right; the GuideLiner was revolutionary. Where the strategy before was "push as hard as you can and see if you can force the stent into the artery," GuideLiner now allowed doctors to easily deploy stents like a Push Pop into areas they couldn't before access. Today, I'd say that 99% of interventional cardiologists know how to use GuideLiner to deliver a stent, and you wouldn't want to be treated by the other 1%.

But when I invented the GuideLiner in 2006, doodling in the audience of a boring medical meeting, I never imagined it would be used how it is today. I thought I had a $10 million product that would help doctors position their guide catheter into the opening of the coronary artery. But shortly after we released the product in 2009, I watched it go viral. One doctor used it to place a stent, then told another, who told his colleagues, then the big conference speech, and all of a sudden it was 2012 and I had a $20 million monster, well on its way to $50 million a year.

As I drove downtown on February 5, 2013, I was thinking about that annual report. But not about the GuideLiner or our sales growth. No, I was thinking about a single paragraph in the "Legal Proceedings" section.

On June 28, 2011, we received a subpoena from the U.S. Attorney's Office for the Western District of Texas requesting documents related to the use of the Vari-Lase® Short Kit for the treatment of perforator veins. The Short Kit has been sold under [FDA] clearance since 2007 with total U.S. sales through December 31, 2011 of approximately $410,000 (0.1% of the Company's total U.S. sales) and has not been the subject of any reported serious adverse clinical event. We are fully complying with this inquiry.

I wanted that paragraph gone. And I was headed to the Minneapolis U.S. Attorney's Office to see what it would take to make that happen.

Although no federal prosecutors from Minnesota would be attending, the Minneapolis federal courthouse was chosen for our convenience. An early sign of good will and cooperation, perhaps. With my Dorsey legal team of Bill Michael and Tom Vitt at my side, we arrived at the obsidian courthouse and made our way up to the U.S. Attorney's Office, whose quarters were even nicer than Dorsey's. After waiting 18 months and getting stood up on my offer to meet to explain this matter, I was finally getting my first date with the suits behind the government's investigation, even if it was only to hear what they wanted from us.

Waiting for us in the conference room was Charles Biro, a dour-faced junior lawyer with DOJ's Civil Frauds Section. Kimberly Johnson, his Texas partner who'd sent us the subpoena, joined in by videoconference.

Biro led things off with his theory of what happened. VSI's indications didn't cover perforators, he said, but our competitor – VNUS Medical – had the word "perforator" right there in their indications. Because VNUS had it, Biro nervously argued, we needed it. We asked FDA to add the word, but when FDA said we needed a study before putting "perforator" on our label, and we didn't have one with good enough data, he claimed that high-ranking executives (read: me) hatched this secret plot: keep the label the same, but tell the sales force, through coded instructions, to illegally market the new Short Kit for perforators anyway.

Biro proudly announced that he'd personally combed through the sales records and sales reps' weekly activity reports and determined that there were hundreds of potentially fraudulent Medicare claims. Biro had a habit of pausing when he got to a number, seemingly impressed with himself for wielding power over a case in which literally *hundreds of thousands of dollars* were at stake. And then he got to his final number – the one he said represented Vascular Solutions' total civil liability in this case ...

Twenty million dollars.

There it was again. *The number.* I looked over at Bill Michael, whose face wrinkled in disbelief. "How'd you get that?" he asked, knowing the answer was that they'd ripped it from DeSalle's "information and belief." Biro fumbled through his spreadsheets, before Kimberly Johnson piped up to assist him. In contrast to Biro, Johnson seemed confident in her grip on both the process and the facts. "That's not our resolution offer," she clarified. "That's what we believe a verdict could bring at trial, worst-case scenario." Bill Michael's brow remained furrowed.

Next up was a 30-something government attorney with a prematurely receding hairline, seated at the end of the table. He'd introduced himself when we walked in but hadn't said a word since then. Frankly, I'd forgotten he was there. "I'm Tim Finley," he said, re-introducing himself as a trial attorney from DOJ's Consumer Protection Branch. Bill Michael had explained to me that these guys usually handle things like fireworks safety and lottery fraud, but a jurisdictional quirk also gives them power over criminal violations of FDA laws.

Finley didn't have much to say, admitting he'd just been assigned to the case because the hot-tempered Lauren Hash Bell was on maternity leave. He nevertheless agreed with Biro's analysis. After that borrowed conclusion, Finley speculated as to what it would take to resolve the criminal case. With a $2.3 million fine and a criminal misdemeanor plea, he said, the case *might* go away. But he was at pains to say he was waiting for Hash Bell to return before making any real offer – those figures were just his personal impression.

I had the numbers written down on a pad in front of me. Twenty for the civil lawsuit, two-and-change for the criminal penalty, plus a federal criminal guilty plea. They added up to a shakedown.

It was our turn now to talk, and the plan was for Bill Michael to lead a charge of reason that would convince the government to back off. He began by saying that in his many years as a prosecutor and private attorney, he'd never seen a prosecution – civil or criminal – reach the terms described over half a million in sales and no patient harm. "As you'll see from the documents," he told them, "this is an insignificant product in every sense of the word."

But as I measured the faces across the table, they had the look of poker players who didn't care what their opponent's hand was, because they were holding aces. *What's going on here?* Sensing Bill Michael's failure to get traction, Tom Vitt chimed in to remind the prosecutors that they were meeting with a company that, in over 15 years, had no criminal history and never so much as received a warning letter from FDA, usually the first step in this sort of case. Again, they didn't care. Johnson checked her watch and announced through the slight lag of the videoconference that our time was up. We concluded the meeting with tepid handshakes, unmoved prosecutors, and no real settlement offers. Not good.

This was getting hairy. We'd given them the documents, plead our case in person, and we were still no closer to reaching a resolution or even building up good will with the other side.

On paper, Bill Michael was the perfect defense lawyer. He knew the process, knew the law, and commanded credibility. But he wasn't a charmer. In fact, in our meeting with the government, he was kind of a jerk. I was beginning to worry that a career calling shots in a prosecutor's uniform meant he'd never developed the soft negotiating (read: ego-stroking) skills that even a small-time criminal defense attorney needs.

But I still needed him, somehow, to get these government attorneys to come to their senses before it was too late.

CHAPTER 5

GLOBAL CRISIS

Late 2013

Aer the fruitless meeting in downtown Minneapolis, we finally caught a break when a new government attorney took over the civil lawsuit. John LoCurto informed us that he would be replacing Kimberly Johnson and overseeing the lawsuit started by DeSalle, and along with his entrance came a welcome message.

In one of his first conversations with our lawyers, LoCurto said that "if [he] had been handling this case from the beginning, it would have been settled by now." Clearly, it seemed, LoCurto didn't have the same zeal for dogging companies over small-dollar controversies as did his less-experienced colleagues. "I'm going to come back with a settlement number with fewer zeros in it," LoCurto told us, indicating that it was now him in San Antonio – not Charles Biro in D.C. – calling the shots on the civil side.

As promised, LoCurto returned in September 2013 with an offer that moved the decimal place to the left … and then some. Far from Biro's $20 million delusion, LoCorto's opening offer came in at $975,000, the largest price drop I'd ever seen in a negotiation, ever. Fighting this thing through trial would cost VSI way more than a million, so as long as we didn't have to admit that we'd done anything wrong, I would've signed on the dotted line right then and there.

But Tom Vitt, who was leading our civil lawsuit defense, thought we could do better. On Tom's post-offer call with his new counterpart, LoCurto signaled that the offer was just an "opening salvo." Translation: they'd accept less, and probably a lot less.

So on Tom went, always blocking out half-hour teleconferences to give the always-talkative LoCurto enough time to babble on. And after each call, the number went down. Our initial counteroffer of $210,000 (a mostly-random but intriguingly-precise figure) knocked the government's counter down to $775,000. Next, Tom got LoCurto to $725,000, then $650,000, then $535,000. Once we got to $520,000 (still without any admission of misconduct), I told Tom to cut the nickel-and-diming and take the offer. We had our "cost of business" deal.

LoCurto's folding was an acknowledgement that the government's case was weak, which it was. And if the civil case was weak, surely his counterpart Tim Finley's fermenting criminal case, with its higher, "beyond a reasonable doubt" burden, was even weaker. Maybe the criminal guys would just go away, or perhaps they'd cut their lines and settle for one of those "Deferred Prosecution Agreements" or "Non-Prosecution Agreements" that I kept seeing the big banks getting in the news. "Non-Prosecution" sounded pretty good to me.

But hope is not a plan, and wishing on the criminal case to go away was a big risk. The safer play, Bill Michael told me, was to fold a resolution of the criminal case into the civil settlement we'd already negotiated, a so-called global settlement. That's how all the big pharma companies coffined their investigations when the Feds came knocking. In the end, these global settlements result in global happiness: DOJ gets a press release bragging about all the money it recovered, and the company gets to stop paying its lawyers. I could have used a break from the six-figure monthly legal bills about now, so I asked Tom Vitt to work with Bill Michael to see if they could make it happen.

But the winds were changing in Main Justice – the nickname of DOJ's massive limestone headquarters on Pennsylvania Avenue. The political left was furious that Wall Street escaped the financial collapse of 2008 scot-free. Sure, banks paid billion-dollar fines to resolve their corporate liability, but no one had gone to jail. Occupy Wall Street squatted on the nightly news, putting pressure on Obama-appointed Attorney General Eric Holder to "hold individuals accountable," as the often-repeated phrase goes.

And for the first time in a decade, the winds also were changing in the Western District of Texas criminal division. Walter Paulissen Jr., a 50-year-old man who asks to be called "Bud," was relieved of his post as head of major crimes (think murder) and white-collar crimes (think Ponzi schemes) and sent back to "the line." According to a source familiar with the demotion, "It wasn't that Bud did anything wrong, it's that he didn't do anything at all. Cases would go to him and die – he became known as kind of this departmental black hole."

But now back as a line prosecutor, Bud didn't have the luxury of simply letting cases die, because now he had a boss and a caseload of his own. One of the first investigations he got was an orphan – left behind by one Kimberly Johnson, who had since left the office. It was the criminal side of a small civil case that no one else in the office wanted … the perfect first case for Bud's return to action. The target was a little Minnesota company called Vascular Solutions.

The scouting report we had on Bud was that he would open with folksy small-talk, then quickly pivot to aggressive hard-talk. A two-faced Texan, you might say. I feared how that was going to mix with Bill Michael, who lacked the folksy face but was similarly bull-headed.

Bud lived up to his billing. After some jolly commentary on the weather, Bud told Bill Michael in their initial meeting that if the company wanted to get off with "just" a corporate misdemeanor plea, it needed to start cooperating against individuals. If the company didn't "accept responsibility" soon, Bud threatened, he'd "drag the investigation out for years and bring all [its] sales reps before a grand jury."

Another grand jury threat. Evidently Bud had yet to realize that at best he was chasing a regulatory ambiguity involving a miniscule product sold by a company with a spotless compliance record. But maybe this was just another empty boast, so we decided to give Bud a little time to cool down and maybe even learn something about the case.

In October 2013, now with the civil settlement committed to writing, Bill Michael returned to San Antonio to see if he could turn our deal into a global settlement. At least, that's what I thought he was going there to do. But according to an email Bill Michael sent me recapping the meeting, he told Bud "that the civil side would be discussing a resolution without the company seeking a global resolution based upon the government's stated requirements for the criminal resolution." In other words, "Pound sand." Which is a lot less tactful than what I was expecting, something along the lines of "We have a settlement on the civil side, should we talk again?"

Bud would later claim that during this October 2013 meeting, he offered to personally negotiate a cease-fire. In a story he told defense lawyers almost a year later, Bud said he told Bill Michael that although he didn't have authority to offer a settlement anchored around a corporate misdemeanor and no individual charges, he would be willing to take the proposition to his superiors. A day later, Bill Michael reportedly called back and said, "Don't bother." Irked, Bud crossed the Rubicon, saying that he would now investigate the case "in the traditional 'white-collar' fashion." Bill Michael allegedly responded: "You do what you have to do."[2]

And that's exactly what Bud did.

This wasn't the first time Vascular Solutions had been thrown into crisis mode.

In 2002, less than two years after we completed our IPO at $12 a share, VSI's stock had cratered to just 67 cents. Our only product at the time was a two-component medical device named Duett that was used to seal the entry puncture doctors made in the femoral artery to implant coronary stents. The Duett was getting crushed in the market by our much-larger neighbor St. Jude Medical's rival product. I had projected that my co-founder Dr. Gary Gershony's invention would capture 20% of the market, but in reality we only got to 4%. As a result, we lost $15 million in 2001 alone. And I wish that were the worst part.

The few sales we did have were exposing the Achilles' heel of our product. The Duett used an inflatable balloon inside the artery to temporarily seal the puncture, while a blood-clotting glue went over the top of the artery to create a permanent fix. But if the doctor failed to keep the balloon pulled taut against the artery wall, the glue could seep in. That was bad news – possibly

---

[2] I don't know how much of Bud's version to believe, because as you will come to see, Bud Paulissen is not to be trusted. I don't know if Bud really made an offer-to-offer-to-discuss-with-his-superiors a "misdemeanor and no individuals" resolution, but I never heard about it. I doubt we would have accepted an offer like that, but it would've been nice to know about (if it were actually made).

causing a nasty blockage that would require an extensive surgery to fix.

Or worse, I discovered. Our long-time regulatory V.P., Charmaine Sutton, walked into my office one morning with a spooked look and shut the door. "Did you hear about the complication Gary had yesterday in Atlanta?" I told her I'd already heard he had an arterial blockage during his last training case, right before he flew home. "Yes," Charmaine continued, "and the patient died last night."

The news rocked me. I closed my eyes, hoping it would just go away.[3] If the inventor could have a complication with his device that killed a patient, what were we doing selling this thing? I immediately called Dr. Gershony, who also seemed shaken, but defiant. "I'm going to personally stamp out arterial occlusions," Gary exclaimed, struggling to come to grips with his own role in the tragic complication. "We need to have a meeting with all of the sales reps out here in the Bay Area this Saturday."

He wanted to train his way out of the risk, but his device, even with *his* training, was the risk.

We'd reached a fork in a muddy, potholed road, leaving us two obvious choices. Continue selling the device on a limited basis with a big warning, or shut down the company and leave our 100 employees jobless. The latter would surely mean shareholder lawsuits and the end of my short career as a CEO, but I wasn't going to push a medical device that killed people. I tossed and turned that night, trying to envision a future I could stomach. I have only spent two sleepless nights at Vascular Solutions, and that was the second one.

Over the next week I called each of my bosses on our board of directors. I told them about the patient death and our two choices, calling the first one "harvest mode" Duett – only supplying it to experienced doctors who were already using it with success. And while harvesting Duett, I proposed planting other crops. We had built a clinically-focused sales force, and our development folks had shown we could nimbly bring a product to the market. Most important, we had $40 million in cash reserves from our IPO that would cover payroll for two-plus years. In short, we had all the trappings of

---

[3] It turned out the patient had other substantial factors that contributed to the death. So although the Duett wasn't the cause, it was a precipitating factor. And that was more than enough, in my mind, to do what I was about to do.

a successful device company; we just didn't have a successful device. So why not develop one? After all, we were Vascular Solutions – let's solve something.

I'll admit to having no idea that day about what new medical device we'd develop – but I had 100 co-workers to help me figure it out. To have a chance, though, I needed the board's approval to move forward and not fire me – at the time probably the worst-performing CEO in America based on our stock price. Having faith that exceeded our results, they backed me and my Hail Mary plan by a vote of 6 to 1.

The "1" was Dr. Gary Gershony, of course. He thought his expanded training would solve our problem in the short term, and that we should continue actively promoting his device until a big medical device company bought us. After voting "no" to my plan at the board meeting, Dr. Gary voted "no" with his feet. He left VSI and sold all of his stock.

My board victory was temporary ... about as long as it took me to re-member I was the CEO of a company with (effectively) zero products. We needed new solutions, I didn't have any, and my physician co-founder just left. I put out an APB within the company – "Calling all ideas ..."

Our Italian distributor knew a doctor in Milan who had one. And Dr. Pedro Silva just so happened to be coming to Chicago for an international medical meeting. I drove seven hours there, met Dr. Silva in a bar, and he used a napkin to sketch his idea for a catheter that suctioned out blood clots from heart attack patients. We negotiated a royalty, I took the napkin back to Minneapolis, and I worked with our design people to bring it to life. The Pronto, as our Italian-designed device became known, was launched in late 2003 to rave reviews and financial success. And Dr. Silva? He ultimately made over $5 million off that napkin.

Back in our lab, two of VSI's scientists, Steve Penegor and Jim Murto, cooked up another idea. Use thrombin – the blood-clotting agent we were already using for Duett – to create a turbocharged bandage we could sell for $50 a pop. Twice I found reasons to shoot the idea down, but on the third pitch I relented. "Okay. Go for it." They made it work, and in July 2003 we launched our super-Band-Aid under the name D-Stat Dry. It did $1 million in sales the first quarter it was on the market.

Our third new product concept came from an employee whose job it actually was to spot new business opportunities, Nancy Arnold. She'd previously worked for a laser company and encouraged me to look into a new technology using laser energy to seal varicose veins. A few small companies were already (struggling) in the market, but Nancy thought we could quickly leapfrog them with our clinically-trained sales force and a few improvements in the components. I said "yes" to this one, too. We picked the name Vari-Lase, completed development, and got FDA clearance – all in 2003.

By 2004, with Pronto, D-Stat Dry, and Vari-Lase all launched, we finally had the promising products our sales reps were itching for. Sales almost doubled that year to $22 million. And in 2005, sales jumped again to $34 million. With the success of these three new products – especially the Pronto, which saved the lives of patients who were dying from heart attacks – we'd survived our crisis, and I was the CEO of a company I could truly be proud of.

But now, in 2013, we had another type of crisis to survive.

CHAPTER 6

MY LAWYER BILL

Early 2014

As I worried that it had now been over two years since we received the subpoena and the criminal investigation wasn't even close to going away? Of course. But we had the facts on our side, and Bill Michael had advised me that "with prosecutors like these, deals get better closer to trial." With that in mind, I instructed him to continue kicking the investigation down the road to minimize our legal expenses. Under the federal Speedy Trial Act, the government has to be ready to start the trial 70 days from the date an indictment is handed down. If we got that far, Bill assured me, we'd be ready, Bud wouldn't be, and he'd blink.

Confidence was never a thing Bill Michael lacked, but I was starting to question some of his techniques. It started in March 2012, when he accepted a rumored million-dollar-a-year bounty to move from Dorsey to the law firm Mayer Brown in Chicago. Around that time, he began taking regular trips to Japan and Korea, trying to build a book of business to justify his lofty new comp package.

So he was busy. That was fine – every good lawyer is. But I got the sense Vascular Solutions wasn't exactly a top priority for him. Even when he was working our case, he didn't seem to have a sense of urgency or appreciation for the havoc it was wreaking on my company. In early 2014, for example, he escorted one of our top sales reps, Glen Holden, on his trip to the grand jury. It had begun; there was really a San Antonio grand jury, and Bud really was following through with his threats of a scorched-earth investigation. While there, the prosecutors alleged that Glen had perjured himself, and now weeks later they were threatening to indict him for obstruction of justice if he didn't come back and change his testimony. I asked Bill to deliver the news to Glen. His plan: "Let's wait until next week. We don't want to ruin Glen's weekend." *His weekend?*

Or the next week, when the government told Bill Michael that they wanted to bring five more employees before the grand jury and wanted them each to have separate lawyers. He didn't seem worried that Bud's dragnet was rapidly expanding, nor did he have any plan to avoid needing 70 lawyers for our 70 sales reps. Instead, he asked who two of the employees were, anyway.

Or, incredibly, when I heard back from him three days later and he asked, "Can you have your HR director send me contact numbers for these three sales reps?" Three days, and he was just now starting to make progress ... on their cell phone numbers.

But what upset me most about Bill Michael was his cozy alliance with the attorney he'd hired to represent our employees, Jon Hopeman. This guy Hopeman, like Bill Michael, was a creature of the smoky prosecutors' offices of the '80s. He fancied himself an ornery intellectual, everybody's least favorite type of lawyer. So disagreeable was Hopeman that when they built the new Minneapolis federal courthouse, the judges joked that the reason they demanded window cut-outs be added to the courtroom doors was so they could see Hopeman flipping them off as he walked down the hallway.

In January 2014, Hopeman hit me with a $91,000 legal bill. One month! One in which none of the employees he represented even went before the grand jury – just 182 hours of Hopeman at the bargain rate of $500 an hour. These lawyer bills were all rabbit holes, but I dug into this one if for no other reason than its lunacy. A curious exact-half of his hours were spent on "review of documents." I understood that he didn't want to give away too much because the government might one day get a hold of our bills, but this was ridiculous – it didn't even say which of his dozen employee-clients he was doing work for. I had never met the guy, but here he was, leisurely perusing documents for as many hours each day as he pleased, then invoicing me at the end of each month the price of a new Porsche. The worst part was that I couldn't really say anything, because Hopeman represented our employees, not the company, and the company couldn't be seen as interfering with our employees' defense – we just paid the bills.

I emailed Bill Michael and requested a call for a full update on the case and a discussion about Hopeman's parody of a legal bill. He informed me that he had approved Hopeman's billing rate and said, as to the call, "I will look at my calendar when I get back to Chicago this weekend and send you some proposed times/dates." This raised some questions. Why did Bill Michael have to be in Chicago to check his calendar? Did he have a novelty-sized Franklin Planner he left in his office? Couldn't somebody else look for him? This was Wednesday, so I guessed I'd have to wait a few days until he could consult his calendar, at which point he'd tell me how many additional days I'd have to wait to talk to my lawyer. When he finally did so, he emailed me and said that we could talk on the phone next Wednesday. Okay, fine, a week for a call …

Except it wasn't fine, because the long-awaited call was nothing but a rehashing of vague plans we'd already discussed. An alarming trend was developing – Bill Michael wasn't prepared. It was the one thing I couldn't tolerate, especially not from my $650-an-hour lawyer. I cut off the call early. "Bill," I told him sternly, "I want an all-hands meeting ASAP to cover this matter in detail." I sent a follow-up email with a laundry list of topics I wanted addressed.

This time he apparently had his calendar with him, because that night he set up an "all hands on deck" meeting with Tom Vitt, Hopeman, and the pool lawyer for the company's former employees who'd been dragged into the government's investigation. That was Dan Scott – hilariously touted on his firm's website as "the best defense lawyer nobody has heard of." Bill Michael even sent out a 16-point agenda to the group. Hey, maybe an organizational kick in the pants was all he needed.

$$-\hspace{-0.3em}\wedge\hspace{-0.6em}\wedge\hspace{-0.3em}-$$

We met two days later, on a cold February morning, in Hopeman's office. It was actually the same office space that Dorsey used to occupy in the days I worked there as a young lawyer. Newer carpet, fresh paint, but still that boxy '80s feel I remembered. I arrived 10 minutes early to a conference room I'd closed many a stock offering in, but we weren't ready to start yet. Bill Michael and Hopeman were down the hallway chatting – no doubt about how to pacify this crazy client of theirs. As everyone else trickled in, including our chairman, John Erb, the Hopeman-Michael sidebar continued out of earshot.

Once they stepped in and the meeting began, my hopes that Bill Michael had self-corrected ended. He opened by handing me a copy of a draft indictment the government had delivered to bully our former V.P. of marketing Fred Reuning. Unfortunately, when I looked at it after the meeting, he'd only managed to copy the odd-numbered pages. Tone-setting, to say the least.

Later, Bill Michael circulated a set of research topics that included items like "figure out who [witness name redacted] is" – facts that could easily be ascertained through a quick Google search. Tom Vitt, who looked uncomfortable throughout his ex-partner's meandering briefing, later told me it "looked like something he jotted on an airplane napkin on the way back from Korea."

As I steamed, Bill Michael turned the floor over to Hopeman, who gave a flowery report on the grand jury testimony that had already been given. None of our employees who'd been dragged down to San Antonio were breaking, he said, even though the government had pushed them hard. That gave me some comfort, but the fact that there were another six employees on the government's grand jury hit-list didn't. We were sinking cash into this investigation, losing time, and I didn't feel like we had anything to show for it. As the group got lost in the minutiae of coordinating witness travel for the next grand jury date, I jumped in to refocus our legal defense team on what mattered.

"Are we ready to take advantage of the Speedy Trial Act if we get indicted this summer?"

I looked around. Nothing but silence and searching eyes. Hopeman glanced at Dan Scott, both expressing disbelief. They'd apparently never even heard of this. Hopeman spoke for the group. "We haven't even started to prepare a defense. There's no way we would be ready in 70 days if we got indicted. It would be more like a year." I glared at Bill Michael, who sat there playing dumb and avoiding eye contact.

It was obvious to me what had happened. Bill thought there would be a settlement, and because of that, he wasn't preparing. He was, in essence, doing the very thing we were banking on the prosecutors doing. His associates were churning away at hour-filling tasks of legal research, but there was no coherent defense strategy. Just Bill, on a plane, dropping in to triage this case between his new, more important Asian work.

I'd reserved the last half of the meeting for an updated background presentation, including what I now saw as potential defenses. It'd been over two-and-a-half years since that first PowerPoint presentation I gave to Bill and

Tom, and neither Hopeman nor Scott had even seen it yet. I handed a copy of my presentation slides to Hopeman on a thumb drive. He looked at it quizzically, then slid it to his junior partner, Marnie Fearon, to figure out what to do with it.

I had a captive, if not receptive, audience. As I began my presentation, Hopeman looked bored in that angry way, Dan Scott listened politely but seemed to be lost, and Bill Michael kept rising and pacing to relieve his back pain. When an audience is fidgeting like that, my instinct is to speed up. But even moving quickly, I wasn't fast enough for Bill Michael. Half-an-hour into a presentation that I told him would take at least an hour, he announced that he had to leave for another meeting. I was left stunned, holding the wireless clicker. The first substantive full-team meeting on this case, and my lead lawyer just walked out on me.

The "all hands" meeting made it clear that I couldn't afford to sit back and blindly trust Bill Michael anymore. If we were going to have any chance at a favorable resolution, I needed to actively manage him and the other lawyers. So I sent him this email:

Bill,

As you could tell, I was troubled by the meeting on Friday. I didn't see a good work plan, I didn't see a budget, but I did see a lot of time being spent by a lot of attorneys who have not been fully briefed on the background facts.

After thinking about it more this weekend, I have concluded that Mayer Brown needs to stop essentially all work on this matter until you can get a plan in place with a budget created and approved by me with an appropriate division of responsibilities between Mayer Brown and Dorsey and the other firms.

Since it will very likely be months now before the government takes any formal action, we have the time now to get organized, and you should be able to create a plan that is much better organized in a short period of time.

Howard

P.S. The draft indictment you provided me was only the odd number

pages. Could you please email me a complete copy of that document as well?

I got a response the next day. Here it is, in full:

See attached.

Bill Michael attached a copy of that draft indictment of our marketing V.P. Reuning – now with the even pages included. Strangely, though, he provided no comment on the substance of the email, which I know he read because the request for the draft indictment was in the last line. *Maybe he's steaming*, I thought. *I'll give him a few days to cool down.*

I waited 23. Here's his response on the 24th day, copied to my chairman of the board, John Erb:

Howard and John:

Pursuant to Howard's direction we stopped all work, with the exception of getting some materials to Jon Hopeman's office recently.

For a host of reasons I think it appropriate to move up the timing of a transfer of the corporate criminal representation to Dorsey. While Howard may not have liked the work plan developed, it was developed through the combined efforts of three of the most experienced white-collar lawyers in Minnesota and had built into it the earlier limitations that he had set forth. As I have told both of you, as well as the board on my recent call, the need to get the company into a position to defend itself and any individuals within the Speedy Trial timeframe would necessitate effort and the attendant costs, especially as we had not been authorized to take a proactive defense strategy throughout the past three years, at the company's direction. I have not re-drafted a work plan as I do not think it appropriate for me to develop further a defense work plan for Dorsey's use.

Additionally, the current billing requirements are not something I am comfortable with due to the vagaries of any criminal investigation, which are not addressed. Lastly, as Howard is clearly not comfortable with my firm's billing rates, having me oversee the defense is not an effective means of representation of the company, nor is it efficient or effective for either Dorsey or Mayer Brown. Accordingly,

it seems that making a change to Dorsey now as counsel in the criminal investigation of the company would be appropriate.

Bill Michael

This arrogant prick. His incompetence got us into a big mess, and when I ask him for a plan to get out of it, he quits and calls me cheap for taking his advice that "deals always get better closer to trial." I took a deep breath and started to wonder what was happening in secret before that San Antonio grand jury. I had no idea, but our V.P. of marketing Carrie Powers did …

CHAPTER 7

GRAND FURY

As Told by Carrie Powers

October 2005 – First Impressions

These medical meetings were a grind. And this one, the 2005 Transcatheter Cardiovascular Therapeutics conference in Washington, D.C., was only my first one. The past two days had been a whirlwind of doctor talks, finger food, and smiley handshakes. All in a skirt suit instead of the washed-out baby blue scrubs us nurses wore every day back at the cardiac cath lab in Madison, Wisconsin.

It was a nice change of pace from the stress of being on-call all night waiting for the next heart attack patient to present, I guess, but tiring in a different way. And after three straight nights of marathon, industry-sponsored dinners at fancy restaurants, I was glad to have tonight free. I don't know if I was craving the burger or the jeans I was going to wear while I ate that burger, but I was ready for it.

As I grabbed my room key to leave, though, I got a call. It was Jason, who used to work with me in the cath lab. We had planned to grab a beer in Georgetown tonight, but now he was saying he had to eat with one of his co-workers. He asked me to join them. "That's okay," I said, "I'll just grab dinner on my own."

"Well, I already said you would come and he's already made the reservation," Jason said. Being forced into small talk with a stranger was the last thing I wanted to do tonight. *Be strong, Carrie.* Again, I told Jason no.

"Come onnnnnn," he whined.

"Fine." I opened the closet door and changed back into my starchy business clothes.

As I walked into the restaurant, I gave myself a pep talk. *Let's just get this over with. Eat dinner, avoid blunders, go home.* Over dinner, Jason's high-energy co-worker asked a ton of questions. Conservatively 50 questions, in short, excited bursts, throughout the hour-long meal. Which products we liked, how we were treating our patients, how we could tell a good sales rep from a bad one, and which companies we didn't like. After three days of pleasantries, I was happy to be me again and let loose with my unvarnished opinion. I wasn't worried about offending the third wheel, and I certainly wasn't there to impress anyone. That said, I found Jason's co-worker surprisingly easy to talk to. So just before dessert was served, I asked a question I probably should have asked him up-front. "By the way, what do *you* do at Vascular Solutions?"

"Well, in 1997 I founded the company, and I'm the CEO."

I turned to Jason, who was purposely staring down at his empty plate. "You idiot!" I scolded him. I had failed my no-blunder goal and resigned myself to choking down dessert in humiliation.

The next day, Jason texted me and asked to meet between conference sessions. When I found him amidst the crowd, he said Howard wanted to know if I would ever consider moving back home to Minnesota and working for VSI. I honestly thought it was a joke after so spectacularly embarrassing myself less than 12 hours before. I said something deflective like "maybe someday, but it's not the right time now" and told Jason to thank Howard for dinner, the conversation, and the offer. I had to run to my next session.

A month later, Howard called me himself. He asked me to move to Minneapolis and join VSI … in its *marketing* department. "I don't have any marketing experience," I told him.

"I don't care," he replied, reassuringly. "You know what doctors want, and they're the customer, so that's all you need to know." It made sense, and

I did eventually want to move from Wisconsin back home to Minnesota, but still I hesitated. "And don't ask for more money," Howard interjected before I could. "You're not worth more than $70,000, *yet*. I'm going to lose money on you the first year." With a pitch like that – how could I refuse?

April 2014 – The Voicemail

As I pulled into work, tan off of vacation from my now $500,000 a year job, I reflected on how far I'd come over the last nine years. The opinionated RN was now the V.P. of marketing. I walked through the hall, past the displays of the Vascular Solutions products I'd helped launch, past the cubes of employees I now supervised, all the way back to my corner office.

I asked my assistant, Marty, to push back my morning meetings so I could catch up on the blitz of emails that came through while I was in Panama with my husband and two young kids. But that little red light was flashing on the phone, so I started with the voicemail, given its persistence.

Junk. Call her back later. Kids stuff. Kids stuff. Kids stuff. Lawyer – wait, lawyer?

Carrie, my name is Marnie Fearon. I work with Jon Hopeman, and we represent current employees of Vascular Solutions. Please give me a call when you get this. I have just accepted service for a subpoena requiring you to testify before a grand jury in San Antonio, Texas, in connection with an investigation into a product called the Short Kit. My number is ...

I tuned out the rest of the message and sat frozen. I looked around the room, half-expecting a SWAT team to rush through the door. I got up and closed it, just in case.

A subpoena? San Antonio? Howard had talked about the Short Kit investigation a couple of times in our Monday ops meetings, but I didn't have anything to do with the Short Kit launch, so why would they want me? *And what is a grand jury, anyway?*

May 2014 – The "Grand" Jury

Here's what I learned in the five weeks I had to prepare for my trip to Texas. A grand jury is like a test trial prosecutors have to get through before they're allowed to bring felony charges. That meant this was a criminal thing. To my relief, though, none of the criminal charges being discussed were against me. This was all about what the company did or didn't do seven years ago, and they just wanted to interview me as a witness.

I also learned that, like the other employee witnesses, Jon Hopeman and Marnie Fearon would be my lawyers. I hadn't spent much time with Mr. Hopeman in those five weeks, but enough to know that his detached expression this morning wasn't a reaction to the mildew-tinted courthouse waiting room I now shared with his other clients.

Waiting with us under the harsh fluorescent lights was Susan Christian (our V.P. of sales operations), Chris Harrelson (one of our Texas sales reps), and Dick Steitzer (our Eastern regional manager). Each of us brought computers to do work on, but there were no desks and no Internet – just chairs bordering an empty room. Work was the last thing I was thinking of, anyway. We were all waiting in silence to see who'd be called first, and my mind was running wild with thoughts of – *wait, the door just popped open.*

It was the somewhat swollen man I'd been introduced to that morning as "Bud," one of the prosecutors in the case. He poked his golf-bronzed neck in just enough to pluck one of us out. "Mr. Steitzer," he said, propping the door open. I saw the fear in Dick's eyes as he rose, flashed a nervous half-smile to the rest of us, and disappeared into the grand jury room across the hall.

Passing hours next to Chris and Susan only made me more nervous. Susan and I hadn't been close before this experience, but I could already tell we would be after. We sat, not knowing who was up next or when. I was glad I wasn't first, but I also didn't want to be last and risk the prosecutors running out of time and making me come back.

As a former gymnast, I know when I'm ready for a routine. And I knew I wasn't as ready as I wanted to be now, a fact that made the wait all the more excruciating. I'd only had a 10-minute prep session that morning with my lawyers, and I didn't even know what the room looked like. That sounds like a little thing, but to me it was big – something I always went out of my way to learn before doing any sort of public speaking.

I clung to one lifeline Hopeman threw me. "You have immunity," he said, "which means that anything truthful you say in there can't be used against you down the road." I wasn't worried about that, because I had almost nothing to do with this Short Kit product, but it was still comforting to know.

All I had to do was go in there, tell the truth, and move on. I was sure the company would move on, too. It seemed like these government investigations were hitting every medical device company nowadays, and VSI was always extremely buttoned-up when it came to compliance. We'd be fine. I was sure this was all just a misunderstanding – *wait, the doorman's back.*

"Ms. Powers," Bud said, in his heavy Southern drawl that made it seem like slow motion. "Please come with me."

Let's just get this over with.

—ᴧᴧ—

The grand jury was nothing like what I'd pictured. For starters, there wasn't anything grand about the room itself, which I expected to be a courtroom. Instead, I found myself lost in a bland conference room with low-hung drop ceilings. The grand jurors didn't sit in a box, instead they sat behind tables arranged in a horseshoe pattern. They were sleepy, and one appeared to be covertly reading the paper. I expected to be led in and seated at a witness stand, maybe with some water, but there was no witness stand, and no water either. *Where do I go?*

Bud urged me toward a lone chair, Witness Island, between the tips of the horseshoe. So that's where I sat, forced to uncomfortably cross my legs because there was no desk or anything in front of me. I tried to hide how anxious I was to be suddenly thrust into this totally foreign environment, but I suspected I wasn't doing a very good job.

What surprised me most was that there was no judge. Hopeman told me that defense lawyers weren't allowed in the grand jury room, and I suppose the judge thing is something I should've known, but I didn't. It was just me, the grand jurors, a court reporter, Bud, and the other prosecutor – a curious guy by the name of Tim Finley, who had the same crew cut as my eight-year-old son. Finley did most of the talking, camped out on the left tip of the horseshoe, asking questions while seated behind stacks of three-ring binders. I had to torque my neck and lift my head to even see him.

But it wasn't until 12 minutes into questioning that I realized just how different this was going to be from what I'd imagined.

> **FINLEY: What did you tell the sales force about how to handle questions about off-label uses?**
>
> **ME: We told the sales force that they needed to know the indications for all our products. If they got a question on the use of a product that was off-label, that they needed to instruct the physician that that was an off-label use of the product.**
>
> **FINLEY: Did the sales force get trained that selling for unapproved use was prohibited?**
>
> **ME: We did not say it was prohibited.**
>
> **FINLEY: So, the way you are describing it to me, the sales force was not prohibited from selling off-label. All they had to do was say that it's off-label?**
>
> **ME: They had to instruct the user that it was off-label, correct.**
>
> **FINLEY: And then they could go ahead and promote off-label?**
>
> **ME: They weren't promoting off-label.**

Finley had been rushing out his questions. But now he paused, jerked his head in my direction, and lowered his otherwise-yappy voice.

> **FINLEY: The sales force wasn't promoting off-label?**
>
> **ME: No … that wasn't promoting off-label.**

I felt like I was being attacked … just for explaining my understanding of a tricky concept. And the confusing part was, I thought I was right.

In my mind, there was an important difference between *promoting* for an off-label use and *selling* a doctor a product she might use off-label. Promoting wasn't allowed under company policy, but taking sales orders from a doctor who used off-label was. It had to be. After all, doctors were free to use devices off-label, and we didn't expect our sales rep to sprint out of the hospital if a doctor said the word "perforator." But before I could explain all this, Finley took his attack up a notch.

> **FINLEY: Wait. Are you saying that on your watch, the sales force never promoted Vari-Lase for perforator use?**

> **ME: I did not say that.**

> **FINLEY: Okay, so what did you mean when you said they didn't promote off-label?**

> **ME: What I mean is that the sales force wasn't going out actively to the community and saying that you can sell the Short Kit for perforator use.**

> **FINLEY: Did VSI ever tell the sales force, don't promote off-label?**

> **ME: I believe [so], yes.**

> **FINLEY: So that would be another rule – that you're not supposed to promote off-label, right?**

Finley looked at me like he'd caught me in a lie. *That's what I've been saying!* This wasn't an interview, this was an interrogation.

Finley's focus then shifted to getting me to agree with him that perforators weren't covered under Vari-Lase's indications. "This use for perforators is not approved," he said, followed by a one-word question, "correct?"

I should know this. I'm the head of marketing, so I should know this. On any other day, I could stop, go find out the answer, and come back so I could have an informed conversation. But this wasn't any day, and I was a long way from my desk. Finley gave me a look like he wanted an answer now.

Okay, stay calm. Let's see: I hadn't seen the indications recently, and Finley never showed it to me. I should've looked at this last night. If this were a meeting with Howard, I would've never been so unprepared. *Focus. Think about it.* These were government lawyers working with the FDA. They should know whether it was covered, and it sure sounded like they did.

I agreed with Finley: perforators weren't covered.

My answer left Finley oddly pleased. At the time, I didn't understand it. Was that even at issue here? He made it seem so obvious. I mean, if we were all in this grand jury room talking about off-label promotion and perforators, I assumed there was a reason.

But it wasn't until he started handing me documents that I fully grasped how unprepared I was. Document after document, Finley pushed at me. I'd get the paper copy, while the grand jury saw the document projected on a big screen behind me that I couldn't see. I was never sure if I was looking at the right document or the right part of it, and by the time I figured it out, the next one was in front of me. Of the nine documents he showed me, I think I'd seen two of them before, and I didn't write any of them.

With each document came a series of pointed questions. Finley was always leading me one way or another, but I couldn't always tell where or why. When I didn't answer the way he apparently wanted me to, he'd turn his head to the side, squint, and slap me with a little comment like, "So the answer to my question is yes?" (even when it wasn't) or snarky barbs like, "Yeah, I know. You say that."

And when he started showing me weekly reports from sales reps talking about "working to get the perf biz" and throwing "perforator parties," I found it troubling. I certainly didn't think there was some secret plot among management to sell the Short Kit for perforators, but how could I know what was going on at every doctor's office across the country? I had access to all of the trip reports our sales reps filled out each week documenting their sales calls, but nobody in the home office had time to read all those. That's why we had regional managers in the field.

Each time Finley showed me a trip report, he asked the same question.

FINLEY: Would this be an example of illegal conduct?

I found it a little backward for a federal prosecutor to be asking me what was illegal, but maybe it was a test. He just wanted to see if I was being cooperative. *Okay, let's work through this.*

I hadn't read the laws, but I knew this was a criminal proceeding. I'd already agreed that perforators were off-label and that the company instructed against off-label promotion. So if our sales reps looked like they were out there promoting for perforators, then that would be against the law, right? It felt weird – wrong – to say that our sales reps had done something illegal, but I didn't see any way around it. Once again, it seemed obvious. And once again, I said yes.

ME: Yes, it would be.

Five times I said that the company broke the law, including twice when I agreed that a sales rep's contact with doctors was "clearly illegal," and another time when I agreed it was "blatantly illegal." But apparently even that – my repeated incrimination of the company I worked for – wasn't enough.

Finley wanted me to agree that the company's instruction to promote the Short Kit for "short veins" or "short vein segments" was just code for "perforator." He wanted me to admit I'd led trainings where this message was secretly handed down. I told him I didn't think that was the message at all. And he didn't like that, at all.

FINLEY: Okay. Well, we have dozens of marketing documents – slide decks, trip reports – where "short veins" are used interchangeably with "perforator veins." The witnesses have all said, "We used it interchangeably." If the company taught the sales force that the term "short vein" includes perforator, then the plan all along is to market the thing for perforators, right?

ME: I don't believe that was the intent or the plan. I think that was the documents not being clear and the sales people interpreting them that way.

It didn't take long to learn that there were penalties for "wrong" answers like this. The worst penalty of all was Bud. When he didn't like what I said, Bud would sit, hands pressed on the table like he was trying to push it through the floor, growing redder and redder. And once he boiled over, he'd tag out Finley and play the worse-cop role. So before Finley could get out his next question, Bud stood up and put his hands on his hips, glowering my way.

BUD: Question for you: Could you go back to the company and do a bit of research for us? Would you send us a slide from any deck that refers to using the Short Kit on anything other than perforators?

I couldn't tell if he was joking. Was this a rhetorical thing? I paused.

ME: A slide deck?

BUD: Out of any slide deck.

Each time Bud spoke, he took a step toward me. Each time, his voice grew a little louder and his tone a little more strained.

ME: Communication?

BUD: I beg your pardon?

ME: Communication or slide deck or—

BUD: Yeah, just anything.

I sat in silence, confused, looking around the room to see if anyone else was. A few were napping, and the others didn't seem alarmed.

BUD: Did you hear me?![4]

I laughed. Nervously, awkwardly, out of reflex. It probably wasn't appropriate, but we'd just had this confusing back-and-forth. I must've misheard something along the way, because I had no idea what he was asking for, or *if* he was even asking for anything.

BUD: It's not really a joke. It's what did you tell the sales force they could tell their customers the Short Kit could be used for? I mean, are there slides out there telling them, "promote it for use in the great saphenous vein"?

ME: I'm not certain.

BUD: It doesn't exist, does it?

ME: I don't know.

BUD: Okay. Well, you're the director of marketing. And witnesses as recently as – well, very recently – have told the grand jury that the terms "perf kit, perforator kit, and Short Kit" were all used interchangeably in the company. Do you agree with that?

---

[4]I vividly remember Bud asking me this question and angrily snapping me back to his attention. But when I eventually got the transcript of my testimony, this question had mysteriously vanished.

**ME: I have heard the terms used. I don't think they were used inter-
changeably in education provided by the home office.**

BUD: No, but they were used!

He pointed his finger at me, his face tomato red. He kept talking, but I was
lost in shock at his sing-songy smack-down.

The way he stared at me, I don't know how to describe it … it felt like he
wanted something bad to happen to me. It was all surreal, like an overdone
episode of *Law & Order*. Is this how it's supposed to be? I looked around at
the grand jurors. None of them looked at all disgusted by Bud's nasty tone.
Maybe they were used to it by now.

Finley grabbed back the reins, sighing "Okay …" to settle things down.
He asked less contentious questions for the next 10 minutes and then announced that we'd break for lunch. As the grand jurors poured out, Bud
looked at me.

**BUD: If you will wait outside, we'll let you know what time we'll
resume.**

I met my lawyer Hopeman outside of the courtroom, in the rotunda of the
courthouse's third floor, struggling to process what had just happened. Bud
walked out behind me and asked to speak with Hopeman privately. I hadn't
walked more than three steps away from them when I heard it.

"Her testimony is pissing us off!" I glanced back to see Bud standing with
his hands on his hips again, exasperated, as Hopeman seemingly tried to calm
him down in a hushed voice.

Hopeman saw me peeking, paused the conversation, and walked over to
me and said, "Go farther away. You don't need to hear all this." *Wait – was I
in trouble?* I kept walking, as far away as I could get.

As we left the courthouse for lunch at a nearby taco shack, Hopeman
told me that Bud had taken issue with my "uncooperative behavior." When
Hopeman asked if he thought I was lying, Bud said, "I don't believe she is
lying, but I do believe she isn't telling the truth."

"They think you're hiding something for the company," Hopeman told
me. Bud said that I should take lunch to "think about my actions and my

attitude," but all I could think of was: *What just happened in there?*

And then, as we were discussing all this, Bud and Finley strolled up to the taco shack. "Let's get out of here," Hopeman said, pulling me away from the rest of the group. It was the first time I felt protected all day.

When we returned to the courthouse after lunch, I sat in the hallway, mentally preparing myself to go back in. I imagined the tone I'd use, where I'd put my hands, and what I'd do if they raised their voices at me again. Bud walked back into the small holding room, and I rose slightly from my seat, assuming it was game time.

But instead, he called Hopeman into the hallway for another huddle. Bud said that they were going to skip over me and bring in Chris Harrelson. That way, I'd have time to "marinate" and decide whether to cooperate. If I didn't, they said, they would consider recommending that the company fire me.

Could they even do that? I didn't know, but since they were saying it, I assumed they could. For what, I wondered, as I sat for an hour-and-a-half at the corner table in the rotunda Bud pointed me to. My focus was gone now, drifting from the testimony I was about to give. *What did I say that was wrong? How am I going to explain why I lost my job?*

I saw Chris Harrelson walk out of the grand jury room, lips pursed, lost in his own world, looking like one word would send him to tears. I locked eyes with Susan, a mutual recognition that things hadn't gone well in there. And then I realized – I was up again.

But once more, they wanted to talk to Hopeman, not me. Hopeman told me later that Bud asked, "Where's Ms. Powers at?"

"Over there," he replied, gesturing to my time-out bench.

"No!" Bud snapped. "Where's her head at?"

"She believes she's telling the truth," Hopeman said, and I did.

Bud walked right over to where I was sitting. "Sorry for keeping you waiting," he said in that fake Southern hospitality way of his. "We've decided to let you go home."

It was hard to go back to the office after that. To act like nothing happened. I'd kind of blacked out in the grand jury room, and I spent my next few afternoons daydreaming, trying to remember what I'd even said. I mostly remembered how I felt, that terrifying feeling of being attacked.

I wondered what the government really had on the company. *Was everybody around me about to lose their jobs? Would it be over something I'd said?* As I walked around the office, seeing friends, co-workers and people wrapped up in their own little problems, I felt the pressure of being one of the few people in the company who even knew what was going on. I couldn't talk about it with anyone, Hopeman said. Especially not what happened in the grand jury. And especially not with Howard.

I kept watching the door for the SWAT guys. If they ever came, I told my assistant, Marty, he should call my lawyers and my husband, in that order. But they never showed up. Instead, all I got was a phone call from my lawyer Marnie Fearon.

I just spoke with the prosecutors. They'd like you to "fix" your grand jury testimony, as they put it. If you don't, they will consider making you a target of the federal criminal investigation. And if the company is convicted or takes a plea deal, they will recommend that you be banned from working in the healthcare industry for at least five years.

The healthcare industry was the only place I'd ever worked. Now, federal prosecutors want me fired and banned from it? *What else could I do?* I closed my office door and thought about it – scared at first, then furious.

CHAPTER 8

I NEED A LAWYER, BUD NEEDS A BODY

Spring 2014

C arrie and Susan returned from their grand jury session looking like they'd seen a ghost. The lawyers said we couldn't talk about what went on down there, so I could only speculate why. But suffice to say, having my officers dragged down to San Antonio and watching them return shell-shocked wasn't something I'd planned for.

I also hadn't planned on my lawyer up and quitting. I say "my" lawyer for a reason, even though Bill Michael before his desertion was representing the company, not me personally. In the early days of the investigation, I viewed myself as being inseparable from the company, so by representing the company, Bill was representing me.

As the tides of the investigation turned to "holding individuals account-able," though, Bill Michael explained to me that if I was indicted as the "re-sponsible corporate officer," I would need to get in my own boat, with my own lawyer. The plan we came up with was for Bill Michael to shift over and represent me, a move that would not-so-coincidentally push his Chica-go-sized legal fees onto our directors and officers liability insurance. His team would do the heavy lifting (and billing), while Tom Vitt and Dorsey would sing backup as the company's counsel to keep legal costs down. It was a good plan, decimated by Bill Michael spiking the mic and walking off the defense stage.

Time for a new plan. First things first: I needed a new lawyer to represent the company – like, today. The most obvious option was for Dorsey, the only firm that knew the case, to go back to running the show. And if so, I really wanted Tom Vitt to step into the lead-lawyer role. He knew the case, had my trust, and his work on our past lawsuits proved him to be a courtroom dynamo. But Dorsey wouldn't let him. Even though he had nearly 30 years of civil litigation experience, the firm wouldn't allow him to run a criminal case, fearing malpractice claims if things went south. So now, instead of having the insurers foot the growing legal bills like I planned, I'd need to hire a new lead lawyer for the company and pay even more legal fees getting him or her up to speed. Thanks, Bill Michael.

"Well who else is on Dorsey's bench?" I asked Tom. He told me about a former federal prosecutor Dorsey had hired to take over Bill Michael's caseload. The guy had tried over 50 criminal cases to verdict. And he even had a cool name: RJ Zayed. "Okay," I said, "is RJ the guy?" Tom said he'd have to check.

RJ had been doing a lot of patent litigation since joining Dorsey, and Tom wasn't sure if he'd even want a high-pressure, drop-everything criminal case like this. But Tom called back later that day and said RJ was up for it. That was all I needed to hear. "I don't have a lot of options right now, so it looks like RJ's the guy. But I need you on the team as well, Tom, because you're the only litigator I trust." I sat down with RJ and gave him my PowerPoint presentation and told him to get up-to-speed on the documents and key players.

The top spot on the ticket now was filled, but I also needed a lawyer for myself. My immediate thought was to go with Jon Hopeman. He was the independent attorney representing each of the current employees, after all, and I was a current employee.

But then I got an email from Jon Hopeman. Check that – Hopeman's secretary. Attached to that email was a scan of a hard copy letter, which he was also sending by regular mail so I'd have the pleasure of receiving it again two days later. A weird use of technology, but I already knew from the way Hopeman ogled at that thumb drive that he was old school. I'd find out from the letter that he was also a pompous windbag.

He opened with a weighty meditation.

I have reflected on the way this matter is being managed, and have some worries that I wanted to share with you. I think the way the billing policies and practices are now, we are headed for disaster.

A disaster? For the company's bank account, maybe. But I paid Hopeman's Porsche-sized bill in full, so what was he so "reflective" about? I soon found out.

> **We began work on this case believing that William Michael of Mayer Brown would be involved to spearhead the case as either counsel for the company or as counsel to you personally, when you are indicted.**

"*When* you are indicted." That was nice. If Hopeman thought there was no chance of me avoiding indictment, maybe he wasn't the right lawyer for me. He continued:

> **Mr. Michael informed us on March 20, 2014 that he may withdraw from any involvement with the case. He told us he was instructed to stand down and stop billing. We were also informed that, at present, there is no one working on the case at any law firm on behalf of the company who has experience with defending major white-collar criminal cases in federal court.**

Wow. Bill Michael told Hopeman that he was quitting 22 days *before* he told me, his client, and then trashed me and the team he was leaving behind. All unauthorized communications, all against his client's best interest, and all childishly spiteful. I knew that money had to factor into this protest somehow, and Hopeman did not disappoint.

> **We have a problem with submitting a rolling three month Work Plan/Budget. We are not retained by VSI. We are retained by the loyal gentlemen employees listed above. Our obligation is to them, not to VSI. VSI has no right to determine the scope of the work needed to protect these men.**

So if the all-knowing Jon Hopeman says it takes a million dollars to defend each *loyal gentleman employee,* then by golly, we must pay. How dare we, a frivolous enterprise, ask the great Jon Hopeman to predict his expenses? He was busy, good sir, doing a great job *protecting these men*, something that we didn't ask him about, but about which he gladly told us.

> **We know it went well in San Antonio. Our witnesses were prepared, not intimidated, and gave us good debriefings afterwards. We developed a good relationship with the two prosecutors assigned to the case. In short, we provided efficient, competent representation to our clients.**

That arrogance was more than enough to cross Hopeman off my list. After I cooled down, I realized I should still stop by his office to smooth things over and correct the record on a few points. He wasn't going to be my lawyer, but we still needed him to fiercely represent his gentlemen *and gentlewomen* clients when Bud came knocking. I dropped by for a brief, frosty, conciliatory meeting, and told him that RJ would be running the show from here on out. Hopefully RJ's 25 years of experience was enough for Hopeman.

I still needed to find a lawyer for myself, and with Hopeman out, I had three leads. I started with The Big Name.

Tom Hefflefinger is a former U.S. Attorney for Minnesota, meaning he was appointed by the president to run one of the nation's 93 U.S. Attorney's Offices. He was just the sort of connected guy our case could use, someone who could shake a hand or two and restore consciousness to this lingering nightmare. But before I could even shake *his* hand, he let me know over the phone that he was too busy. While he had me on the line, though, he told me something chilling. "I made a call down to an old friend in the Department of Justice," he said. "There's someone in D.C. who doesn't like you. They see this as a much bigger case than it appears, and you're the target."

Whoa. Up until that point, I figured this had been all about a petulant duo of line prosecutors. Guys out to make a name for themselves, or in Bud's case, restore a name for himself. It never occurred to me that my case could hold some symbolic quality that a DOJ bigwig in Washington fetishized. It didn't make sense, so I chose to ignore it – at least for now – because I still had a lawyer to find.

The second lawyer on my list was The Veteran. Peter Wold had a criminal defense practice located across the street from the Minneapolis courthouse and 35 years of experience. Unfortunately, when I arrived at his office, it was part of a shared workspace for defense lawyers fronted by a waiting room that felt more like a barber shop than a law firm. I was the only guy in a suit, and judging by the clientele's familiarity with the receptionist, the only one who wasn't a repeat customer.

When I was finally escorted back to see Peter, he greeted me with a hurried hesitation in his voice that showed his age. "I may have to cut this meeting short," he said. "We're waiting for the jury to come back with a verdict in a case we just tried." Good – this guy was still active. "We argued an insanity defense." I wasn't expecting that. I needed someone to argue that the government's decision to prosecute me was insane, or maybe that the vague regulatory system was insane, not that *I* was.

My last meeting was with The Professor – John Lundquist. If ever an attorney had a spirit animal, it was John Lundquist and a bespectacled turtle. He had the lineage and temperament of a Minnesota Swede: even-keeled, always pleasant. And unlike my other two candidates, he had availability and experience trying healthcare fraud cases.[5] Like Peter Wold, Lundquist was also on the "experienced" side, but he was still game for trial. Plus, he had a real office and a formidable team behind him, starting with his much-younger partner, Dulce Foster, a sharp litigator with a take-no-shit personality and a science background.

I hired Professor Lundquist the next day, and my team was set. One of the great things about having Lundquist on board was that I knew he wouldn't, as Bill Michael so extravagantly did, put his own interests and vanities before my defense. That would prove crucial if, heaven forbid, we ended up at trial.

$$\perp\!\!\bigwedge\!\!\perp$$

Our April 2014 board of directors' dinner was my first chance to see RJ in action and hear his appraisal of our case. But when seven o'clock hit at our favorite cheap Italian dining spot, RJ and Tom Vitt were nowhere to be found. Then I got a call from Tom. "We're here. Where are you?" he asked.

"Where is here?" I asked back.

"Biaggi's ... by your office."

Wrong Biaggi's. We were at the one closer to the airport, for the convenience of two board members who'd just flown in from Chicago. Understandable Biaggi's mistake, and no big deal – we'd order some appetizers and

---

[5]In 2004, Lundquist represented medical device inventor Dr. Scott Augustine in a criminal healthcare fraud trial. Midway through trial, the lead prosecutor reportedly passed out at the counsel's table due to stress and had to spend the night in the hospital, leading the government to float an attractive settlement offer to Lundquist's client. I always questioned why Dr. Augustine took the plea offer when he was seemingly bound to win outright, and the answer he and Lundquist gave was that it took the risk of prison off the table. That's not the way I was going to play this game.

discuss other items first.

They arrived mid-bruschetta, and I asked RJ to jump right into his presentation. I had given RJ the heads-up that these were relatively informal affairs, but he nevertheless insisted on giving his presentation while standing. "Whatever makes you comfortable," I said.

As soon as RJ stood over the dining table and began, I got the sinking feeling that this wouldn't be the man to save my company in court. He passed around print-outs of his slides, but for some reason the order wasn't synched with his presentation. Since they also didn't have page numbers, the board members were forced to flip quizzically through the binder for "the one with the chart," while RJ mumbled and *uhh*-ed his way through his speech.

While the cosmetic stuff was off-putting, my real issue with RJ was with what he said. Under RJ's analysis, the government had us dead-to-rights. At this point, he said, our best bet was to suck up to them, beg for the best plea deal possible, and thank them as we took it.

He assumed FDA *didn't* give us permission to market for perforator treatment, without so much as flagging it as an issue. He ignored that I'd specifically told our reps not to promote the Short Kit for perforators. And he brushed off *United States v. Caronia*, a recent, highly-publicized case that said companies and individuals can't be convicted for truthful speech about off-label uses. Our reps' speech, he insisted, wouldn't be on trial – it would be the *intent* of their speech, which the government would use to show that we were illegally marketing the product. And if that sounds like a thought crime end-around to the First Amendment, it was, and it was exactly what the U.S. Court of Appeals for the Second Circuit rejected in *Caronia*. RJ, however, poo-pooed that decision as nonbinding on Texas federal courts. It didn't look like my defense attorney had much defense in him.

"If Howard pleads guilty, I think we should be able to get him off with no prison time," RJ said, "but we'll have to fight hard to keep him from getting banned from working in the healthcare industry." He announced it proudly, as if that would be some grand accomplishment.

The way RJ saw the case, it probably would be. RJ didn't think the case was triable for the company, and with him at the helm, I had to agree. Any "guilty" verdict against the company would be a disaster, allowing the U.S.

Department of Health and Human Services ("HHS") to ban the company from selling any of our now 100 medical devices to U.S. hospitals that take Medicare patients. Which is every U.S. hospital. So, in effect, any conviction meant the company could face the death penalty. And under the law, a felony conviction would make it mandatory. The same rules applied to me: a misdemeanor conviction would probably mean forced retirement, and a felony would guarantee it, on top of years of prison time.

To his credit, RJ worked hard to reset our relationship with the prosecutors in the wake of Bill Michael's flame-stoking. In his initial overtures at cooperation, just days before the board dinner, RJ told Bud and Finley that "we weren't running from the documents" and were "willing to take responsibility." I didn't love that negotiating position, but I was anxious to hear RJ describe the prosecutors' response to my board for the first time.

Still standing, RJ reported that since the time Bill Michael spoke those immortal words ("You do what you have to do"), Bud and Tim had poured their "blood, sweat, and tears" into the criminal case, according to Bud. Their misdemeanor case was strong, Bud said, and the felony case was "progressing." The old deal – a corporate misdemeanor plea with no individual responsibility – was now off the table. Bottom line, Bud said, at this point they "need a body."

Bud added that witnesses were lining up against the company, including the man Bud described as a "poor piece of roadkill." That was Danny McIff, the Utah sales rep I had fired for deleting that enthusiastically-titled Power-Point "TREATING PERFORATOR VEINS!!!" The few witnesses who denied that the conduct took place, Bud warned, were doing so at their own risk. Like our salesman Glen Holden, who Bud described as "a poor fucker" who was "a coat of paint away from perjury." Bud said they were going to indict Glen for felony obstruction of justice unless he came in "on bended knee" to "fix" his grand jury testimony and admit that he'd lied. After all those years of managerial complacency, Bud was back on the warpath and clearing out anything in his way with a flamethrower.

All that was the setup, it seemed, to Bud's next salvo. The government might be willing to argue on the company's behalf against exclusion by HHS, he said, if VSI pled guilty and gave the prosecutors its "full cooperation." Which begged the question, conveniently answered by a Bud Paulissen email that RJ relayed to the board.

> **Hello, RJ. In response to your inquiry last week about what VSI could do to cooperate with the government, Tim Finley and I suggest the following:**
>
> 1. **Hold accountable the individuals who are most responsible for the violations**
>
> 2. **Cooperate in our investigation of Howard Root and in any prosecution of him**
>
> 3. **Take appropriate steps to correct false statements or testimony by VSI employees (*e.g.* Glen Holden, Shane Carlson)**
>
> **Tim and I look forward to speaking to you after you meet with the company's board of directors.**

I looked around at the table of board members and saw the fear. The very fear on which Bud and Tim were preying. I am one member of the board of directors, but the other six are collectively my boss. And their duty of loyalty isn't to me; it's to the shareholders. Saying "yes" to Bud's conditions by throwing me under the bus would keep the company in business and eliminate the biggest risk to *their* bosses, the shareholders. As I stepped out of the private dining room so the board could start the independent section of the meeting, it was now absolutely clear what was needed to settle this case. That "body" Bud needed was mine. And if the company didn't hand it over to him, he'd take down the whole company. Or at least try.

—ᴧᴫ—

RJ's performance at the board dinner made it clear he wasn't the guy I wanted representing the company, but I didn't have anyone to replace him. At least not yet. I talked to Tom Vitt about switching roles with RJ, but he reiterated that Dorsey wouldn't let him, and he added that RJ wouldn't accept a "second chair" role "at this stage in his career." Another arrogant attorney. Great.

So for now, I had no choice but to run RJ out there to see if he could coax a less-predatory deal from Bud and Tim. If it worked, great – we'd move on and be done with this. If it didn't, I'd shake up our legal team, again.

In June 2014, after a two-month settlement dance with RJ, Bud presented his final, "no-haggle" offer:

1. **VSI agrees to plea to a misdemeanor.**

2. **Howard agrees to plea to a misdemeanor.**

3. **VSI agrees to pay a "7 figure fine."**

4. **VSI implements a robust compliance program and agrees to remediation; and**

5. **VSI agrees to terminate Glen Holden and Beth Matthews and discipline Shane Carlson, Carrie Powers, and Susan Christian for their off-label promotion activities as part of the remediation.**

Misdemeanors, remediation, terminations, and discipline – *was Bud trying to cast a spell on us?* If you consider the strings attached, Bud's "best offer" was decidedly worse than his first. The money was irrelevant, it always had been. And at this point, even max seven figures ($9,999,999) would have been okay with us. Separate from Bud's offer letter was a yet-to-come statement of facts we'd have to agree to as a condition of the deal. When Bud finally sent it over, it was chocked full of incendiary allegations and clear that signing it would mean HHS would bar me from the healthcare industry for at least five years. I'd have to be fired from VSI. And the company wouldn't be safe, either.

So much for cooperation. RJ's submissive approach seemed only to embolden Bud, who must have assumed that the board was wilting under the government's pressure. Quite the opposite; the board quickly and unanimously voted to reject Bud's "best" offer.

And with that, our last faint hope of a global settlement finally died. So the next month, in July 2014, we paid $520,000 to end the civil case, without admitting any wrongdoing, and without any companion criminal settlement. DeSalle Bui received his 20% whistleblower share – not the $4 million he wanted, but $104,000 … which his ex-wife's lawyer siphoned off before a cent ever reached DeSalle's bank account.

In any rational world, our civil settlement would have been the end of this story. But rational left the station a long time ago. We were on the crazy train, and it was speeding toward a criminal indictment. To have any chance of stopping this train now, I'd need a new approach … and a new lawyer.

CHAPTER 9

NEXT STOP: INDICTMENT

Summer 2014

With Bud and Tim firmly dug in, escaping indictment would require going over their heads. Despite The Big Name's warning, I still thought we could get one of the real DOJ decision-makers to see the lunacy of trying to wipe out an innovative American company over literally nothing – no crime, no patient harm, no financial gain. This thing could still go away quietly, I thought, but my defense lawyers in Minnesota were a long way away, in distance and influence, from Main Justice in D.C.

My problem was, unlike the Medtronics and Goldman Sachs of the world, I didn't have a team of lobbyists to pressure the politicians or close the deal with an impromptu DOJ drop-in. I knew Senator Amy Klobuchar from our '80s days working together at Dorsey, and she was coincidentally on the Senate Judiciary Committee, but allegations of prosecutorial misconduct inside her own party's DOJ seemed like a political non-starter. I tried anyway, but all I got was a curt email from her chief of staff: "It has been a long-standing rule of the Senate that senators cannot get involved in ongoing investigations at the Department of Justice." Actually, there's no such rule, according to our former DOJ lawyers who told me they'd experienced inquiries from senators first-hand. But politically, this was the easiest way for the senator nicknamed "small stuff" to tell a constituent "I can't" instead of "I won't."

I might not have a lobbyist, but we did pay over $50,000 a year to be part of a group called MDMA – the Medical Device Manufacturers Association, based in D.C. So I called its president, Mark Leahey, and asked him to point me to the most well-connected lawyers in town. "The best firm for this sort of thing is King & Spalding, and the lawyer you want to talk with is Dan Donovan," he said, naming a former aide to Senate healthcare watchdog Chuck Grassley.

"The best" sounded good enough for me, and I didn't have time for a second opinion. An indictment could drop any time, and I had no faith that RJ could prevent or handle it. I needed a new legal team that could take this case to the DOJ pooh-bahs, and then trial, if necessary. So on the same June afternoon that Tom Vitt and RJ arrived in San Antonio to try to haggle with Bud over his "final offer," I touched down in D.C. to interview their replacements.

I arrived at King & Spalding's 1700 Pennsylvania Avenue office, which is to say, I basically arrived at the White House. If *physical* proximity to power was what I was looking for, then this new firm had it in spades.

Three lawyers were waiting for me in a bleach-white conference room peering across at the balconies of the Eisenhower Executive Office Building. They were Dan Donovan (the Grassley power-broker), Jeff Bucholtz (a Harvard-trained law junkie who'd steered drug company Allergan out of an off-label investigation), and another lawyer who seemingly just had a suit jacket on his hanger and an opening in his schedule. None of the three looked like a trial lawyer, but I hoped together they might be "prevent a trial" lawyers.

I began the meeting with an announcement: "I have something unconventional I want to do." I slid a draft of a hard-hitting press release across the table and told them I wanted to send it out, hold a meeting with our employees to explain DOJ's wrong-headed investigation, and post a recording of that meeting on our company website for the world to see. "If we're going to get indicted," I told them, "we're going to fight, and I need to get our story out before the prosecutors get to tell theirs."

They must have wondered whether they were sitting across the marble-top table from a lunatic. Nobody publicizes that they're about to get indicted, especially not a public company. Anything I said would inflame the prosecutors, color me insolent in the judge's eyes, and could later be introduced against me at trial. Bucholtz's pale, concerned face glanced at the press release quickly and, two paragraphs in, looked back at me. "We'll look it over and give you our comments," which I interpreted as "Yeah, let's not do that." I worried they couldn't – or didn't – understand the biggest risk I saw: that our little public company would be destroyed by the government's allegations before we ever reached the courtroom steps. But that was a worry for another day.

On this day, I was here to find out who these guys were and whether they could help me avoid an indictment altogether. I quickly saw the Capitol Hill veteran Donovan as the facilitator, Bucholtz as the top-drawer wordsmith who would strike fear in the hearts of DOJ brass, and the other guy as someone I'd never see again. Missing from this team was a trial lawyer, in case this team failed and we ended up in court.

"If we do get indicted, who at King & Spalding could represent the company at trial?" I asked. Bucholtz responded for the group. "That would be John Richter, who is out of town on another matter and couldn't be here today. He's the trial lawyer, not us."

As soon as I left the meeting, I Googled the trial lawyer. I found out that Richter had worked his way up to Acting Assistant Attorney General in charge of DOJ's Criminal Division during the George W. Bush years and parachuted into a U.S. Attorney post in the Western District of Oklahoma near the end of that era. He had plenty of trial experience, and his picture showed a chiseled, clean-cut guy who I figured would appeal to a Texas jury.

I connected with Richter by phone the next day. He had already dug into the case and was eager to discuss approaches. He knew how "the Department," as he called it, worked. And without hesitation, his first thought was to "appeal" Bud and Finley's prosecution decision to the people currently holding his old job. I didn't even know you could do that, but Richter rattled off the names of five key individuals who could stop this case and should receive the appeal letter, along with each of their backgrounds and ideological bents. I told him to get started.

In order to avoid another trip to D.C., I recorded my background PowerPoint presentation, the one I'd already given multiple times to new lawyers on the case. I put the recording on a secure part of our website, and then sent a link to Richter so his team could review it. They dove in and came up with something big. Richter had seen something in Vari-Lase's FDA indications statement – the single most important document in the case – that I had somehow missed. And it proved that we had been covered for perforators all along, in a way that even Bud could understand.

I had been reading our indications as consisting of two parts:

> Vari-Lase is indicated for the treatment of varicose veins and varicosities associated with superficial reflux of the great saphenous vein
> **and**
> for the treatment of incompetence and reflux of superficial veins in the lower extremity.

Even based on this reading, I believed that we were covered under both parts. First, varicose perforator veins are "associated with" a diseased great saphenous – owing to the domino effect one failed vein can have on surrounding veins. And second, perforator veins are treated in their "superficial" portion, in other words, above the muscle fascia.

But Richter and his team were reading it to have three parts:

> Vari-Lase is indicated for the treatment of varicose veins
> **and**
> varicosities associated with superficial reflux of the great saphenous vein
> **and**
> for the treatment of incompetence and reflux of superficial veins in the lower extremity.

I was happy to admit that Richter's reading, not mine, was the correct grammatical construction. Because "varicose veins" and "varicosities" are the same thing, reading it as one clause would render the first part of the sentence – "varicose veins and" – meaningless, or at least completely redundant. And since varicose perforator veins are undeniably varicose veins, this Richter-discovered first clause of our indications clearly covered the treatment of perforators. Promoting the Short Kit for perforator treatment wasn't off-label, so it couldn't be a crime.

It was another arrow in our quiver, and this one, like my new legal team, was the sharpest I'd ever had. The guys at King & Spalding were exactly what I needed: aggressive, intelligent, and most important, *advocates* for VSI.

I called Tom Vitt and gave him the news that King & Spalding would be taking over, but that I still wanted Dorsey to play an assisting role, at least in the transition. Tom said that he understood my decision, that he'd break the news to RJ, and that the handoff would be professional. Tom later modified that slightly, calling me back to say that my decision had made RJ a *"pissed off"* professional." He said RJ was upset because he had cleared his calendar for our case, thought he was doing a great job, and had gotten the company the best offer available. That selfish reaction, unsupported by the results, only confirmed my decision that, although RJ may have at one point been *the guy*, he wasn't *my guy*, the one I needed to defend my company.

Our legal team was finally set. *Let's see what you've got, King & Spalding.*

After getting up to speed, Richter told me that in all the off-label investigations he'd seen over the years, never had he seen so much unchecked prosecutorial aggression over something so insignificant.

Richter was confident that it would not stand. Within a month, he said he could accomplish two goals: First, he could get DOJ management to look into Bud and Finley's conduct and provide some adult supervision. Second, and more critically, he said he could get us a settlement offer that would completely take criminal pleas for me and the company off the table. I don't know if it was just my standard period of initial infatuation with new hires, but I was buzzing off second-hand Richter confidence.

His team, composed of attorneys from King & Spalding's mysteriously-titled "Special Matters" group, was deeper than the ones that Dorsey and Mayer Brown had assembled, combined. For the first time, I felt my case was getting the attention it – a special matter – deserved. It wasn't until later that I'd find out how much that feeling was costing me, but for now, I was relieved to know that we were truly preparing for battle and not just going along for an expensive government goose chase.

One of the top-billing lieutenants under Richter's command was a petite man with a bare-knuckle attitude named Mike Pauzé (rhymes with Rosé). Don't forget the é. Pauzé had been pulled in by Richter as the guy with the experience managing fact-intensive cases. And with 250,000 entries in our sales reps' weekly reports to comb through, this was definitely going to be one of those cases. After cutting his teeth as a federal prosecutor in Maryland, Pauzé was selected as a trial attorney for the Enron Task Force in 2000, a veritable all-star team of government lawyers working one of the most complex criminal cases in recent history. Now I needed him to put those skills toward defending the most complex case in my company's now-18-year history.

Richter and Pauzé weren't impressed by Bud's supposed "best offer," and that description wasn't going to stop them from trying to get a better one. But instead of playing dead in hopes the prosecutors would ease up, my new guys' plan was to play like the prosecutors were dead and go to their bosses. And on October 3, 2014, just hours before they did, they broke the news to Finley, in what would become known as "The Call."

"Howard," Pauzé informed me in a post-The-Call call. "Something just happened that's really good for you. Tim Finley just lost it on the phone."

Pauzé explained that when he and Richter called Finley to let him know about the formal appeal letter that was on its way out the door, Finley went ballistic. "We had a deal!" Finley protested, referencing a supposed agreement between him and RJ, under which Finley would go to bat with HHS to prevent the company from being excluded, as long as RJ didn't go over Finley's head to Main Justice. I had never heard of this oddly-specific deal (and Tom Vitt later told me it never happened), but clearly Finley was taking its dissolution poorly. For an inexperienced prosecutor who weeks ago thought he had his weary adversary on the ropes, watching us punch back stronger than ever was evidently meltdown-inducing.

"We would not look positively on sending in the appeal letter," Finley said, according to Pauzé, "so I would think about that." When Pauzé told him they had thought about it, Finley added one (more) final warning. "Send the letter if you want," he said, voice growing tense, "but if you do, it will be a mistake." Like an adult dragging out a kid's prank call, Richter tried to bait Finley into fleshing out his inappropriate threats, but he was cut off. "You've been talking a long time," Finley said, "I have to go."

"And then he slammed down the phone," Pauzé told me, holding back schoolyard giggles. "We're editing the appeal letter now. It's all going in."

$$\_\wedge\!\!\wedge\_$$

The appeal letter went out as planned a few hours later. Addressed to Joyce Branda, second-in-command of DOJ's Criminal Division, it was a brilliant 20-page indictment of the coming indictment. It was a hen's tooth, the rare combination of a document that was 1) written by a lawyer, 2) persuasive, and 3) readable. The reply of our board of directors' resident wordsmith, Paul O'Connell, summarized it perfectly. "I suppose I always knew it would happen; a document so good even I have no edits." We could only hope the Acting Assistant Attorney General agreed.

First, Richter wrote to Ms. Branda, there was no crime.

> **In this case, there is no daylight between the plain language of the indication and the treatment of perforator veins. A reasonable Interpretation of the indication is that it encompasses the treatment of perforator veins.**

But if you choose to go ahead, Richter warned, you will lose on the facts.

> **The evidence does not establish any sort of concerted effort by Company executives to misbrand the product by promoting it for the treatment of perforators. And the vanishingly small contribution of the Short Kit to the bottom line of the Company and the sales representatives' compensation belies any meaningful motive to commit a federal crime.**

And you also will lose on the law.

> **As you know, in 2012, the Second Circuit [in *Caronia*] reversed a misbranding conviction based on so-called off-label promotion, construing the [law] "as not criminalizing the truthful off-label promotion of FDA-approved drugs."**

Should you somehow happen to win, the letter cautioned, it'll only be because your guys played dirty.

The investigatory tactics in this case raise serious questions about the credibility of the investigatory conclusions. Witnesses were threatened with perjury charges and asked to change their testimony to conform to the government's theory. Grand jury subpoenas were used to induce witnesses to agree to private interviews. The method of questioning also has been designed not to elicit the facts, and then shape the theory, but to shape the facts to conform to the theory. As former Department of Justice officials, we appreciate the gravity of raising these issues. We do not do so lightly.

Finally, to drive it all home, Richter recounted Finley's bizarre attempt to stop the appeal in its tracks during that afternoon's phone call, saying that it mirrored the unethical tactics employed in the case.

Richter closed his letter with a request to be heard out in person, and a "cc" line indicating that it had been sent to "William Paulissen, Esq.," which is notably not the name of Walter "Bud" Paulissen. It could have been a simple mistake, but I wasn't ruling out the possibility that Richter was playing some elite-level mind games here.

A week and a half after the letter went out, Richter got his meeting with Joyce Branda, Acting Assistant Attorney General for the United States Department of Justice. This new access-based strategy was going famously, it seemed.

I wanted to go to the meeting at Main Justice. I wanted to pass that inscription on the side of the building reading "To Render Every Man His Due." I wanted to walk through the Great Hall, past that big aluminum Lady Justice, and into the conference room where Bud and Finley would finally become accountable to someone. And I really wanted to see the disgust on Joyce Branda's face when Richter recounted the details of his call with Finley.

But I wasn't invited. Instead, I waited anxiously for the recap call from Richter. It came at 11:59 a.m., less than an hour after the meeting's scheduled start. "Howard, we're out. Do you have time for a call at 2 p.m.?"

Not a good sign. I hadn't known Richter for very long, but long enough to know that his meetings take longer than one hour, especially something big like this. So I knew the meeting didn't end because Richter was done – it ended because the government was done.

Richter confirmed my worst fears – he couldn't shake them. To our surprise, Finley himself had shown up, and he sat there like his bosses had his back, not like he was in detention. Branda didn't seem bothered by hearing that the off-label crime theory her prosecutors were selling her concerned an on-label use. Nor did she bat an eye when Richter awkwardly read through a battery of prosecutorial misconduct allegations an arm's length from the perpetrator. In an effort to meet the government half-way, Richter even dangled the possibility of the company pleading guilty to a misdemeanor as long as no individuals (including me) were included in the plea. But after all that, all Richter got was a vanilla statement from Branda. She would consider what we had to say and get back to us.

I don't know why I expected more, but finally making it to the big boss after four years, only to get her knee-jerk endorsement of what was happening, hurt. We told her that they were trying to ruin me and my company over something that wasn't a crime and she effectively said, "I have to go to another meeting, but I'll think about it." Worse yet, we'd shown all our cards in that meeting to avoid an indictment, and now we looked naïve for doing so. I should've listened to Hefflefinger – this wasn't just about a couple of line prosecutors on a scent they couldn't shake. Somebody in the Department of Justice didn't like me.

The official DOJ response came a week later:

> **Thank you for your offer. While we are pleased that the company is willing to accept responsibility by agreeing to a misdemeanor plea, the government cannot accept as a term that it would not prosecute any VSI employees. Specifically, and most importantly, we cannot accept a resolution of our investigation of Mr. Root's conduct unless Mr. Root also agrees to a misdemeanor plea.**

It was now painfully obvious that there were only two ways forward for me. Confess to a crime that never happened, or get indicted and risk complete personal destruction. If I took the deal, the only thing the government would promise me was no prison time. I'd be fired, banned, fined, and shamed.

Still, I can't say I didn't think about it. But the answer was always "no." That is, *unless* the company made me do it. They couldn't actually *force* me to plead guilty, of course, but if the company took a deal, fired me, and agreed to "cooperate" against its fired CEO, I wouldn't have much of a chance at trial.

How the company responded was the board of directors' decision, not mine. And even though I had a seat, I wasn't allowed to vote on the settlement offer, for obvious reasons. So it was Richter – representing the company, not me – on the November 8 call to talk them through their options.

After giving my perspective to the entire board, I hung up so the independent deliberations could begin. With a queasy feeling in my stomach, I passed the time by imagining how the call was going, hoping for a few things. I hoped Richter told them that we could win this fight. I hoped they remembered how we'd made it through the near-extinction experience with the Duett. And I hoped that when they finally voted, they didn't destroy me to save the company I founded.

John Erb called me back as soon as the meeting concluded. "We unanimously voted … to reject the government's offer." For lots of reasons, he said, but what made it easy for the board was one compliance provision Bud slipped into the settlement offer. Under it, Bud's office alone would determine whether we failed to meet any future obligation in the five-year compliance agreement, and we'd be left with no right to appeal. The board generally watched this matter from a 30,000-foot view, but even from that distance they'd seen enough to know not to trust Bud. So they didn't.

Bud's overreaching saved me, at least for now. I felt good, energized by the unified support of my board. And then, two days later, I got the email from Richter.

I spoke with Bud and told him we could not accept this offer. He stated that he would expect the grand jury to return an indictment on Thursday.

It was Monday.

Step 2

DIAGNOSIS

CHAPTER 10

THE HAM SANDWICH

November 13, 2014

I n 1985, Chief Judge of the New York Court of Appeals Sol Wachtler fed a reporter a delectable sound bite. Arguing that the state's criminal charging system should be overhauled, Judge Wachtler explained that prosecutors have so much sway over grand juries that they could "indict a ham sandwich." The phrase has proven enduring, even if Wachtler, a practicing Jew, later wrote that he wished he'd have gone with "pastrami."

The fact that Wachtler himself was later indicted[6] does not detract from the statement's wisdom. With the underlying dynamics unchanged, the *ham sandwich* remains as true today as it was in 1985. The grand jury process, purportedly designed to protect innocent defendants from public ruin and wrongful prosecution, goes about it in a way that can only be described as a sham.

Prosecutors tell the jury a one-sided story, unconstrained by the rules of evidence, unofficiated by a judge, and unanswered by a defense lawyer. As an unneeded bonus, the grand jury isn't saddled with the weighty duty of finding guilt beyond all reasonable doubt. "That'll happen down the line," the prosecutors tell them. "Right now, all you need to find is 'probable cause for arrest,'" a phrase meaningless to your average juror. Stacking these ingredients atop one another, the result is predictable. Of the 162,000 federal and state grand juries seated in 2010, just 11 declined to return an indictment. Not 11 percent. Eleven.

As a defendant, there's nothing you can do. You're playing a basketball game where the home team is the ref, their rim is lowered and, worst of all,

---

[6]In 1993 Wachtler was indicted for extortion, after he wrote threatening letters to his well-known mistress, a political fundraiser, and mailed her 14-year-old daughter an explicit note affixed with a condom. He pled guilty and was sentenced to 15 months in federal prison.

your team isn't even allowed in the gym. And if, for some reason, the home team doesn't win, it won't be reported (it's secret, remember), and they can schedule another game the next day. No matter how many games they've already played and lost, if the prosecutors win just one, you better believe there will be an all-caps headline trumpeting your devastating defeat.

It is with this as background that on November 13, 2014, a federal grand jury returned indictments against me, my company, and our sales rep, Glen Holden.

It was November 12. I knew the indictments were coming, but there was no time for moping. I had a company to protect. It wasn't going to be easy, but the absurd length of the investigation had given me plenty of time to devise a post-indictment strategy. On my mental chalkboard, I saw three categories of people I'd have to win over in order to keep the company together and with me as its CEO through trial: our shareholders, our board of directors, and our employees.

Of these three groups, the most important to keep happy was our shareholders. That's not because shareholders were the most important contributors to our business; in reality, while they had everything to do with our beginning, they had nothing to do with our future success. Even with the gigantic monthly legal bills we were incurring, the company still was comfortably profitable with over $40 million in the bank and no debt. We wouldn't need to raise money and I didn't need to sell any of my holdings, so a low stock price wouldn't affect anything we did, at least not directly.

But, indirectly, a falling stock price would send an unmistakable signal to the other two categories of important people – our employees and board – that we were facing existential danger. The board and employees' response could trigger a cascade into collapse, gradually at first, and then suddenly.

Here's how I pictured it happening. If our shareholders lost confidence in our defense strategy, they'd sell off stock and our share price would drop. Our employees would see our falling stock price, see the value of their stock grants decline, and worry that the company would go out of business. Many would leave. At the same time, the publicity around our indictment would make it difficult to re-fill the ranks with new employees. Investors who held onto their stock would start to pressure the board to do something to bump the stock price back up, and lawsuits would be filed as a cudgel for doing so. If the board blinked and threw me out to appease the shareholders, more employees would get distracted or leave, our performance would suffer, sales would decline, more shareholders would sell, and the downward spiral would continue. Repeat to zero.

On the flip side, if our stock price avoided freefall, it would be viewed as a clear sign that the indictment was a hurdle that we'd eventually clear. On November 12, 2014, our stock hit an all-time high of $30.49 – the market apparently unmoved by our warnings of a potential indictment – way up from the year's low of $19. We didn't need the stock price to hold its all-time high; no, all I needed and could reasonably hope for was for it to stay above $25. If our stock stabilized there, I was sure I could keep our shareholders from revolting. So that was my hope – keep the stock north of $25 and the shareholders happy, and the board of directors and employees would come along for the ride to trial.

But how could we keep the stock price from falling after the government branded us a criminal enterprise? I came up with a two-step fortification plan. The first step was substantive – a stock repurchase program. In the same press release announcing the indictment, we would announce that the company planned to buy back up to $20 million of our stock. This would be the company betting on itself, saying "If you want to sell, we're here to buy, because we think the price is too low." A repurchase program would also help cut down on short-selling, as betting for a stock to drop off a cliff becomes less attractive if there's a net there waiting to catch it. But the truly beautiful thing about the stock repurchase announcement is that you don't actually have to buy any shares unless the stock price falls below the secret "price net" you set. We only wound up repurchasing $2.6 million of stock out of the "up to $20 million" we authorized, in part because the show of strength pushed our stock price back above our goal of $25.

The second step was explaining to the whole world why we were innocent. Our press release announcing the indictment was our best chance to tell that story and show confidence in our defense. The typical company's press release in this situation consists of bland comments that the company denies the allegations but can't comment on pending litigation. That wouldn't get the job done.

We needed to answer the only question that mattered: Why would federal prosecutors bring criminal charges if we hadn't done anything wrong? Thankfully, the answer to that question was already laid out in Richter's appeal letter to Main Justice. I sprinkled excerpts throughout the press release I'd brought to that first meeting at King & Spalding (and had since revised dozens of times). With a hard-hitting denial and specifics to back it up, I was convinced I had what I needed to buoy investor confidence.

And then, two nights before I planned to issue the press release, the lawyers said I couldn't do it. "That's not how it's done," Richter told me in more words, leaning on external excuses to get his message across. *It'll piss off the judge! The DOJ bosses won't like it! There's a special local rule we just found that prohibits you from doing it!* In its place, Richter proposed a single-paragraph release that began with "The indictment filed today is the fruit of an unfair investigation." *Right, that'll do the trick.*

I emerged from my home office to tell my wife, Beth, of Richter's veto. She didn't like it. "You said you weren't going to let them roll over you. Now you're going to be in the same position as everyone else who's charged with a crime – everyone will think you're guilty."

She was right. These were false charges, and I had to see if I could push back against Richter's reluctance to take our defense to the court of public opinion. I asked him to email me the special local rule so I could review it. I read it, but something didn't seem right. I called my personal lawyer, Lundquist, to confirm. "Howard, that's the same rule as in every federal district," Lundquist said. "And it only prevents the lawyers from issuing pretrial publicity. It doesn't even apply to you."

I was pissed. I knew I'd have to fight distortions from the government lawyers; I just didn't expect to have the same fight with my own lawyers.

I told Richter we were going back to my draft, but that I'd make some of the revisions he insisted on. He controlled King & Spalding's appeal letter, so I took those quotes out. I knocked down my descriptions of Bud and Finley's misconduct to the bare minimum I thought I'd need to get my point across.

But he still wasn't comfortable with my final draft, and he sent me a long email ending, "I, therefore, cannot authorize you to issue the press release." *Okay, Richter – you're covered.* But I didn't need a lawyer to authorize a press release.

The next morning, our PR consultant, Jon Austin, scheduled a meeting for me and Lundquist with Joe Carlson, the Minneapolis Star Tribune newspaper reporter on the medical device beat. The idea was to sit down with him before the indictment to arm him with the facts he could use to prepare a balanced story. According to LinkedIn, Joe Carlson is the only reporter ever to win NIHCM's Journalism Award for best trade story three times, whatever that is. While I didn't know him and he didn't know me, with his trade press history, I figured he'd be receptive to the company's side and attuned to the nuances of the case.

I regretted showing up to the interview as soon as I got there and realized I didn't have anything to talk about. With all the facts I'd stripped out of the press release, and without being able to show the reporter King & Spalding's appeal letter, I was left with a big bag of nothing. All I could offer up was vague promises that the government's abuses would come to light in future court filings – not the sort of thing Joe Carlson could base an award-winning story around. Worse yet, he was throwing me irrelevant questions like, "Did the whistleblower quit or was he fired?" Clearly he was skeptical of our innocence, and now I'd given him an extra day to polish his take on the coming indictment. I wasn't looking forward to the paper's Friday edition.

—◁/\◁—

On Thursday afternoon, I got indicted. So did the company. And so did our sales rep, Glen Holden.

You would think that federal agents would show up at your door and take you away when you are charged with a felony, but I learned that's not always how it happens. Your lawyer can get a copy of the indictment and bring you in, or DOJ's PR department can publicly shame you with a flaming press release at the same time you're reading the indictment they just dropped. I got the flame.

VASCULAR SOLUTIONS AND ITS CEO CHARGED WITH SELLING UNAPPROVED MEDICAL DEVICES AND CONSPIRING TO DEFRAUD THE UNITED STATES

"These charges involve a deceptive sales campaign led by the CEO of a public company," said [Acting Assistant Attorney General Joyce] Branda. "We will take action to hold corporations and their leaders responsible when they violate laws intended to protect public health."

Root is charged with leading the illegal sales campaign, which lasted from 2007 until 2014, and conspiring with others to hide it from the FDA. With Root's approval, the sales continued even after the company [failed to obtain FDA clearance to change their indication and] sponsored an unsuccessful clinical trial that showed that the Vari-Lase system was less safe and effective than a competing device that the FDA had cleared for perforator vein treatment. The sales continued even after a whistleblower complained to Root in 2009 and the government told the company about its investigation in 2011.

The indictment also charges VSI and Root with deceiving the FDA. In late 2007, Root decided to launch a special "Short Kit" designed for perforator vein treatment, despite the lack of FDA marketing authorization, by claiming that the product was intended for "short vein segments" or "short veins." At the same time, internal company documents approved by Root taught the sales force that these terms included perforator veins and urged salespeople to suggest to health care providers that Vari-Lase devices could be used to treat perforator veins.

Two members of the sales force are alleged to have misled investigators; in addition, the indictment charges that one member falsely denied his conduct and another tried to scapegoat a low-level salesman.

An indictment is merely an allegation, and every defendant is presumed innocent until proven guilty beyond a reasonable doubt.

It was "merely an allegation" after paragraphs and paragraphs of what looked like a public conviction. I wondered how Acting Assistant Attorney General Branda got around that "special local rule" in San Antonio prohibiting lawyer pretrial publicity …

Ten minutes *after* the indictment was filed, Bud emailed Richter to give him a "heads-up" on the indictment, which isn't how a "heads-up" works. I didn't have much time to scan the indictment before I needed to blast out our own press release, so after one quick read-through, I hit send.

STATEMENT OF VASCULAR SOLUTIONS ON GRAND JURY INDICTMENT

The allegations against us are false and we will contest them vigorously. This indictment is the profoundly flawed product of government attorneys who have conducted a misguided and abusive investigation. Without the company being able to present any information to the grand jury, today's action is not surprising. It is, however, fundamentally wrong and profoundly unjust.

We vehemently disagree with both allegations: we did not engage in any illegal off-label promotion of the Short Kit, nor did we engage in any false or misleading conduct.

The discrepancy between the insignificance of our Short Kit product and the severity of the government's actions in this matter is simply astonishing. The reason for that discrepancy will become readily apparent when the government attorneys' stated motives and abusive conduct in this investigation are disclosed in our upcoming court filings.

We will defend our company and our employees against these improper and false allegations through trial where we are confident of prevailing. We have the resources to vigorously contest the allegations and an excellent legal team in place.

While proceeding with our legal defense, we plan to make no change to our business operations or personnel as a result of this matter.

In other words, "We're fighting, we're going to win, and I'm not stepping down."

After spending the afternoon fielding shareholder calls and a frenzy of emails, I got home and decided I should take a closer look at these federal criminal charges. The government's press release told a story they hoped to prove at trial, but the indictment – the actual document, not the event – was the road map they'd need to get there. Nine charges for me, nine for the company – we were once again joined at the hip.

Misbranding – Four Counts

The indictment said we sent four shipments of Vari-Lase products to a clinic in Austin, Texas, that were "misbranded." That sounded like somebody slapped the wrong label on our products. But DOJ's press release was all about us selling devices "without FDA approval" or "off-label." That didn't sound like the same crime. So what was going on here?

Here are the linguistic gymnastics it takes to get from "off-label" to "misbranded." The indictment alleged that a few of our sales reps talked with doctors about using our Vari-Lase Short Kit to treat perforator veins. That discussion, it alleged, *transformed* the intended use of the product to treating perforator veins. And because the indictment claimed we didn't have FDA clearance for treating perforator veins, sales based on that discussion were "misbranded" for the allegedly off-label use.

Adulteration – Four Counts

As confusing as misbranding is, adulteration is worse. Traditionally, adulteration is about selling a medical device that's either not manufactured in a sanitary environment or is sold without ever getting FDA approval. But Vari-Lase was always made in our cleanroom, and we had 12 separate FDA clearances allowing us to sell it in the U.S. So what was happening here? I had no idea. In our research, we couldn't find a single instance of "off-label" adulteration being advanced as a legal theory, and eventually the prosecutors must have figured this out because (spoiler alert) they dropped their four adulteration charges before trial. You can forget about adulteration now.

Conspiracy – One Count

Here's the big one. The felony. It's just a single count, but a closer look revealed it as having three parts: 1) a conspiracy to commit misbranding, 2) a conspiracy to commit adulteration (also later dropped), and 3) a conspiracy to defraud the U.S. and its agencies by concealing their sale of ... *yes, this is a mouthful* … medical devices for unapproved use on perforator veins in order to impair and defeat … *yep, still going* … the lawful function of the FDA and other law enforcement agencies. If they proved any of those three prongs, they'd get their deathblow felony conviction.

The first two prongs were obvious, but it wasn't clear what they were going for on the third one. Was this the "code word" theory, the alleged employee perjury, or some hybrid allegation of Medicare fraud? Neither I nor our lawyers could make sense of it, meaning we'd have to wait for pre-trial motions, or trial itself, to smoke out the prosecutors' catch-all conspiracy.

The day after the indictment, I shot out of bed at 6 a.m. to grab the newspaper from the driveway. On a slow walk back into the house, I read the article in the Star Tribune. It was a purée of clunky explanations, uninformed quotes, and alarmist allegations ripped from the indictment. The reporter, Joe Carlson, only used one quote from me, a statement about how few the sales of the Short Kit were, and put it at the end of the article. There was nothing about the prosecutors' misconduct.

I walked into the bedroom, where Beth had turned on the TV. "I've got some good news and bad news," I said.

"Good news," she requested – it'd been a while since we'd gotten any of that.

"They didn't use that picture of me from when I was fat – the one they always use." She looked like she was expecting something better.

"The bad news," I continued, "is that it's on the front page."

Beth dismissed this as well. "So what?" she said. "We always knew it would be on the front page of the business section."

"No," I said as I showed her the paper, "The front page of the whole paper. It's the lead."

By the time I got to the office that morning, everyone had already had their coffee and read about how the federal government was about to crush our company. Despite this, the employees seemed to be taking the news pretty well, or at least hiding it well from me. One V.P., Susan Christian, told me she sat her teenage son down that morning and showed him the paper in case he'd hear about it from his friends at school. He reportedly shrugged it off and said, "Mom. Nobody reads the paper."

Still, I thought I should call a meeting to discuss the indictment with the employees, in case a few of them were more worried than Susan's 16-year-old son. Our 400 home-office employees crowded into our lunch room that afternoon for a 15-minute rundown of an investigation that had lasted four years. I told them that we'd done nothing wrong and that we had $40 million in the bank to pay top-flight lawyers to fight this thing. We had survived the worst day – our indictment, and now we'd get the chance to go after the prosecutors and their misconduct. Everyone could help, I told them, by continuing to do their jobs. I'd be in my office every day doing mine.

Our stock price closed at $23.74 that day, a $117 million haircut off the company's value the day before. It wasn't good, but it wasn't a complete collapse, and the volume wasn't breaking the levees. Our stock repurchase plan had already kicked in to help push us back above $25, and if we could keep it there, I knew we'd be in good shape.

The other part of my plan, the press release, also worked. After seeing it, our most experienced stock analyst, Thom Gunderson at Piper Jaffray, wrote in a note to investors: "We believe that Vascular Solutions will weather this tempest in a teapot, and stock valuation will be unaffected in the long term." When I called Thom to thank him, he congratulated me on the strong words in the press release. Knowing me well, though, he added, "I'd like to see the first draft."

A decade ago, there was no way a stock analyst would have come to our defense. But in the intervening period, DOJ had cried wolf so many times on American corporations that government shakedowns were viewed as the norm. To investors, DOJ run-ins were just part of the business cycle. And this time, for once, a company and its CEO were willing to fight back.

CHAPTER 11

AN IMPROBABLE CEO

I wasn't supposed to be a CEO. In fact, if you told me in high school that I'd start a medical device company and invent its top-selling cardiology product that made "impossible cases possible," I'd have told you I was more likely to play in the NFL ... I don't know, as a kicker or something. And I couldn't kick.

I was supposed to be a lawyer. Growing up in the '60s, there weren't a lot of channels on TV. But Perry Mason was the coolest guy on any channel. His calm. The way each week he outsmarted someone who was trying to outsmart him. He even described himself in a cool way.

You'll find that I'm a lawyer who has specialized in trial work. I'm a specialist on getting people out of trouble. If you look me up through some family lawyer or some corporation lawyer, he'll probably tell you that I'm a shyster. If you look me up through some chap in the District Attorney's office, he'll tell you that I'm a dangerous antagonist, but he doesn't know very much about me.

I wanted to be like him – a trial lawyer. And in the summer after my junior year at St. Anthony Village High School, after my best friend Mike Sage told me that his debate partner quit the team, I signed up for a crash course in stand-up advocacy. As a senior rookie, I started off taking weekly beat-downs from experienced opponents, but by the end of the year I'd figured it out, and we even qualified for the state debate tournament. With that taste of oratorical success, I locked in my three-step life plan:

1. Get through college.

2. Dominate law school.

3. Be Perry Mason.

Growing up in a middle class suburb as the fourth child in five years meant I'd be on my own when it came to paying for college. That was fine – I sure wasn't going to complain to my "no drama mamma" or my father, who was raised during the Great Depression and lost his own father at the age of 12. By 15, he was forced to move to a neighboring farm and work before *and* after school to help out back home. So at 17, surely I could sacrifice a little prestige and pick an affordable college to keep costs to what I could afford.

That somewhere wound up being the University of Minnesota, the same somewhere my three older siblings (and eventually my younger, caboose sister) had chosen. I decided to major in economics, figuring that it would be easy enough to pull the grades I'd need to get into law school, and sciencey enough to exempt me from the foreign language classes I hated. My college advisor – economics professor Ed Coen, father of the film-legend Coen brothers – saw my law school path as a trivial waste and advised me to get a doctorate in economics instead. But I wasn't sold on being a professor (and apparently neither were his sons).

I quickly found that being a Golden Gopher undergrad wasn't as lustrous as I'd hoped. The classes were stale and the professors seemed more interested in their research than their students. College debate became my outlet, passion, and identity. With each rep of preparation, logic, and public speaking, I felt like I was inching closer to Perry-Mason-hood. I penciled in my junior year as the one where I'd make my mark on the national debate scene, and I spent two weeks during the summer of 1981 sharpening my skills at a monk-like Arizona debate camp.

I arrived back on campus that August to find the rug pulled out from under me. My debate coach had quit and our budget had been slashed. Air travel was now out, meaning my dreams of national competition were extinguished. Or were they?

In Arizona, I'd met Norm Nichols, a college debate coach with flush program coffers (by debate standards) and a desire to compete nationally, but no debaters. He proposed I join him at San Joaquin Delta Community College in Stockton, California. It seemed preposterous at first, but when I looked into it, I discovered that I could take enough Gen-Ed classes during my junior year to transfer back to the University of Minnesota for my senior year and still graduate in four.

So I packed my car and drove across the Rockies to balmy Stockton, California. There I scooped up a debate partner – Gordon Hart, a bright but awkward high school senior who had enrolled in a community college math class. Together, we traveled the country, competing with the big schools at Northwestern, West Point, and UCLA. We even realized my dream of qualifying for nationals – and then proceeded to get torched.

When I returned to the Great North for my senior year, the debate budget had been restored (at least partially) and a new coach had been hired, so I rejoined my former partner and we won the region and finished with a bang – taking ninth place at nationals. But by then, I was less focused on debate and more focused on winning the law school admissions game.

The time-pressured logic of debate, it turned out, had trained me well for conquering law school's notorious admissions test. My scores were good enough to get me accepted to Minnesota and Columbia, but apparently not enough to overcome the whole "junior at a junior college" issue, leading to rejections from Harvard and Yale. Although I was anxious to leave Minnesota, and Columbia had the national cache, I also had an empty bank account and a local girlfriend. So, University of Minnesota it was (again).

With no more debate distraction, I aced my first-year law school classes, setting me up for a second-year summer internship (read: three-month party) at one of the top firms in the nation – Cahill Gordon & Reindel in New York City. At $1,000 a week, it paid a little better than my previous summer's $4 an hour gig at Burger King.

The summer of 1984 in Manhattan was an eye-opening experience: a trip to Belmont Park with an envelope of cash to bet horses, cocktail hours atop the World Trade Center, and softball games where our 300-lawyer office mysteriously and frequently failed to field a full lineup. I soon found out why. The associates were keeping their heads down and clocks running, grinding out hours long after I left at six for the day's social safari.

I was drawn to Cahill for its legendary litigation practice, but I was finding that the prospects for the lawyers working under superstar Floyd Abrams weren't so bright. One disheartened partner, who'd been at Cahill for a decade and a cocktail hour for a little too long, complained about having yet to see a courtroom himself. Despite his assumed seniority, he still spent his days making prep binders for his grey-haired elders. Not Perry-Mason-like at all, I thought. If I wanted my day in court, I'd have to go elsewhere.

Then I rotated into Cahill's corporate finance section and realized that maybe I didn't need my day in court. In the '80s, corporate finance was the Wild West, Cahill was Main Street, and my third-year associate officemate Vinnie was a gunslinger. Throughout the summer, I'd walk in to find him closing deals over the phone for one of the firm's biggest clients, with his feet kicked up on the desk and no partner on the line to babysit. That client, it turned out, was Drexel Burnham Lambert, operating under the now-disgraced junk-bond maven Michael Milken. The excitement, pace, and independence of corporate finance ended my dream of being Perry Mason right there, and my fortuitously-chosen economics degree meant I could handle the spreadsheet work.

As glamorous as Cahill's Wall Street offices were, they were in New York City, and I preferred air-conditioned cars to sweaty subways. Any Minnesotan will tell you that the 10,000 lakes have a way of luring back those who stray from their shores, and I knew I wanted to return almost as soon as I left. I chose Dorsey, the biggest law firm in town, after a partner there gave me a personal pitch and promised me a spot in the corporate finance department. With that, and a "pass" on the bar exam, I was a real lawyer.

–⅃⅂⅃–

I lived a good life in the late '80s at Dorsey. The deals were exciting, I was paid well, and I liked the fun group of associates we had – even if being a Reaganite put me in the minority in a law firm that listed Walter Mondale on its letterhead. Most of the associates would be life-long lawyers, but some, like my classmate Amy Klobuchar, would end up as restrained politicians on Capitol Hill, while others were more suited to be unrestrained business leaders. Here's proof from my 1986 party:

Future Sen. Amy Klobuchar   **Future CEO Howard Root**

I would eventually settle down, but not quite yet. I bought an 80-year-old house on Lake Minnetonka and hosted an annual blowout party that drew progressively larger crowds each year. Beth, my charmingly-feisty future wife, even got dragged to one of these summer functions, although I didn't get a chance to meet her because the power line came down mid-party and I was too busy rigging the house with candles. Good first impression. It wasn't until a couple of years later that I'd be introduced to her in the light of day, and today we live on the same Lake Minnetonka lot she showed up at for the "surprise candlelight" party – except gone is the old tinderbox, replaced by a house with a more dependable power supply.

At Dorsey, I was assigned to handle public offerings and cut my teeth on Tonka Corporation – of yellow toy truck fame. At $25 million, it was a weighty public offering by '80s standards, and my job was to look after its most menial tasks. Most crucially, I was to watch the prospectus proofs come off the printer and make sure that there was no period after the "Inc" in "Solomon Brothers Inc" in order to match the firm's legal name. Our eager-to-please proofreader routinely insisted otherwise, and I watched vigilantly to make sure she wasn't "helping" too much, lest I get branded with the scarlet phrase for lawyers – "lacks attention to detail."

Somehow, the Tonka deal wasn't the only time I had to police the use of periods after the letter "C" during my Big Law career. A senior partner at Dorsey had the name of Reese C Johnson. His middle name was "C" – that's it, so there was no period. And I proudly made sure everyone got it right in the closing documents.

I was noticing a connecting thread between the corner offices of the partners I worked for. They were mostly overworked, largely unhappy, and always preoccupied with immaterial nonsense. That wasn't the future I wanted. But I needed a way out before my paycheck turned to golden handcuffs, so I took some advice I heard on every plane flight – "Look around. Your closest exit may be behind you."

A few months into my fifth year at Dorsey, my secretary, Kristi Niday, handed me one of those little pink phone message slips (this, kids, is how it worked before voicemail and email). It was from Manny Villifaña – the Elon Musk of the Minnesota medical device community at the time. He wasn't even 50, but Manny had already started three successful medical device companies, including industry whales Cardiac Pacemakers and St. Jude Medical.[7] A month earlier, I'd worked on the initial public offering for his new venture, Helix BioCore, and for some reason, Kristi said, Manny now wanted to have lunch with me.

I could only assume my law firm was getting fired. The IPO was done, both partners working on the account had left the firm, and one had shown up inebriated to the closing party at Manny's house – which Manny called "The Bronx" – having apparently pre-gamed, for some reason. I was the only one left, and it now looked like I'd be stuck holding the bag. Running that bad news up the flagpole wasn't going to be good for my career at Dorsey, and because of Manny's visibility, the word of him dumping us would spread around town quickly.

"Howard, I've done over 20 public offerings in my career," Manny said after we'd ordered, "and this was the smoothest one I have ever done, thanks to you." Here it comes, I thought. Manny's next word will be "but," and then he'll add, "I'm firing your law firm." But the *but* never came.

---

[7] Later in his career, Manny became the king of failed medical ventures when his last two endeavors, CABG Medical and Kips Bay Medical, were shut down and liquidated in succession. But, having the Midas touch, Manny still managed to pocket $6 million in the liquidation of CABG Medical alone.

Manny continued, "It's early, and I've got big plans for Helix. I'm going to develop a new mechanical heart valve to compete with St. Jude Medical." Interesting, but I wasn't really sure why he was telling me this. "And I want to make a hostile takeover bid for Molecular Genetics." More stuff out of left field. That sounded like fun, but Molecular Genetics was a client, so I knew I couldn't help with that one. Where was this heading?

"I want you to consider taking a year's leave of absence from Dorsey to work at Helix." Oh, that's why I was here. "If this company is half as success-ful as St. Jude Medical, you'll be a millionaire. Every officer in every one of my companies has made at least a million dollars."

That sounded pretty good to me. No more proofing punctuation, no more tracking billable hours in six-minute increments, and a chance to do exciting work alongside a real-life entrepreneur. On top of all that, I'd be a millionaire. I had already begun plotting how to ask my friend and client Greg Herrick for a job at his personal computer company Zeos International, but Manny asked first. And as I'd heard Manny say many times already (and would plenty more), "Sometimes you get kissed, and sometimes you get slapped. But you have to ask."

—∿—

So I asked, and Dorsey agreed to the one-year sabbatical to keep Manny happy. All of a sudden I was general counsel of a publicly-traded company, where I quickly realized I had stepped into a … hot mess. Within six months of going public as a mammalian cell biotech business, Manny decided to entirely reinvent the company to focus on the mechanical heart valve he'd told me about over lunch. That meant firing a lot of people, including the director of human resources, who was in charge of firing people. And that left the executioner duties to me, the general counsel, along with a backlog of 30 heads for the chopping block.

I spaced them out in 15-minute intervals, just enough time to present the termination letter, go over the exit instructions, and explain their COBRA benefits. Each time I called back to the lab to summon the next employee to my office, I heard background groans of "Normmmmm," a reference to "The Executive's Executioner" episode of *Cheers* where Norm is hired solely to fire a bunch of employees.

Manny's hostile takeover scheme fizzled out, in part because the target company's stock price started to rise. So with the mechanical heart valve development project left as our only business, Manny decided to shake things up with a name change. We now became ATS Medical, standing for Advancing the Standard (of heart valves), and my stock options grew to be worth $50,000. I definitely wasn't the millionaire Manny predicted I'd become, but it was enough that I decided to stay on permanently with Helix-now-ATS. Goodbye, law firm life.

Over the next four years at ATS, my legal duties slowed to a crawl. FDA approval for the mechanical heart valve was stalled, so to keep busy, I volunteered for (more) non-legal activities. I didn't fully know it at the time, but ATS was my medical device dojo. I managed purchasing and shipping and even printed new business cards with "Howard Root, Materials Manager" on them so as not to scare off vendors with the whole lawyer thing. I wiggled my way into working on the European sales brochure, leveraging that into traveling with Manny to a German medical meeting and on sales calls to heart surgeons in France.

Those experiences made it clear that I needed to learn more about the medical side of the business. So when I met a cardiovascular nurse from a local hospital at a bar one night (pre-Beth), I asked her if I could go to her place and … watch an open heart surgery. Her doctor agreed, and I scrubbed in, tried not to pass out, and watched a six-hour procedure to replace three heart valves in one patient. Dr. Demetre Nicoloff was an absolute magician, fascinating me as he narrated every cut and stitch. As I walked out of the hospital, stock offerings now seemed as dry as the paper they were printed on – I was hooked on medical devices.

And then, in 1995, Manny fired me. "Howard, we just don't have enough legal work to keep you on payroll," he said. "So we're going to terminate your employment effective three months from now and give you three-months' severance. After we finish this meeting, I'll ask you to pack up your belongings and leave the company."

Stunned, I immediately packed up my stuff, got in my car, and drove to Graceland. I don't know, it just seemed like a good thing to do. When I got back home, I sat down for a personality career assessment, something Manny offered to pay for. The analyst concluded that I should stay in a supportive role as a general counsel or go back to an established law firm, and – pointedly – that I should not try to start my own business.

I took the advice and interviewed for an associate general counsel position at Deluxe, a check-printing company. But I crashed and burned when I overstepped my place in the interview, asking my prospective boss why he didn't embed lawyers in each business unit in order to be more proactive than reactive. "That's not how we do it here," he bristled, and the interview functionally ended.

With my sabbatical long expired, Dorsey was out as an option, and there wasn't any other local law firm I could think of that would accommodate my now-hardened independent streak. So I ignored the personality test and started my first business.

The plan was to be a one-man law firm that provided on-site legal services to companies that were too small to afford a full-time general counsel. To pick up clients, I'd drastically undercut the inflated rates of brick-and-mortar law firms. It worked, kind of. The first client I landed was a small diabetes management company called Chronimed, whose CFO, Norm Cocke, loudly and proudly pronounced his last name with a silent "e." I pronounce my last name to rhyme with "foot" and not "boot," so I'm all for letting people choose what they're called – but this was embarrassing on a professional level.

Then I got a good lead on where to find another client. While I was doubling as the HR guy at Helix-ATS, I interviewed a well-coiffed (yes, I was jealous), wide-smiled guy named Mike Nagel for a marketing position. Manny didn't hire Nagel because he looked too young, but I still kept in touch with him. Nagel called me up and said his former boss had started a business incubator and needed someone to do its legal work.

Enter Wendell King, a 50-year-old man who grooved to The Doors and summered at "run naked through the woods" festivals. Wendell used to give out audio cassettes of his original poetry, which one of his secretaries made the mistake of popping into her tape deck while driving her daughter to school. A few minutes in, she desperately punched the eject button to stop what she described as "CEO-narrated soft porn."

The concept of Wendell's incubator was to take an idea, create a business plan, hire a management team, pitch the financing, and run the business until it was big enough to run itself. Which was a good idea, if Wendell or his team knew how to do any of that. Instead, he had a finance guy who couldn't do accounting, a former check-printing executive who knew nothing about start-ups, and a warehouse office across the street from a business called "House of Balls."[8] They couldn't pay me any money for my legal services, but the free office space and theoretical equity was enough for me to join their rag-tag enterprise in late 1995.

The first incubatee Wendell wanted me to work with was RAVE Sports. The plan was to combine a few one-off sporting goods companies (think water trampolines and floating, electric-powered lounge chairs) and merge them into something that could scale.

I put together the offering documents, and we raised $1 million to get RAVE Sports off the ground. Wendell was looking for someone to run this new lake-toy conglomerate and even hinted that it could be me, but thankfully I didn't volunteer. Wendell found another check-printing guy to do it, and after years of puttering along at two miles an hour, the company folded, losing all the investors' money and my sweat-equity in the process.

$$\text{---}\mathord{\wedge}\mathord{\vee}\mathord{\wedge}\text{---}$$

My CEO sights were set elsewhere. I knew I could pull together a start-up medical device company, and Wendell's incubator provided the office and letterhead to do it from. Now I just needed a medical device.

Once again, Mike Nagel played matchmaker. He led me to Dr. Gary Gershony, a cardiologist in Sacramento with a solution for closing the entry puncture doctors make in the femoral artery when implanting a coronary stent. Dr. Gershony's idea was pretty simple, economical and, according to

---

[8] House of Balls, from what I learned by peering through the windows, was a gallery of large and small balls the owner had turned into decorative art. Down the street were different sets of balls in a building with no windows – the Deja Vu exotic dance club. It was a mixed-use area, to say the least.

the multiple animal studies that he had already performed in his lab at University of California, Davis, very effective.

Dr. Gershony agreed to co-found the business with me under one condition – sorry, I meant six conditions.

Dr. Gershony's Conditions

1. Raise at least $750,000 from investors
2. Pay Dr. Gershony $150,000 for his idea
3. Pay $40,000 to a company that did prior development work for Dr. Gershony
4. Pay Dr. Gershony $50,000 a year to consult while he still continues working full-time as a cardiologist in Sacramento
5. Pay Howard $75,000 a year as full-time CEO
6. Give Dr. Gershony 800,000 shares of founders' stock and Howard 262,500 shares

It was a windfall for Dr. Gershony, but nothing that would scare off investors. And at the end of the day, this was my best shot at running a medical device company. Manny wasn't going to give me a chance after firing me, and my thin resume meant getting hired as the CEO of an established medical device company was not an option. I had to create my opportunity, and this was it. We signed the term sheet, and Dr. Gershony gave the company a name – Vascular Solutions. It seemed a bit presumptuous to add the "s" at the end of "Solution," given that we only had a single idea for a single product, but now 20 years and 100 medical devices later, the name fits perfectly.

My first task: find the money. Three-quarters of a million dollars, in fact, just to get started. I put in $262.50 for my founders' shares and was willing to throw in another $15,000 to buy more stock, but what was the point? My parents kicked in $15,000 and my local stock broker friend Joe Buska forked over $75,000. Even combined and doubled, it was hardly a dent. If this was going to work, I'd need the local investment bank I'd worked with at Dorsey to come through and back me in my new role as CEO.

But Paul Kuehn – my heavy-hitting connection at the investment bank Miller, Johnson & Kuehn – was ducking my calls. It turned out he thought I was calling about "that stupid water toy company" that I had helped put together for Wendell. But once our mutual friend (and later VSI board member) Dick Nigon cleared up that misunderstanding, I had Paul's ear.

"Are you the CEO for this company?" Paul asked, skeptically.

"Yes," I told him in the most confident tone I could muster.

"Okay. Well the deal you cut with the doctor is way more generous than I would ever do, but that just cuts your share."[9]

After nailing a pitch I'd rehearsed compulsively in the days leading up to the meeting, Paul and his partner Dave Johnson agreed to push their wealthy customers to invest in my speculative company. But, Paul added, "You have to get rid of Wendell King from the board. We can't raise money for the company if his name is anywhere in the document." I didn't like having to part ways with the free spirit Wendell before we'd even started, but since that was what it would take to get this off the ground, even Wendell agreed it was the right thing to do.

Four weeks after I signed the term sheet with Dr. Gershony – January 27, 1997 – Vascular Solutions closed on our first $1.5 million financing (twice what we needed), and I called our first Monday morning operations meeting.

Improbably, I was now a CEO.

(clockwise from left) Me, Charmaine Sutton, Carol DeSain, Dr. Gary Gershony, Meryl Codner, Tim Deraney, Wendell King, Mike Nagel

---

[9]Dr. Gershony later sold all his founders' stock at between $1 and $2 per share, a decision he later told me was "the worst decision [he] ever made," since our stock rose to over $50 in 2016.

CHAPTER 12

RUN

December 2014

Q: Do you have a job?

A: Yes, CEO of Vascular Solutions.

Q: How much do you make?

A: My base salary is around $500,000, plus a bonus that last year was around $125,000.

Q: What is your net worth?

A: Around $20 million.

Q: Any mortgage?

A: No.

Q: Do you own any guns?

I had to think about that one. I was sitting in a glorified closet in San Antonio being interviewed by my "probation officer in advance," Craig Pair. Lundquist was sitting next to me, and his associate was standing by the door to conserve space. Pair explained to me, from behind his 1970s-issued government desk, that he wasn't a member of the prosecution team. His job was only to process me into the system. "If you are guilty, I hope you get a just sentence," he said. "And if you're not guilty, I hope you beat the charges." I liked that.

While the prosecutors decided that they didn't need to send someone to my home to arrest me, criminal procedure still required that there be a formal court appearance to kick off the proceedings. That's what's known as an arraignment, something I had learned about way back in law school and never thought I'd use professionally, much less personally.

So on December 9, almost a month after the indictment hit, I flew down to San Antonio for my first appearance in court. Before the arraignment, though, Pair needed to interview me so he could advise the judge whether I'd be safe to release back into the general population pending trial. Hence, the gun question.

The reason I had to think before answering was because a few years ago I had a woodpecker problem. They loved to bore into the deteriorating wood siding of my 80-year-old house. So I decided to protect my homestead. I bought a gun. A pellet gun. I doubt I actually hit anything, and it was really just to scare the woodpeckers, but now I was worried I'd have to disclose it as a weapon. Did something that looked like an assault rifle, had a scope, but was only spring-powered and shot pellets, not bullets, count as a gun? In Texas? I figured I better disclose it anyway.

ME: No … I don't have any guns. Unless you count BB guns as a gun.

Pair peered at me like I was a sissy and continued running down his checklist.

PAIR: Have you ever taken any illegal drugs?

ME: I smoked marijuana once or twice in college, but that's it.

Again, Pair … not real impressed by my criminal bona fides.

PAIR: Do you have any children?

ME: No, it's just me and my wife, Beth.

PAIR: Where's your family?

ME: I have a father in St. Paul, a brother in L.A. and a sister in D.C., and a brother and a sister in the Twin Cities.

PAIR: Are you close?

ME: Yes.

That's what I said, but I still don't know if it was the right answer. I don't see my siblings that often, but we don't fight. Is that close or is that distant? The "yes," I thought, would at least move this inquisition along.

I was right. Pair put his pen down, scrunched his face, and looked right at me. "You are one of the few people I've met here who could leave the country and live happily ever after." He picked up the indictment and scanned it. "But these charges aren't that serious. If they were, I'd tell you to run."

With the interview now over and me uninterested in extending my trip south to Mexico, there were just two more things Pair needed. The first, he said, was to confirm my answers with Beth over the phone, and the second was to stand beside me while I peed in a cup. I wish I'd gotten a heads up on both, because Beth was out shopping, and I'd just emptied the tank. But with a text message and a bottle of water, both problems were solved. I was ready for my first ever appearance in criminal court.

$$-\!\!\wedge\!\!\wedge\!\!-$$

In order to lessen the workload on the rarely-overworked, lifetime-appointed federal judges, procedural motions like arraignments are heard by U.S. magistrate judges, in this case the silver-haired Henry J. Bemporad. He began with the easy stuff. "How do you plead?"

"Not guilty," I answered with the polite yet defiant voice I'd practiced. He asked the same of Glen Holden, who was being arraigned in the same courtroom on perjury and obstruction of justice charges, and who responded in kind.

And then it was the company's turn. Our new general counsel, Gordon Weber, having traveled 1,200 miles to say two words, responded, less defiantly, "Not guilty."

Judge Bemporad said he was inclined to release me and Glen on $50,000 unsecured bonds (a signature on a sheet of paper instead of the customary 10% in cash) and that we wouldn't need to turn over our passports. It appeared Pair had concluded that I, a gun-free wimp, wasn't a menace to society. Bud also didn't object to either of us being released, but now it was the company's turn.

Judge Bemporad thumbed through his papers for a minute and raised his head in confusion. "I'm not really sure how to handle this. How do we release a corporation?" I knew this wasn't a run-of-the-mill case for the Western District of Texas, but now I got the idea that it was almost unprecedented, at least for this Judge. "What I'm looking for is a little help," he said, stirring the sedentary lawyers on each side. Richter stood up, pointed the Court to the relevant procedure, and effectively said, "The company can't run, and you can't put it in jail, so there's really nothing to do." Bud mumbled in agreement.

Judge Bemporad shrugged and wrapped up the hearing. Next it was time for Glen and me to get booked. "There were two deputies here that were supposed to escort you to booking," Pair said, "but they were so unconcerned with you guys they decided to leave and go have lunch. Can you just walk yourselves down to the second floor and check in at the window?"

"Sure," I replied. And with that, Glen and I perp-walked each other down to the booking room.

When we got there, the door was locked, but there was a window next to it, and a bell right below that. I rang it twice, and a man half-way through his sandwich poked his head out like the doorman in *The Wizard of Oz*. "Yes?"

"We're here for booking," I told him.

He looked at me, looked at Glen, looked at our suits, and asked, "So where's your clients?"

"No," I explained, "We're the defendants." He opened the door with mild puzzlement and handed us off to a burly marshal.

I was first to be processed. While Glen waited, I followed the marshal through another door, into the bowels of the criminal processing unit. It was a real jail. As we walked the stained concrete floors toward the fingerprinting stations, we came to a holding cell with metal bars and a few benches. Inside stood a handful of prisoners in orange jumpsuits, speaking Spanish to each other.

I really don't want to get put into that cell, even if just for five minutes while they're running the paperwork. I took my eyes off the prisoners to see if the marshal was stopping at the gate, but fortunately he kept walking.

After posing for mugshots and thumbing out a few prints, the questions started up again.

MARSHAL: Address?

ME: 6464 Sycamore Court.

MARSHAL: Is that in San Antonio?

ME: No, Minnesota.

MARSHAL: Oh, were you on the base?

ME: No. I'm not in the military.

MARSHAL: Were you arrested by the FBI?

ME: No, the FDA.

MARSHAL: What's the alleged crime?

ME: Conspiracy to sell an adulterated and misbranded medical device.

The marshal's eyes narrowed in confusion as he scrolled through a dropdown menu on his computer screen. I'm guessing my charges weren't listed there and he settled on "Other." Curiosity getting the better of him, he turned to me and asked one last question.

MARSHAL: So what are you doing here in San Antonio?

ME: That's a good question.

After I was released, I called Beth, who'd already spoken with Craig Pair. "How'd it go with my pre-probation officer?" I asked, in a discussion I never imagined having with my wife.

"*You* have to be polite," she snipped back, "but I don't." Uh oh. Like me, when Beth was upset about something, she made it known. "So after he asked me a bunch of questions, I asked him, 'Do you know how ridiculous these charges are?'"

Okay … probably not what a federal officer wants to be asked by the wife of a defendant.

"And then he said, 'Ma'am, all I can say is that your husband doesn't belong here. I respect what your husband has done, and he doesn't belong here.'"

That was sweet of him, I thought. Craig Pair was the nicest man I'd met in San Antonio. Hopefully Beth left it there and I could leave town with at least one guy on my side. But she couldn't resist.

"So I told him, 'Someone should lose their job when this is over.' And he replied, 'Ma'am, I just hope it isn't me.'"

CHAPTER 13

HOW'D WE END UP HERE?

December 2014

I always thought I would leave Minnesota and its long, cold winters. But once I did, I knew I wanted to go back. It's how I felt as a college student in California and as a summer associate in New York City, and it's the same way I now felt about this case. What were we doing in Texas?

The practical answer was that San Antonio was where DeSalle Bui filed his whistleblower suit, so that's where the civil prosecutors took it over, and that's where it got referred to the criminal side and piqued someone's interest.

Regardless of why our case started in Texas, now that it was really happening, I wanted it back in Minnesota where it belonged. I wanted a local jury who would appreciate the significance of fellow Minnesotans losing their jobs over a medical-regulatory disagreement with the FDA. There were other reasons. The flights alone – for me, Lundquist's team, Hopeman, and the witnesses – were going to be a significant expense, as for some reason San Antonio is one of the priciest airports to fly to from Minnesota.

We could bear the extra flights and even a Texas jury, but the real risk was the disruption to our business. I'd be gone for over a month during trial, a longer stretch away from the company than I'd ever taken. And it wouldn't just be me who'd be absent. We'd seen during the 16-month grand jury sideshow that the prosecutors were perfectly comfortable telling witnesses to show up in San Antonio, before cancelling their trips at the last minute, or worse, making them sit around without being called. I figured this would only get worse at trial, where the situation would be more fluid. And for a lean company whose key personnel would be doubling as trial witnesses, it could be a disaster. With me and our key employees out of the picture, I feared we wouldn't be able to remain the perpetual-growth-machine that kept our company a Wall Street darling. If business floundered, so too would our stock price.

So on the day of my arraignment, our lawyers filed a motion to move the trial to Minneapolis, citing the increased expenses, disruption to our business, and glut of Minnesota witnesses as reasons to do so. On top of that, we noted, the Western District of Texas was mired in a declared state of "Judicial Emergency," with vacancies on the bench exacerbating an already-overburdened immigration docket.

This all seemed persuasive, especially when there wasn't any good reason for keeping the case in San Antonio. The prosecutors, however, weren't excited about the idea. In their response brief, they said it should stay in Texas because we had orchestrated a nationwide conspiracy, were rich enough to fund a trial away from home, and would have no problem running the business remotely. *Easy for Bud to say.* They also accused us of making "inaccurate assumptions about who the prosecution will call at trial," and claimed that "the United States intends to call at least 10 witnesses who reside in Texas." Ten! I could think of three, maybe. But I'd never find out who the 10 were, because although they submitted a list of anticipated witnesses to the court, they did so in secret to block us from seeing it.[10]

I still figured we'd win our transfer to Minnesota. We had a secret weapon. And he wore a robe. Federal judges are assigned their cases randomly by a computer, and we just happened to draw the judge who would be most, let's say, *sympathetic* to transferring the case out of the district.

The Honorable Fred Biery Jr., as I understand it, is not a judge who particularly likes the law. He does, however, like being addressed as "Chief Judge" of the Western District, his title at the time. As soon we drew him, I found and read his most notable decision from his 22 years on the bench: *The Case of the Itsy Bitsy Teeny Weeny Bikini Top v. The (More) Itsy Bitsy Teeny Weeny Pastie.* Seriously, that's how he styled it. That case centered on an ordinance directing proper attire for semi-nude dancers, which Judge Biery gleefully noted had "once again fallen on the Court's lap." Never one for subtlety, he followed that rib-tickler by cramming 16 more double-entendres into an eight-page opinion, which was fairly long by Biery standards.

Like all federal trial court and appellate judges, Biery had a lifetime appointment. So as long as the job didn't interfere with his lunchtime basketball

---

[10]Of the 18 witnesses the prosecutors actually called to testify at trial, only four resided in Texas and none resided in the Western District.

and afternoon gardening,[11] he continued to show up. Knowing that Judge Biery wasn't really into all that legal stuff, our transfer motion described the case as "extremely complex," which was true, but, you know, tailored to Judge Biery's *interests*. Under the law, transfer decisions are essentially left to the judge's discretion, so with one stroke of his pen, Biery could clear our "complex" case from his docket.

But he didn't. Judge Biery decided to keep the case, saying VSI and I had the resources to contest a trial in San Antonio and that we should wait and see as to the number of witnesses called from Texas. I couldn't understand why Judge Biery would want to keep this unusual (by San Antonio standards) FDA regulatory trial and all the work it would require. Was he doing Bud, his fellow San Antonian, a favor by not making him travel to Minnesota for trial? Was he just bored with immigration cases? Whatever the reason, Texas it was. Think I could pull off a cowboy hat? No, probably not.

Knowing that the trial would be in San Antonio meant Judge Biery could now set a trial date: September 2015. If trial is like a time bomb, this date becomes 0:00 on the movie-sized digital readout. And along the way, as the clock ticks down, the rules of criminal procedure trigger smaller explosions.

The first to detonate was discovery.

In a criminal case, the most important discovery obligation belongs to the government: to give the defendants all of the documents that are material to their innocence. This Brady material – named after the Supreme Court case holding that the Constitution's Due Process Clause requires handing it over – is hugely helpful in framing defense strategies. As Joe Pesci, playing a rookie criminal defense attorney, fantasized in *My Cousin Vinny*, "If he'd let me look at his files; oh boy." To which Marissa Tomei responded: "He has to, by law – you're entitled. It's called disclosure, you dickhead!"

Documents in Brady productions can be silver bullets, like the no-match DNA report in a sexual assault case. That is, if you can find the documents.

---

[11]Paraphernalia from both hobbies is prominently featured in his judicial portrait, hanging in the San Antonio federal courthouse.

In a misleading display of "broad discovery," a prosecutor can bury meaningful documents in millions of pages of irrelevant documents, nowadays most often slipped into a series of 300-page scans of documents collected in hard-copy form.

Of course, that assumes that the prosecutors turn over the gems at all. In a now-famous dissent, U.S. Circuit Court Judge Alex Kozinski warned in 2013 that "there is an epidemic of Brady violations abroad in the land." Take the political-judicial persecution of the late U.S. Senator Ted Stevens on charges that he accepted discounted repairs to his modest Alaska cabin. Sen. Stevens' prosecutors got their conviction but withheld information that the government's star witness had contradicted his story, and separately, had suborned perjury from an underage prostitute. Stevens lost his Senate seat eight days after he was convicted in 2008, and he died in a plane crash before the full extent of the prosecutorial improprieties was revealed.

Knowing what unsupervised federal prosecutors were capable of, and knowing some of the strong-arm techniques that our prosecutors had already trotted out, we were on the lookout for any Brady horseplay. King & Spalding drafted a remarkably tedious 14-page Brady request letter, basically a wish list of documents and information we wanted.

And on February 13, 2015, Charles Biro, DOJ Trial Attorney, sent us this early Valentine's Day present: 58,637 pages in total; 22 grand jury transcripts; six "statement under oath" transcripts (whatever those were); 73 interview memos; 55 notes of interviews; and tens of thousands of pages of FDA files and hospital records.

With this document dump, I understood why Bud referred to the prosecutors as having invested their "blood, sweat, and tears" in this investigation – they had interviewed virtually every physician who ever had purchased a Short Kit, and many who had not. In the end, they talked to about as many doctors about perforators as our 70+ sales reps did, combined. Factoring in DOJ's desire to calculate a return on investment for their investigations, I now realized why our settlement negotiations had been futile. These prosecutors were all in and needed a big win – a corporate admission and my head on a government-issued platter.

The discovery dump helpfully included a table of contents – essentially a menu for the documents I'd binge-read at home over the coming weeks. All the witnesses' names were right there, pointing me to their grand jury testimony transcript. Board member Paul O'Connell advised that I take it slow and just read a couple of transcripts each night so I could still focus on my day job. I agreed, and with my fingers figuratively crossed, went straight to Carrie Powers' grand jury transcript.

It hurt to read. I knew Carrie was smart and had a steel backbone, but it didn't exactly shine through in her grand jury transcript. She was falling for entry-level lawyer tricks. Bud or Finley would say something as if everyone knew it were true, and then ask Carrie if she agreed with it. Instead of saying "I don't know" (which she didn't), she would agree.

After page upon page of this, and damning statement after damning statement, I put down the transcript, fuming. It was as if Hopeman hadn't prepared Carrie at all. Whenever you take the stand, Rule #1 is *don't assume anything.* That means you don't guess, you don't offer legal conclusions, and you only testify about what you know. If you don't know something, *say that* – it's usually a great answer.

How did Hopeman, an attorney for over 30 years, miss this stuff? My mind went back to the condescending letter he sent to me after Bill Michael quit: "We know it went well in San Antonio. Our witnesses were prepared, not intimidated . . . ." I call B.S. on all of it.

I moved from one transcript to the next, unable to put them down as the clock wound well past midnight. The rest of Hopeman's clients had gotten similarly jumped (just not as badly) using the prosecutors' same game plan: lure the witness in with some misleading question about how off-label use is illegal, get the witness to agree that perforators are off-label, and then broadside them with a stack of trip reports to "prove" we'd committed a crime. It worked almost every time on salespeople whose very nature is to please, like our Eastern regional manager, Dick Steitzer, who kicked off his 2014 grand jury session like it was open mic night at the local comedy club.

STEITZER: Well, it's a pleasure to be here. By the way, congratulations on – on the Spurs. I was rooting for them all the way. I'm a Celtics fan, but I was rooting for the Spurs all the way, I was.

The one salesmen who wasn't buying it was Glen Holden, our top-performing sales rep out of Connecticut. Glen was equally unprepared for the fight but, unlike Carrie, he was willing to push back. That fightin' spirit only served to get the prosecutors upset to the point it ultimately got Glen indicted on perjury and obstruction of justice charges.

Here's one of the "lies" that the prosecutors claimed Glen used to "obstruct" their investigation.

FINLEY: So is the answer to my question a no, then? You weren't trying to increase business?

GLEN: No. I – I would say I'm trying to help the patient population. That's first and foremost. That's – that's my job.

If that's obstruction, I'm Santa Claus. Glen was opining on why he was selling medical devices, and these prosecutors thought if he didn't say it was all about the money, he was lying and should go to prison. Perhaps not so coincidentally, though, Glen being indicted meant he wouldn't testify in our trial – as he would likely exercise his Fifth Amendment right against self-incrimination. So even if the charges against him were bogus, and they were, they had the effect of silencing a witness who had proven to be one of our strongest.

Later in my reading binge, I got around to the transcripts of those weird "statements under oath." They looked like grand jury transcripts, but they weren't. Instead of taking place before the grand jury in San Antonio, these interviews had taken place where the witness lived (Connecticut, Chicago, etc.). Same swearing of the oath beforehand, same misleading questions once it began. I had never heard of this "grand jury road trip" process, so I asked Richter, who had years of experience as a prosecutor, if it was common.

"I've never seen it," Richter replied. "I don't even know if there's a rule that permits it. But I don't know if there's one that prohibits it, either." Richter had one of his many associates research it, and they found neither. Was Tim Finley inventing a new rule of criminal procedure? And why?

Here's why, I discovered. If you have a witness statement that is sworn and transcribed, you can use the transcript later in court. Prosecutors like to collect these statements, and the normal way to get them is by bringing the witness in front of the grand jury. But bringing a witness down to San Antonio and putting them in front of the grand jury ran the risk that the jury would hear exonerating testimony. Any incriminating statements in a "statement under oath," on the other hand, could later be read word-for-word to the grand jury by the investigating FDA agent, with the exonerating parts excluded. So what Finley had created was a process with all the benefits of the grand jury, and none of the risks.

They called it a "statement under oath" interview, but let's call it what it really was, a kangaroo court. To get the witness to agree to this was itself a process: Bud would go to a judge in San Antonio and ask him to issue a grand jury subpoena. Then, he'd call the witness and say, "Hey, I have a subpoena in my hand ordering you to appear in San Antonio before a grand jury. Now, you can either come down here, or for your convenience, we could hop over to your hometown and take a quick statement. Which would you prefer?"

As you might imagine, the witnesses overwhelmingly preferred avoiding Texas. So around the country Finley hopped on his unlimited Main Justice budget. The witnesses didn't really get it. Take Dr. Daniel Pepper, for instance. He was the vascular surgeon who conducted our clinical study on perforators (the RELIEVE study) that the government had now publicly branded a dangerous failure. From the emails we'd produced to the government, though, they knew that Dr. Pepper believed that laser perforator treatment was safe and effective, and that the subpar RELIEVE results were attributable to unrelated treatments he had performed at the same time he treated patients' perforators. Not the type of guy they wanted the grand jury to hear. Here is the transcript from the beginning of his interview, which took place just outside of Seattle.

> **FINLEY: And you've agreed very graciously to give your statement under oath here today?**
>
> **DR. PEPPER: That's correct. I understand this is a grand jury testimony. Is that correct?**
>
> **FINLEY: Well, we are doing a grand jury investigation, but this isn't grand jury testimony.**
>
> **DR. PEPPER: Okay.**

FINLEY: This is just testimony outside of the grand jury –

DR. PEPPER: Okay.

FINLEY: – because the grand jury is in San Antonio, Texas, and you're all the way over here in Bellevue, Washington so –

DR. PEPPER: Thank you.

FINLEY: – we'll try to do it this way.

DR. PEPPER: I appreciate that.

Six witnesses wound up being selected to participate in Finley's kangaroo court, including our former V.P. of regulatory Deborah Schmalz, the one who wrote the FDA application that was at the center of our case. The prosecutors would call her as witness #2 at trial, but they used the kangaroo court to shield the grand jury from hearing about how she thought our FDA indications covered perforators all along.

As I descended even deeper into my document binge, it became obvious that all Bud's talk in settlement negotiations about having this airtight case was a bluff. As I flipped through the doctor interview memos, I was disgusted to find that the doctors had dismantled each and every major government theory.

Government Theory: The only use for the Short Kit was to treat perforators.
Dr. Duncan Belcher Interview Memo: "Of all the times Dr. Belcher has used the Short Kit, he estimates that he's used it to treat perforator veins 15% of the time."

Government Theory: Perforators are extremely difficult to treat, unlike superficial veins.
Dr. Timothy Manoni Interview Memo: "Dr. Manoni stated that he does not find it difficult to ablate a perforator vein versus a saphenous vein."

Government Theory: DVT complications in the RELIEVE study are extremely dangerous.
Dr. Daniel Pepper Statement: "If you asked me, is a [small DVT like those

in the RELIEVE study] a significant event, I don't think so … [W]e've done over 8,000. No deaths … We don't treat them, these are really very benign."

Government Theory: Medicare doesn't cover perforator treatment.
Dr. Sean Roddy Statement: The physician group that writes the Medicare codes looked into adding a specific code for perforators but found that "the current coding covered perforator use."

And then I read the big one. The one that proved they had nothing.

Government Theory: Vascular Solutions' indications doesn't cover perforator treatment.
FDA Medical Director Dr. Pablo Morales Statement: "[I]n some sense VSI may be right that the indications would include [perforator veins]."

It was incredible. The prosecutors, in their own files, knew that their indictment was built out of Swiss cheese. Bud and Finley should have halted construction, but they didn't. They kept building, kept pushing forward. Interview more doctors! The witnesses say the walls smell like cheese? Threaten them with perjury!

$$\pmb{\_\wedge\!\!\upharpoonright\!\!\_}$$

For all the documents that Biro turned over, way more were missing. Over a million pages, we'd later find out. But to get those pages, we first had to call them out for not turning them over. Among other gaps, Pauzé zeroed in on the government's failure to respond to one of my favorite categories in his "hand it over" letter that kicked-off discovery:

> **A detailed description of all communications by the government to any potential witnesses regarding threats, or other statements that could be construed as threatening or having a tendency to be coercive, made to any potential prosecution witness.**

A few months later, like a mail-order item, it arrived: Exactly what we asked for. A nine-page letter jammed with narrative descriptions of Bud and Finley's interactions with 26 witnesses they admittedly threatened or "warned." Reading through them one by one revealed clearly the prosecutors' strategy, which we'd only pieced together anecdotally. *Interview everyone, flip the unhelpful ones with threats.* Our Midwest regional manager, Beth Matthews, was a textbook mark, as documented in Biro's own words:

Shortly after her testimony, we informed Matthews' counsel that we thought she had given false testimony. Matthews initially declined to correct her testimony and asserted that she had been truthful.

Matthews gave [another] interview in September 2014. Before the interview, Trial Attorney Finley told Matthews that if she did not correct her testimony, he would:

> **(i) recommend to Department of Justice management that perjury and obstruction of justice charges be brought against her;**

> **(ii) refer her to HHS as a candidate for possible exclusion from [the healthcare industry]; and**

> **(iii) ask VSI to terminate her employment.**

"Well, Howard," Richter gleefully told me after reading this paragraph, "We might just get up at trial and read this." As if that list of terribles wouldn't be enough to win Matthews' cooperation, the prosecutors also "told her that many VSI employees had admitted engaging in this conduct."

This wasn't some passing reference to other witnesses' admissions, either – Bud and Finley cherry-picked secret grand jury transcripts and read excerpts aloud to teach Matthews the testimony they wanted to hear. They violated the law to leak these grand jury transcripts, and, in the end, they got what they wanted.

Following the interview, Matthews signed a sworn [admission].

Biro's production showed that the government coaxed this same type of prosecutor-written admission out of four other witnesses. It was a disgusting desplay: take all the things you want the witness to say "yes" to, type them up one after another, and have the witness sign it *or else*. It looked like a rock solid admission – just leave out all that original exculpatory stuff.

I wondered, as I put down the last interview summary, were all these hollow trophies – the admissions, kangaroo court transcripts, and cherry-picked doctor interviews –the way Bud and Finley were able to convince their bosses they had a case? *We've got five solid doctors* (I'm not telling you about the other 50), *five witness admissions* (who cares about their statements before we threatened them), *and eight grand-jury-crucified sales reps* (forget that we hid the indictions from them).

Even in the days leading up to the indictment, I couldn't comprehend how this investigation had gotten so far off track. But now, with everything in front of me, I saw. When I lined up the interviews chronologically, I could see how these prosecutors told a tall tale to posture for settlement, and then, when talks fell through, they were forced to manufacture evidence to support it. Now, with both sides locked in and a date on the court's calendar, the time bomb was ticking.

CHAPTER 14

TIME

April 2015 – 6 Months to Trial

Perry Mason was a lie. It all happened too fast. One 60-minute episode went from crime to arrest to trial, glossing over the prep work that I, now six months away from our September 2015 trial, found myself mired in. While we were scouring the documents, generating reams of legal research, and cobbling together witness outlines, Perry magically had it all at his fingertips ... right after the commercial break.

Actually, that's the way it's supposed to be, minus the magic and commercial break. The Sixth Amendment, after all, guarantees that "in all criminal prosecutions, the accused shall enjoy the right to a speedy and public trial." The eponymous 1972 law (the "Speedy Trial Act") that breathes life into this amendment gives "speedy" a concrete definition: 70 days. Seventy days from the time of indictment, it says, the prosecution must be ready to give its opening statement.

Like water, time to prepare is something everyone needs. But too much time, the Speedy Trial Act recognizes, can drown a defendant. Under the dark cloud of prosecution, a defendant is often isolated from society and employment, financially destitute, and, for the many who can't afford bail, physically restrained by the state.

Unfortunately, the Speedy Trial Act wasn't a choice in our case anymore. Our original "shock and awe" strategy was to demand that our trial commence 10 weeks after indictment, forcing the unprepared government to deliver their sloppy and legally-incorrect case on the fly. But after Bill Michael quit and made us the unprepared ones, that plan went out the window. We had to waive speedy trial.

So here I was, half a year away from 0:00, drowning in time.

Time Is Money

Tick, tick. Do you hear that? That's the sound of my lawyers, a thousand miles away, billing.

An hour of John Richter's time costs $1,080. The first time I heard that, I have to admit I kind of liked it. There's an odd sense of pride that comes with knowing that the guy defending you commands a MacBook Air for the amount of time it takes to charge one.

That pride, however, faded when I saw that same guy bill the company for a $2,000 plane ticket to San Antonio. First class, I hope. Or that three other people on his team bought the same ticket, and then billed for the time they were in those pricey seats. But the expenses and travel were just appetizers at the legal-expense bacchanal of "trial prep."

It's the steady churn of lawyer-hours that will get you. One young, inexperienced King & Spalding associate who I'd never heard of and whose name I couldn't spell – Saltarelli, the bill said – ran me up for 152 hours at $510 an hour for the month of February alone. And each month, another 12 lawyers and paralegals showed up on the bill, clocking between 80 and 180 premium-priced hours. It added up. King & Spalding's March bill was $628,000, even after a 15% "professional courtesy" discount that Richter offered up when we signed on.

And that was just one firm. Between the current employees' lawyers, the former employees' lawyers, Glen Holden's lawyers, and local counsel in San Antonio for everyone, we had ten firms bombarding us with regular monthly invoices. All told, the lawyers ate up $2.4 million in the first quarter of 2015 alone – and with it, over 40% of our company's profit.

What a great business model these law firms had: Want to make more money? Think of another legal research project!

It didn't work like that at my company. We make things. So every minute spent trying to show a lawyer how to prepare a budget (I finally just gave up on that quest) or fact-checking their work, was a minute I wasn't working on developing our next medical device. Vascular Solutions had flourished by developing and launching new, useful products every year. A few caught on, a few didn't, but steadily the top line grew. But it'd been months since I sat down with engineers to explore a new device idea. And if that continued, pretty soon our once-flush product pipeline would slow to a trickle.

While it wasn't coming out of my wallet, every dollar we spent on lawyers was coming from someone's – in this case, our shareholders. The hemorrhaging of cash to law firms was a sore thumb in our earnings numbers, even though we reported our legal expenses separately and calculated an "adjusted earnings" number without them. *This is your company. This is your company on trial.*

Other lawyers were coming out of the woodwork to get in on the party, too. Although our stock price had climbed all the way back above $30 by April 2015, the vulture shareholder law firms were still circling, waiting for our stock to dive. Through thinly-disguised advertisements called "Investor Alerts," these financial-ambulance-chasers were hunting aggrieved shareholders. "Investigation Over Potential Wrongdoing at Vascular Solutions" read the headline on one of the dozen or so of these things. So far, it didn't look like they'd found a plaintiff. But if we lost at trial, I knew they'd have no problem finding a few hundred.

$$\sim\!\!\bigwedge\!\!\sim$$

Time Reveals All

By now I was used to being pressured by blood-lusty prosecutors to step down from the company I started. And eventually I got used to it coming from Joe Carlson, the Star Tribune's "award-winning" newspaper reporter. One of his recent subheaders read, "[i]n a rare strategy, Howard Root is running a publicly traded company after an indictment," followed by a snarky comment in the body: "could be easier said than done." He even couldn't get the most basic facts straight – reporting that our stock price was seven cents below its yearly low (it was seven dollars above) and that I was the company's majority shareholder (I owned less than 5% of VSI's stock).

I expected all that from a journalist with an agenda. What I didn't expect was for my CEO chair to take friendly fire.

Each year, a ceremonial vote is held to re-elect the board of directors. I say ceremonial because there are seven seats on the board (including mine) and there are only ever seven candidates nominated. So like grade school soccer, everyone's a winner. But as the votes started rolling in before the 2015 annual shareholders' meeting, I noticed something odd.

Somebody had voted 2,520 shares against me. They were registered shares, the type only our original investors had, along with employees who bought stock through our employee stock purchase plan. Those "no" votes were functionally meaningless, but I still wanted to know where they came from. Was this the warning shot in a brooding shareholder lawsuit?

I asked our general counsel, Gordon Weber, to dig into it and figure out who owned precisely 2,520 shares of VSI stock. When I didn't hear back for a couple days, I slipped into his office. "Hey, did you ever get a chance to look into that board vote?" Gordon shut the door and pursed his lips sheepishly, opening the shareholder register to a page he had marked: Tim Slayton – 2,520 Shares.

Tim Slayton was (and still is) our controller, the second-in-command in our finance department under our CFO. Tim had been with us for over five years, and had never expressed any issues with the company or me.

"What is Tim thinking?" I wondered aloud.

Gordon already had the answer. "He said he 'just wanted to see if anyone would notice.'"

Well, Tim, *Mission Accomplished.* I thought about putting a replica of the George W. Bush banner in his office – just to see if he would notice – but didn't. While Tim apparently had time for games, I had more important issues to deal with in the office. The email grapevine said somebody in the company was a little too eager to take my job:

I just spoke with our rep in Houston. He was in a lab with Dr. Grantham from Kansas City who said, 'I was talking with Chad Kugler the other day, your CEO-in-waiting.' When he asked what Grantham meant by that, the doctor said, 'well he'll be your CEO when Howard goes to prison.'

I groaned and shook my head. Chad, the guy I'd tapped as my successor-in-waiting, was already telling customers about my potential imprisonment and his potential promotion – six months before the trial was even scheduled to start. And Dr. Grantham, a cardiologist I knew pretty well, was making me a punch line with my sales reps. If that's what's happening now, I thought, what will happen when I am in San Antonio for two months at trial?

After a talk with Chad to let him know that I was not expecting to lose, he apologized and said it wouldn't happen again. I then shot an email to Dr. Grantham asking him to call me. When we connected, Dr. Grantham started, without any hint of sarcasm, "Do you want me to apologize first or do you want to yell at me?" It had been a bad day in the lab, he said; other sales reps were bothering him; and he just tried to sound in-the-know. With an honest explanation and awareness like that, my anger subsided, but I knew this wouldn't be the last time I'd worry about our employees' adventures.

Time Waits For No Man

Except, evidently, Tim Finley. I got a call from Lundquist – always in a soft tone, but this time with a hint of unease. "Finley wants to push the trial date." The government needed more time to organize the documents, produce the remaining documents we were asking for, and to get their expert witnesses ready. Our "voluminous" discovery requests had cut into their trial prep, Finley would tell the judge if he had to. We were better off just agreeing to move trial to 2016, Lundquist said, because pro-government Judge Biery would surely grant their request anyway.

It was the last thing I wanted to hear. I wished we could have held the trial the next day, just to be done with it. Just to be able to get up on the stand and finally tell a jury what really happened here. I was tired of playing on the government's schedule and having to adjust my business and life accordingly. But once again, there wasn't much of a choice. I agreed to the move, and the judge gave us a new date: February 1, 2016

Fifteen months after the indictment. This was the opposite result of what we would've gotten under the Speedy Trial Act. We were being bled out slowly by legal expenses, facing increased disquiet from employees, and now – the kicker – we had zero chance to catch the government with its metaphorical pants down. With another six months to sharpen their swords and craft their narrative, we'd be getting the best Tim Finley and Bud Paulissen had to offer. Exactly what that was, only time would tell.

CHAPTER 15

DRESS REHEARSAL

August 2015 – 6 Months to Trial (Again)

The government's trial delay play pissed me off, but I decided to look on the bright side. An extra six months of trial prep meant an extra six months to figure out how to explain this case to a jury. It wouldn't be easy, because the story we had to tell – the truth – sounded complicated. It was long, but not just that, it required the listener to understand medical jargon, a tangled FDA clearance processes, nuances of First Amendment law, and even more. Every one of my lawyers had an idea of how we should tell our story to a jury, but that was part of the problem. Which one should I trust?

Welcome to the world of jury consultants – battle-tested professionals who spend their entire careers shaping trial messaging. Their secret? Legal focus groups.

I'd known focus groups for offering a vivid, voyeuristic window into designing and selling a product. Over enough iterations, seeing how even a small group of doctors react to what you're selling can tell you a lot about how the population as a whole will react. In the context of a jury trial, these reactions would be valuable not only in terms of *how* to present our argument (the product), but also to *whom* we should present it (the customer). As they (probably don't) say in Texas, it's like killing two rattlesnakes with one beer can.

Richter didn't just find me a jury consultant, he found me *the* jury consultant. When he asked around, Richter said, the local lawyers reported back that there was only one name when it came to picking Texas juries. This guy was so good, they said, that in civil cases parties hire him even before filing their case and even if they don't intend on using him – just so they won't look up one day and see him on the other side for jury selection.

His name was Robert Hirschhorn. He was in his early 50s and looked like a put-together John Belushi. But hiding behind the greased, midnight hair and the baggy Texas Longhorn gear was the nation's preeminent jury whisperer. He'd picked the jury that let George Zimmerman off in the Trayvon Martin murder case. He also got an acquittal in millionaire Robert Durst's (first) murder trial, memorialized in the HBO mini-series *The Jinx*. Just imagine what he could do with someone likeable.

For Hirschhorn, picking a jury is more than a dark art, it's a process. If that sounds like something a used car salesman would say, you're starting to understand Robert Hirschhorn. The first time we sat down in San Antonio, he explained *the process* to me in the type of frantic, hyper-direct way I'd come to know him for:

> **Any juror can be a great juror. There are no bad jurors, only bad judges and prosecutors. We need to find the jurors who are right for you. The way we do that is through test sessions – isolated experiments with local jurors. Local jurors, that's important. Experiments let us see what jurors are responding to and what they aren't. Each session, we'll test a different part of the case, and see how that changes the result. This process isn't going to be simple, Howard, and it's not going to be cheap. But I promise you: If you put your case in my hands, I'll get you the best jury out there.**

Hirschhorn was in many ways the Anti-Richter. The schlubbiness to Richter's expensive tailored threads. The brutalist efficiency to Richter's charismatic waffling. The St. Mary's School of Law to Richter's prestigious University of Virginia. The self-made scrappy to Richter's blue-blood smooth. This is all to say, I guess, that Hirschhorn reminded me a little of me.

And like me, Hirschhorn had an unconventional (albeit different) path to get to where we were this day – sitting behind a one-way mirror as the mock jurors flooded into a large conference room.

Hirschhorn had been a drug-foggy kid with a penchant for graffiti, he said, before an interventional story from "the smartest man [he] ever met" changed his life forever. That man was his grandfather, who told him that as a young man in the Soviet Union, he'd tipped off villages to the impending attacks from The Imperial Russian Army, allowing the innocent to escape just in time. But his grandfather was caught, and after a sham trial, sentenced to death. He was shipped off to Siberia but was able to escape and navigate his way through Eastern Europe before eventually making it to the States. There was a reason young Robert was here, his grandfather said, and it wasn't to booze and skip school.

The younger Hirschhorn set out to become a defense lawyer. And he did, working nearly a dozen trials before he met a jury consultant who won him a case and changed his life once more. Cathy Bennett, the famed jury expert he'd go on to marry, was described in The New York Times as being "the mother of modern criminal law practice in America." She pioneered asking open-ended questions during jury selection, and agreed to show Hirschhorn her tricks on the condition that he spend a full year learning, keeping his opinions to himself. No small request for Robert Hirschhorn.

He joined up with Cathy Bennett and Associates, where together they formed a team that picked civil trial juries that brought their clients $20 million in recoveries from the Ku Klux Klan. But in the late '80s, Cathy was diagnosed with cancer. She postponed her treatment to finish working the rape trial of William Kennedy Smith. A Kennedy, and another win. Four years later she passed away, and 24 years after that, Hirschhorn was still carrying on her legacy, continuing to run the shop as Cathy Bennett and Associates. He only took a few criminal cases each year, and here I was in his laboratory, eager to take the first step in my process.

$$\rule{1cm}{0pt}\text{---}\bigwedge\text{---}$$

The mock jury had been meticulously curated to reflect the demographics of the San Antonio jury pool I'd soon draw from. As meticulously as could be done, anyway, considering that our pool was limited to people who chose to surrender their Saturday (starting at 7 a.m.) for $300 and a turkey sub.

Here were the rules: Richter would play the defense lawyer, Pauzé the prosecutor. Each would get 30 minutes to argue their case. We'd be testing the government's strongest arguments against our responses. Afterward, the jurors would be polled (anonymously) on who they thought won, then split evenly (by initial conclusion) into three separate jury rooms, where we'd surveil their deliberations. But it wasn't just the jurors who were evaluating the lawyers; it was also my first chance to see our fancy Washington lawyers in (mock) action.

Pauzé was up first, for the government. A svelte 5 feet 6 inches tall, he looked small for the big room. But as soon as he unleashed his croonery voice, he filled it. "This is a case about money," he bellowed, "and about a public company CEO who's rich and doesn't abide by the rules. The FDA told them not to sell their medical device or they would be violating the law, and they did it anyway."

Pauzé paced around the room for the next 25 minutes, stopping to hit his points with a reasoned, no-frills style. "Thank God," he said, "that this millionaire's products haven't killed anyone yet." It was infuriating to sit through, but I couldn't take my eyes off it – it was like watching Perry Mason mixed with the best debater I'd seen on the college circuit. After cutting up my expected defense, he finished by sliding the machete across my jugular. "This is a case about *choices*," Pauzé said, hitting that last word with force. "Mr. Root made the choice to sell the Short Kit even though the FDA told him not to do it." He paused and pointed his finger at the jury. "Ladies and gentlemen, that was not his choice to make."

As he held his tense stare-down of the audience, I thought, "Even I would vote guilty." A majority of the jurors agreed. After hearing only Pauzé's speech, the pool was polled to depressing results. Out of 96 total votes on all charges, we got 56 "guiltys," 39 "don't knows," and only one "not guilty."

While I was watching the instant juror feedback on the control room monitors, Pauzé slinked in with a Scrooge-like grin on his face. "Just so you know, Howard, I didn't enjoy that," to which I shot back, loud enough for everyone in the control room to hear, "Nice job … asshole." What a luxury, though, to have a great back-up quarterback on my team.

Now, however, it was time for the starter – our trial team's "first chair" – former U.S. Attorney John C. Richter. He certainly looked the part, standing tall over the crowd with his power Rolex peeking out just-so from his perfectly-starched cuff. But he was nervous, almost too excited about what he had to say, in a way that made me focus more on the man than the words. The argument itself wasn't bad; it was just a little bland, and as a result I didn't remember a single line of it only 10 minutes after he finished. This wasn't the golden yarn Pauzé had spun. But then again, I'd been told the prosecutor's argument is always easier to make.

Richter brought a few mock jurors back from the guilty brink, but not many. After video-taped testimony of fictional witnesses on each side did little to move the needle either way, the pool was split for deliberations, as we watched on three video monitors from the neighboring conference room.

An hour passed, and each of the three rooms came back guilty (although only two of the nine counts with the unanimity that would be required to convict at trial).

The result was terrifying, but watching them get there was fascinating. Each juror had answered a detailed questionnaire upon arrival, and matching the people to the opinions felt like a kid taking in a baseball game armed with a full set of Topps trading cards.

Take, for instance, Christopher, a 48-year-old Democrat with a business background. When asked for his three most-visited websites, he only wrote one answer: "Porn." He was either uncomfortably honest or incredibly cheeky, and he turned out to be one of the lone holdouts for the defense.

Also in our corner were a diehard libertarian and two retired black men – one in a suit jacket, the other a former probation officer. From the start, neither seemed impressed by the government's case, and I wondered if there was something there. Had generations of law enforcement abuse made African-Americans predisposed to recognize what was happening to me, a rich white guy from Minnesota? I didn't know; that was Hirschhorn's job.

Most hostile to our position was a group Hirschhorn had profiled as the "rule followers." There was Rebecca, in her 30s, a furious note-taker who dressed like a librarian. In the same group was Albert, the veteran with five mothers-in-law (how?) who concluded, about me, "He makes the big bucks. If he doesn't know what's going on, fire him and find me someone who does." And then there was Martha, the aging white secretary with four children, who listed on the questionnaire her most admired person as "Camille Fiorillo." Apparently I was no Camille Fiorillo.

I was simultaneously annoyed and amused watching the jurors on each side work to sell and distort the evidence. The note-taker Rebecca was convinced that I'd forwarded the entire sales force one Danny McIff trip report that discussed planning a "perforator party." I didn't. And in an act of oratory the ancient Greeks would spit at, Rebecca offered a busted syllogism to win over her fellow jurors: "If the sales rep violated company policy, and the company policy is based on an FDA regulation, and the regulation is based on the law, isn't the violation of a company policy a violation of the law?" The answer to that, if you're playing at home, is "no." I'd hate to work at a company run by Rebecca, where missing the cover page on your TPS report has her calling the cops.

Above all others, one comment gave me concern. It was from Rebecca the note-taker, again, but the nods in agreement signaled that it was more universally felt. "Why would the government go through all of this if they didn't break the law?" she asked, suggesting indictment should trigger an automatic conviction.

And with that, the focus group session concluded. I didn't get any acquittals, but we would've gotten some hung juries, and the porn guy was with us. At the end, Hirschhorn sat me down and assured me that this was productive and that we'd "learned a lot" testing the government's best arguments against our soft spots. *Hmm ... not exactly the chipper assessment I was hoping for.*

—⌁—

For the next go-around with a mock trial, I wanted to play with one of those variables Hirschhorn had talked about. The gap between Pauzé's brilliance and Richter's *ehh*-ness irked me. I called up Pauzé to talk about it, under the guise of discussing a missed deadline on a work plan I'd requested. "Between you and me, Mike, I'm having a hard time getting Richter to understand what I need and giving me a plan that I can use."

"Part of that's my fault," Pauzé confessed. "I dropped the ball on that weekly report." Intimating that I wasn't the typical client, he added, "We need to find a way to work better with you and get you what you need."

"Look, what I don't need is the senior partner being the only attorney that I get updates from," referring to Richter and not finishing before Pauzé interrupted me. "Howard," he said. "I don't consider John to be my senior partner. We started at King & Spalding at the same time."

Interesting. I had assumed, based on who was doing most of the talking on the phone calls (and, frankly, Richter's whole aura), that he was the team leader. But what was more surprising, even if Richter wasn't the top guy, was why his fellow partner would go out of his way to make that known to the client.

This was all very illuminating, so I decided to dig deeper and ask the one question I had been afraid to ask. "Mike, tell me, since you've been at King & Spalding, how many criminal trials like this one have you done?"

After a moment of silence, Pauzé replied, "None."

"And what about Richter, how many has he done?"

"None."

I closed my eyes as I asked the obvious follow-up. "So when he says he's had 26 trials, all of those have been while he was working as a prosecutor for the government?"

"Yes," he conceded. "Nobody really takes these cases to trial for the defense."

I felt sick. I, a former lawyer, in the most important legal battle of my life, had hand-picked lawyers who had zero experience doing what I'd hired them to do – to build relationships with witnesses, find experts, and prepare for trial as a defense lawyer, instead of the government's blank check and power of compulsion. I looked at the calendar again as it counted down days to trial.

I was now too midstream to change horses, but perhaps I could change riders. There was something about Pauzé I liked, and it wasn't just his performance. When we'd spoken about how I needed to be in the loop, he didn't just tut-tut me like the lawyers who'd come before him. He told me, convincingly, "You have a lot to add to our defense. I am competitive, and I don't want to lose. And I take it personally what these prosecutors have done to you." Pauzé wasn't just cheering for me – this guy was going to fight for me. I thought he was the guy we needed in the ring, not Richter.

But before I did anything drastic, I wanted to consult the oracle, Hirschhorn.

"Robert," I asked him, "we have to choose who's going to give the opening and closing arguments for the company – Richter or Pauzé. Who do you think?"

Hirschhorn, for some reason, answered my straight-forward question with questions of his own. "How did you hire King & Spalding? Have you worked with Richter before?" He was trying to suss out the political dynamics, I suppose, playing politics with cautious loyalty to Richter, the man who'd hired him.

But that wasn't the type of candid advice I needed from the guy I'd hired to give candid advice, so I backed him into a corner. "Put yourself in my shoes. This is the most important trial I'll ever have. If I lose, my company will be destroyed and I could go to prison. If you were me, who would you choose?"

"That's easy," Hirschhorn said, springing into clarity. "Mike's a star. Richter's not bad, but Mike's better. If it were me, I'd have Mike do the opening and closing." I thanked him and got on the horn with Pauzé the next day.

"Mike," I started, "the opening you gave in San Antonio was simply outstanding. I haven't seen anyone better than you in a courtroom setting."

"Coming from you, Howard, that means a lot to me," he replied, alluding to my reputation as a tough critic, and probably wondering why I was calling to tell him this.

"I spoke with our board chairman, John Erb, and with Hirschhorn, and we decided that we want you to give the company's opening and closing at trial. Richter was fine, but you're better, and we need to plug our best lawyers into the most important roles. For practice, I want you to argue the company's side in our final mock trial." A brief silence.

"Okay, great, I can do that. If that's what you want and it's your final decision, let me give the news to Richter," Pauzé said. "You won't have to worry about him. He'll be disappointed, but he's not going to work any different, unlike some of the problems you had with your previous lawyers. We'll make this work."

A flight delay made me late for the final mock trial a few weeks later, so I arrived late Friday afternoon, halfway through Prosecutor Richter's opening argument. He was more comfortable in this role, but it still sounded like fact-listing, not storytelling. Soliloquies were more Pauzé's thing, it seemed, and I was anxious to hear him work his magic once again. And this time, for my side.

Pauzé, as he always did, hit it hard. The vibrato in his voice bounced off the walls of the conference center as he recounted how this case had been born of misunderstanding and shaped around prosecutorial bulldozing. But something about Pauzé's choreographed outrage fell flat this time. Maybe it was the stale conference room environment. Or that the defense argument was a tougher sell, as I'd been told. He'd be better in the courtroom, I told myself, but we were still missing something, something essential. There was no "not his choice to make" line – nothing that grabbed me and wouldn't let go.

Next up was my lawyer, Lundquist, with an opus on my innocence. I was a little concerned that he hadn't practiced enough and would just read off the script, as he had during a dry run earlier in the week. But even more, I was worried that he'd go off-book and engage in some argument improv. Lundquist did neither, though, delivering a cozy, relatable story to the jury. Something about the sexagenarian's soothing voice made me comfortable with the complicated points in our story, and when he hit a note about being "disturbed" by what the government was doing here, it resonated. When grandpa gets mad, everybody notices.

It was clear to me that Lundquist would be the perfect complement to Pauzé. The pleasant, stately Midwestern gentlemen to spell the sharp, hard-charging New Yorker. Two Pauzés would be too much, two Lundquists too little. But one of each, I estimated, would be just right for our Texas jury.

As Lundquist finished, so did the afternoon. The jurors weighed in on their polling devices, and the results came back an even split. One-third "guilty," one-third "not guilty," and one-third "not sure." Hirschhorn comforted me by saying the "not sure" folks were really "not guilty" votes that didn't know it yet, meaning that there was little risk of a unanimous mock conviction.

But the next day, he said, would be the real test. The same jurors would return, and for the first time, we'd have live testimony from each side. I'd take the stand for the defense, facing Richter – the man I'd just demoted – on cross-examination. And hopefully I wouldn't get embarrassed, because my boss, John Erb, was flying down to play watchful eye for the board.

—⩗—

I looked out at the fake jury. They'd all returned to complete their duty and collect their two-day sum of $575. From the other side of the one-way mirror, they looked even quirkier than I'd noticed the day before. Most eye-catching was Don, whose frequent naps in the front row required a poke from a Hirschhorn staffer to reanimate him.

As I walked to the front of the room wearing the blue button-down shirt Hirschhorn had picked out for me, I was careful not to make eye contact with any of the jurors. The old joke in Minnesota is that the extrovert is the one who looks at the other guy's shoes. But even by those standards, I'm bad at the pupil-to-pupil stuff. Later that day, I'd be told this comes off as insulting in San Antonio.

I didn't have time to worry about that now, because I was running through the checklist of tips Hirschhorn had just given me. *Don't argue, and definitely don't get angry. Smile. Don't be Donald Trump, but also don't be "low energy" Jeb Bush. Act the same on direct as you do on cross. And most importantly, be natural …* which, if I followed, would mean ignoring all the other tips.

I thought my direct examination went pretty well. Lundquist asked the questions, and I'd either seen or written all of them. When I knew the answer, I turned to the jury like I'd been trained and replied in the most casually-sincere manner I could muster. I got to talk about starting the company, about the freeze-dried plasma product we were developing with the U.S. Army, and my history of strict compliance demands on the sales force. "If the speed limit is 70," I explained, "I want my sales reps doing 55, not 70, just to be safe." I got some nods from the jurors, and Don stayed mostly awake, so I considered it a victory.

It was the cross-examination that was the adventure. Richter began by bombarding me with weekly trip reports from our sales reps talking about treating perforator veins. The "perforator party" one, some others – all of which, as CEO, I had access to at the time, but probably hadn't ever read. After each trip report, he'd ask if I'd seen it. And each time, I'd answer, "I see it now, but I didn't write it or remember reading it back when it was sent." Jurors would later say this was evasive, too lawyerly. Richter would follow up that exchange by asking me if the trip report was an example of promotion. "I don't know," I mostly said. "I wasn't there for this visit, so I don't know what actually happened with this doctor." Same thing, too lawyerly, Hirschhorn said. Richter was dishing out papercuts, to be sure, but he couldn't find a seam to really tear me apart.

More worrying was that Richter didn't seem able to find his own documents. He frequently stopped, fussed around with his notebook, and wound up having to show me his personal copies of the fake exhibits. I didn't understand. I was supposed to be the one who was unprepared for this, not him. In one particularly tense moment, he called for Peter Cooch, his young associate running the PowerPoint, to turn to his "side-by-side" slides. To which Cooch, with the look of a late-adolescent Macaulay Culkin, stared back in empty fear. Richter fumed: "The side-by-sides. Bring up the side-by-sides." Cooch clicked around his computer feebly, and then shook his head. Cooch didn't have them.

My eyes bounced between them, realizing that my decision to go with Pauzé had been a good one. Instead of moving on and adapting on the fly,

Richter melted down. By the time he finally got around to asking his next question, a Hirschhorn staffer stepped in. "Counselor, we need to conclude." Richter had gone 25 minutes over his 60 minutes of allotted time, completely blowing the remaining schedule.

After the jurors were sent to deliberations, I stormed back to the control room. There, John Erb was even more upset than I was. "That was embarrassing," Erb told me. "Richter just fumbled for his documents and didn't look prepared. We need to correct that for trial." I agreed, shaking my head and staring into the hushed darkness of the control room.

In charged Richter, palms to the sky, straight toward Macaulay Culkin. "Cooch! Where were my slides?!"

"John," he said in resigned exasperation, "I have no *idea.*"

After my testimony, the results showed that it wasn't just Richter who'd done poorly. Rather than swoop in and save the day like I thought I would, I'd moved the dials *the wrong way.* After Friday's even split, we now had 11 jurors firmly in the "guilty" camp, with only 7 "not guilty" and 13 "not sure." Hirschhorn chopped the pool into three groups, placing Don the snoozer (along with a fidgeter and a groaner) in what I called "the room of misfit toys."

The unfavorable polling response to my testimony was matched by the jurors' savage commentary in deliberations. "It's guys like Howard who have destroyed this country," said Luis, a machinist. An old-school Texan who went by "Skip" complained about my "expensive suit and un-shined shoes," leading me to wonder if I should get a cheaper suit or shine my shoes. Young Estefanía found me to be "an excellent social comedian," which I knew was an insult, but one I couldn't exactly pin down.

A juror appropriately named Breezy offered, unprompted, "I wouldn't want to be married to him." She was no doubt picking up on a mock employee's testimony that I was a control-freak who "wouldn't even let his employees eat lunch at their desks," something we expected one of the government's real witnesses to say at trial. The next day our lawyers asked me what my wife said when I relayed Breezy's comment to her. "She agreed," I answered. Beth hadn't, but I couldn't resist playing along with my reputation.

This wasn't my normal world. I was used to, as CEO, getting a certain benefit of the doubt. In my interactions with employees and at industry conferences, what I said came with a certain credibility. Not anymore. The mock trial had been a depressing lesson in life as a defendant. Your criminality is all-but-explicitly assumed, and sometimes even the "all-but" part goes out the window. "Reasonable doubt is a cop out," said mock juror Corey when reminded of the burden of proof.

While deliberations were proceeding, Hirschhorn sat me down on the bench, and, like a coach, told me what I needed to do better the next time I got in the game. I'd given over 20 depositions in my career, testified in two civil trials, and thought I knew what I was doing. "This is a different planet," Hirschhorn explained. Being precise with words, the skill I'd developed through all those depositions, didn't matter here. The jurors wouldn't be reading the transcript, they'd be watching me. Hearing me. And from that they'd take away a feeling. Right now, that feeling was that I was "sneaky," the adjective most-used by the jurors to describe me. Hirschhorn told me that I was the most important witness, and that when I took the stand for real, it would all come down to my ability to strike a specific emotional tone. Not exactly my strong suit, but I pledged to work at it. I had no other choice.

The mock jury in Room 2 was getting close to a verdict.

NOT GUILTY ON ALL CHARGES. Even with the bad reactions to my testimony, we seemed to be doing better in deliberations. Pauzé and Lundquist's presentations had hatched strong advocates who internalized our talking points, deploying them to win over their detractors one-by-one with logic and a close reading of the fake jury instructions. To explain away me, the unlikable CEO, juror Jacob conceded, "We can agree that Howard's not a great guy, but he didn't commit a crime."

The room of misfit toys also came back with a unanimous NOT GUILTY. We were rolling; and maybe, I thought, these quirky jurors were our bread and butter. They didn't take the government's allegations at face value and generally seemed unmoved by the supposed evil of off-label promotion that the government was peddling.

But the last room remained deadlocked at 5-5. When it was clear that the entrenched sides weren't going to reach a unanimous verdict, and that in real life this would end up as a hung jury, Hirschhorn entered the room for some rapid-fire debriefing. He first asked the jurors, "Does a CEO know everything that goes on at his company?" to which the jurors favoring conviction answered a resounding "yes." Hirschhorn shot back with, "Do you know everything that goes on with your children?" which the same jurors answered by squirming in their seats.

As the jurors collected their checks and set off to enjoy what remained of their weekend, Hirschhorn came up to me and shook my hand. "You've got a triable case, Howard. If you need to, we can win this thing." I knew we needed to, so it was comforting to hear him say that we could.

But if Hirschhorn's process had taught me anything, it's that only one Rebecca, one Luis, or even one Skip, if convincing enough to sway a jury's guilty verdict on just one charge, could send my life crashing down. We still had months before we'd have to win over jurors for real, but we all – Pauzé, Richter, Lundquist and I – needed to get better. Thanks to Finley, we had time.

CHAPTER 16

HAND PICKED

October 2015 – 5 Months to Trial

I called Richter. "Yes, Howard, I've already heard," he said, "one of our guys was there, too."

I'd just started reading the summary email from our V.P. of compliance when I reached out to our D.C. lawyers about what was going on in their own backyard. After all the warnings they gave me about that "special local rule" in Texas prohibiting public statements about our case, how could the government get away with this?

> Howard, I'm at the D.C. medical device conference and the keynote lunch speaker was Julie Taitsman, the Chief Medical Officer for the Department of Health and Human Services' Inspector General. One of the topics she covered was "government perspective on medical device enforcement trends." I almost couldn't believe it, but she said the following:
>
> "Most of you are probably aware of the actions, or as I like to call it, mischief, going on in the Second Circuit [referring to the *Caronia* case]. I'm not going to go into detail on those shenanigans. But I do encourage you all to pay close attention to a case in the Western District of Texas – *U.S. v. Vascular Solutions.*"
>
> "The government chose this case. The government went on the offensive, unlike in [another recent case] *Amarin*. In this case VSI did not have clinical support to promote for perforator veins. In fact, they had a failed clinical trial and promoted for perforators anyway. They did this while knowing that their product was less safe than a competitor's."

It wasn't just "someone" in D.C. who didn't like me, as The Big Name, Tom Hefflefinger, had warned months ago. No, it went way deeper than that.

I suspected something when I read the Yates Memo, released just a month prior. Signed by its namesake, DOJ second-in-command Sally Yates, the seven-page memo was a policy response to calls from the public to get tough on corporate crime. Its solution? "Absent extraordinary circumstances, the Department will not release culpable individuals from civil or criminal liability when resolving a matter with a corporation." Translation: If you're settling with a company, you need to find some employees to take down or have a damn good reason not to. The simple, but obvious, question was *why?*

It's explained right there in Yates' introduction. "Such accountability is important for several reasons: it deters future illegal activity, it ensures that the proper parties are held responsible for their actions, and it promotes the public's confidence in our justice system." That last reason is the one you should be paying attention to here – it's a PR move.

But this business of "holding individuals accountable" for PR headlines gets a little tricky when applied to DOJ's off-label promotion regime, whose translucent purpose is to create an industry-funded ATM that spits out billions to the government each year. If the goal is to get lunch money, and the plan is to bully the kids who will give up their lunch money to avoid getting nose-punched, then saying "I'm going to punch you in the nose either way" is going to make the victims less willing to hand over their money. This, the obvious result of applying the Yates Memo to an amorphous regulatory scheme, was playing out with me as the kid trying to duck the nose-punch.

All of Bud's talk about not being able to settle the case unless I pleaded to a crime seemed like posturing during settlement talks, but now I saw where it came from. The pressure from up-high weighed on Bud and Finley, no doubt frustrating them in their efforts at settlement. Their bosses wouldn't accept a settlement without me pleading guilty, and we wouldn't settle if employees (including me) were destroyed. DOJ bigwigs had us on a trial collision course this whole time, and surviving the impact was our only way out. Or was it?

Our motions to dismiss, filed in late-summer 2015, would be the first time a judge would weigh in on the government's case, and our one chance to get it tossed before trial. There were also consolation prizes up for grabs – confining the government's legal theories and coloring Judge Biery's perception of the facts and the prosecutors.

We filed a barrage of these motions – and I don't even want to guess how much they cost in attorneys' fees – but three were the most important.

1. Motion to Dismiss the Indictment Or, In The Alternative, To Preclude The Government From Using Defendants' Truthful Speech To Prove Misbranding And Adulteration Counts

This was First Amendment conjurer Jeff Bucholtz's baby. It was the main reason the Mark Zuckerberg look-alike was brought onto this case, and having him waiting in the wings, threatening to write it, was one of the main reasons I hired King & Spalding in the first place. Now it was time to unleash him.

Seizing on the opening *Caronia* had provided, Bucholtz's delicately-crafted legal invective was a takedown of the DOJ's off-label shakedown machine. Behind the entire enforcement program, Bucholtz argued, is the criminalization of speech – no matter how much the government tried to characterize lip movements as *action*, not speech.[12]

Because the First Amendment protects truthful corporate speech, and *Caronia* said that truthful speech about off-label uses is not a crime, the prosecutors should have told the grand jury that. But the grand jury transcripts (turned over in discovery) showed that instead of disclosing this salient point of law, they ducked and weaved around it. As Bucholtz explained:

> **When a grand juror asked the prosecutors explicitly whether "the law makes a distinction between if you're selling it . . . honestly or dishonestly as a salesperson if you know it's off-label," the government did not tell the grand jury about *Caronia* or the First Amendment. Instead, the government elicited testimony (of non-lawyer witnesses) that – contrary to *Caronia* – all off-label promotion is prohibited.**

---

[12]A sample: "It was lawful for the defendants to sell Vari-Lase, having obtained FDA's authorization to do so. It was lawful for doctors to use Vari-Lase to treat perforator veins, even under the government's view that treating perforator veins is off-label. And it is the defendants' speech about that lawful conduct that, according to the government, somehow transforms their lawful conduct into a crime."

***See, e.g.* Exhibit 3. ("So, based on your understanding, regardless of whether you tell the doctor it's unapproved or not, you still can't try to sell the unapproved use, right?")**

Left in the dark, the prosecutors asked the grand jury to return an indictment "overwhelmingly based on speech that cannot be characterized as false or misleading." Trip reports, sales meetings slides, and that bootleg Danny McIff PowerPoint. The grand jury's apparent consideration of actually-legal conduct and misleading legal instructions, Bucholtz wrote, "raises a grave doubt about the validity of the indictment." It should therefore be dismissed, Bucholtz argued, or at the very least, Judge Biery should enter an order banning "the government from relying on truthful speech to prove its case at trial."

Bucholtz knew his argument, and he didn't want anyone else diluting it. But Lundquist's team, apparently unbeknownst to the island of King & Spalding, had been working on their own First Amendment motion. And Bucholtz, who ordinarily carried the quiet disposition you'd expect from a *magna cum laude* Harvard law nerd, openly didn't care for it.

Lundquist wanted to argue on my behalf that off-label promotion was constitutionally void for vagueness – you can't be convicted based on a statute no one understands. "One problem with that argument," Bucholtz wrote in an email to Lundquist four days before it was supposed to be filed, "is that it's meritless." The unblessed argument had unearthed The Other Bucholtz – the one who, I later learned, blares death metal in the office on weekends. But because The Other Bucholtz was still a legal enthusiast of the highest magnitude, his rampage was contained to a heady 10-paragraph email. His conclusion:

> **Respectfully, I don't view the vagueness issue as a debatable tactical judgment – I view it as an argument that, at least as framed in your current draft, undermines our First Amendment argument, which I view as the best chance both the company and Howard have to get this case on a favorable footing.**

I read Bucholtz's pleading, but I was still on the fence. "*Ehh*, file the damn thing," I told Lundquist. Why leave a bullet in the chamber?

2. *Motion to Compel Production of Legal Instructions to the Grand Jury*

This one piggy-backed off the First Amendment motion. If the government didn't tell the grand jury that making truthful statements about off-label uses was legal, then what did they tell them just before they returned the indictment? We asked for a transcript of these instructions – essentially the rules the grand jury thought they were playing by – in discovery, but the government refused to turn them over. So we filed a motion to unearth them. And here's where things got weird.

This is from the government's response brief, in which they argued that we shouldn't be allowed to see the grand jury instructions:

> **Because legal instructions to the grand jury are not discoverable absent extraordinary circumstances, the prosecution instructed the court reporter to make an audio recording in lieu of transcribing them. While more than half the instructions were recorded and can be transcribed, the court reporter's audio recording equipment "timed out" – *i.e.* stopped recording due to lack of typing – seven minutes into the reading of the instructions, thus failing to capture approximately the last four minutes of the instructions. The failure to record was inadvertent ...**

What!? The audio recorder stopped because no one was *typing*? That's on par with Nixon's "Rose Mary Woods was stretching" excuse for his 18 ½ minute Watergate recording gap.

But don't worry guys, they said, *we're totally not doing anything fishy.* To show that, they sent the judge a secret set of documents (an *in camera* submission) that included a transcript of the seven minutes before the audio recorder went radio silent and a "handwritten script reflecting the instructions given during the four-minute period when the recording equipment timed out." They added that "Finley read this instruction nearly verbatim," and therefore, "the *in camera* submission is being offered to the Court so that the Court may confirm, if necessary, that the grand jury was properly instructed."

Actually, Finley's unauthenticated "script" that he "nearly" followed couldn't possibly "confirm" what he actually said. And, as we pointed out in our reply brief, they violated Federal Rule of Criminal Procedure 6(e) by failing to ensure that the jury instructions were properly recorded. And yes, following the law is "necessary," even for a federal prosecutor.

3. Motion to Dismiss the Indictment Based on Government Misconduct

This one was *my* baby. I'd been promising our investors "you'll see!" when explaining why the prosecutors brought this case, and now was the time to reveal what we had. In 173 pages of motion and exhibits, we detailed misconduct "so pervasive that it fundamentally undermined the reliability of the grand jury's determination." See for yourself.

The motion documented the government's pattern of:

- **Strong-arming witnesses to influence testimony.** Carrie Powers' testimony was "pissing them off." Susan Christian was spouting the "same line of shit." Glen Holden was a "poor fucker [who] just on principle may be indicted," unless he returned "on bended knee" to change his testimony. We left the profanity in to keep Judge Biery's attention long enough to recognize the threats behind it.

- **Distorting evidence.** FDA Agent George Scavdis falsely testified before the grand jury that VSI "did not have any form of FDA marketing authorization for treatment of perforator veins," even though an FDA medical officer told him during an interview that "VSI may be right" that the indications covers the treatment of perforator veins.

- **Abusing grand jury subpoenas to strip witnesses of counsel**. At one of those kangaroo court interviews, a former employee asked to leave the room and speak to her lawyer, to which Finley responded, "No. The options are, you can answer my questions, you can refuse to answer my question, and if you refuse to answer my question, I might have to bring you [down to San Antonio]." The witness answered the question.

- **Grossly misstating the law.** According to the grand jury transcripts, at one point Bud instructed that it was "unlawful to use the Vari-Lase equipment on perforators, period." *Wrong. Very wrong.* Other times, he said that merely selling a device "with the intent that it be used to treat perforators" was illegal. *Also wrong.*

- **Leaking secret grand jury testimony to influence witness testimony.** Some of the witnesses said things that didn't help the government's case. The prosecutors then threatened to charge those witnesses with perjury for what they said, threatened to have them fired, and threatened to have them banned from the healthcare industry. Then, after all that, they called them back for a second interview. *Hey, we think you got some things wrong the first time, things we need you to "fix." By the way, here's some sealed testimony from the grand jury – this is what others are saying. If you don't say the same, you'll be "practically alone" and we won't consider your testimony "fixed."* A clear violation of the law and Rule 6(e), which says a prosecutor "must not disclose a matter occurring before the grand jury."[13]

To support these allegations, we relied on the transcripts the government gave us and affidavits from Jon Hopeman, RJ Zayed and Dan Scott. Over 100 years of experience among them, all coming to the same conclusion as would someone off the street if you told them these anecdotes: *that seems wrong.* Hopeman didn't want to put his neck out there at first. But after a bizarre conversation in which Finley reportedly told him it'd be a "great idea" to provide an affidavit describing the prosecutors' disclosure of grand jury testimony, Hopeman drafted a 12-page affidavit detailing all of the misconduct he'd witnessed.

I still think Finley's comment must have been sarcasm, because our misconduct motion was bad news for him and Bud. As soon as something like this is filed, I learned from my legal team of ex-government lawyers, DOJ's Office of Professional Responsibility (OPR) opens a file and conducts an investigation. Having an OPR file in itself is a red flag in a prosecutor's employment history, and any findings of misconduct would all but block the violator's chances of career advancement within the Department. But that's just the formal stuff. Informally, Bud and Finley's bosses would see the motion. Should they judge the conduct to be particularly flagrant, either or both could be kicked off the trial team, robbing the government of valuable case knowledge just months before trial. Having seen how sloppy these guys were in the grand jury, though – they seriously struggled to formulate an admissible question – I wondered if maybe we actually wanted them on the other side at trial.

---

[13]This is not a minor, technical violation. In October 2016, former Pennsylvania Attorney General Kathleen Kane was sentenced to 10 to 23 months in prison for leaking grand jury testimony for her own political benefit, among other charges under state law.

With the motions filed and fully briefed, all we could do was wait for Judge Biery's ruling. A good fall gardening season was underway in San Antonio, so I thought the decision would take a while to appear, but that didn't stop me from checking the government-run PACER website daily (and sometimes hourly) for new filings.

On November 2, I saw a new filing – #123 in our case. It had only been two weeks, early by Biery standards, but I clicked on it anyway. At the top, in all caps, I saw:

ORDER DENYING DEFENDANTS' MOTION TO DISMISS BASED ON ALLEGED GOVERNMENT MISCONDUCT

My blood pressure spiked. He'd even retroactively re-titled our motion to slip the word "alleged" in there, rubbing salt in the denial. After a short introduction, there appeared a numbered list of 17 findings – none of which were favorable, and all of which were painful to read. Here's a sampling:

1. The Court finds that this matter does not require a hearing.

3. The record does not demonstrate that the attorneys for the Government forced any witness to lie or that they misshaped the testimony of any witness.

6. The Court further finds that the record does not demonstrate that the attorneys for the Government knowingly provided false and misleading testimony to the grand jury.

9. The Court further finds that any potential violation of Federal Rule of Criminal Procedure 6(e) [disclosure of secret grand jury testimony] was harmless.

10. The Court finds no evidence to support the Defendants argument that the attorneys for the Government misused the grand jury process to induce examinations outside the grand jury.

12. The Court finds that the attorneys for the Government did not endeavor to distort the law when they instructed the grand jury.

13. The Court finds that there is no evidence of any prejudice to Defendants caused by any alleged misconduct by the attorneys for the Government.

15. Even if this Court found the Defendants' allegations of misconduct to be true and conclusively proven, the remedy would not be dismissal of the indictment.

I got to the bottom.

17. Because the Court concludes that the Defendants have not demonstrated intentional prosecutorial misconduct or substantial prejudice to justify dismissal of the indictment, the Defendants are not entitled to any relief.

IT IS SO ORDERED.

Huh. That's weird; it's not dated. Wait – it's not signed, either. Wait – what is this?

I looked back at the description in PACER. "Filed by Paulissen, Bud." *What? Why would Bud file Judge Biery's order? Wait – this isn't Biery's order, this was Bud's wish-list of what he'd like to see in Judge Biery's order.* So why would Bud, unprompted, file a proposed order a full month after he had filed his last response brief?

Then I thought about the judge and realized this probably wasn't unprompted. I remembered the time we had a question about page limits for our briefs, and how easily our San Antonio lawyers were able to get on the phone with Judge Biery himself for an answer. Judges typically frown on these *ex parte* communications (conversations with the judge without all the parties present), but Biery apparently did not.

I don't know for sure, but here's how I imagine it went down.

Judge Biery runs into Bud at the courthouse Halloween party.

Judge Biery (dressed as Chief Judge Fred Biery): Hey there, Bud. Nice costume.

Bud (dressed as a giant strawberry): Well, Your Honor, I know how much you love horticulture, and, well, just thought I'd try to put a smile on your face.

Judge Biery: Righhtttt. Say there, Bud, I read that little motion them Yankees filed.[14] Something 'bout you swearing at some folks …

Bud (turns redder): Well, you know, you can't believe sworn affidavits these days. I mean, maybe I raised my voice once or twice, but—

Judge Biery: Aw, sure. I remember raising my voice when I took the bench in 1979. But then I learned it doesn't matter, any of this. Long as we're all home by 2:30.

Bud smiles awkwardly, rocking on the balls of his feet.

Judge Biery: Tellya'hwhat. You write up one of those little draft order things, put whatever you need in there to keep you and that Finley fella outta trouble, and file it. Never know what'll happen.

Biery winks and walks off, as Bud's floppy leaf-crown pops off in excitement.

Judge Biery's real order came two weeks after Bud's impersonation. In a contorted affront to justice, he brushed away each one of our claims. Every. Last. One. The legal reasoning was superficial at best, often only one or two sentences following a lengthy and rather unlettered recitation of each side's arguments. It looked, and this is no exaggeration, like a middling high school essay.

Biery began by dismissing Bucholtz's First Amendment treatise in a single paragraph. The First Amendment and *Caronia* didn't apply here, he said, because the government alleged that we misled doctors about Medicare and study results. He ignored our request to "preclude the government from using truthful speech to prove" their case, which was, you know, in the title of our brief. Next he teed up Lundquist's unconstitutional vagueness argument and kicked it through the roof with case law. It was a tactical mistake, I now saw, giving Biery enough legal high-ground to disarm our remaining arguments with insultingly-shallow analysis.

---

[14] After we filed our motions to dismiss the indictment, Judge Biery remarked to one of our local San Antonio lawyers, "Those suits sure like to file a lot of motions."

Biery strained to apologize for the government's misconduct allegation-by-allegation, under headings ranging from the letter "A" to "H." It was okay for the prosecutors to threaten witnesses with perjury for disagreeing with the prosecutors' theories because we couldn't prove that Bud and Finley *knew* they were lying. It was okay for them to leak grand jury testimony because the poisoned witnesses didn't testify a second time before the grand jury. Running kangaroo courts across the country was cool because the witnesses could have chosen to go before the grand jury in San Antonio if they'd really wanted to. The FDA agent telling the grand jury perforators weren't covered was okay because that FDA medical officer contradicted himself and "it is not clear what other interviews [the FDA agent] relied on as bases for his testimony." Blocking witnesses from talking to their lawyers might have been bad, but even if it was it didn't make a difference in the end. And finally, systematically soliciting misstatements of the law from unknowing witnesses was legit because "an indictment may not be dismissed on the basis of incompetent evidence." Right.

In the last section of the misconduct ruling, Biery listed 17 findings, all favorable to the government. The same 17 findings Bud had put in his draft order. In the same order. In the same words, without a single change.[15]

Astonishing. How do you even comprehend something like that without the word "conspiracy" darting to the front of your mind? I still hadn't finished the opinion, though, and somehow the worst was yet to come. Biery's final kick in the groin was making sure we never saw those grand jury instructions.

The indictment alleges defendants made false or misleading statements, which are not protected by the First Amendment. Defendants have not shown that any failure to instruct the jury regarding the First Amendment could have had any effect on the grand jury's decision to indict.

Think about that. If the grand jury was falsely led to believe that truthful promotion regarding perforators was illegal, what's to say they didn't indict us for making truthful statements? Look at it this way. If Bud lied to a grand jury and said that turning left was illegal, then presented evidence of you turning left, and you got indicted, the fact that he made an off-hand claim about you

---

[15]That's not completely true. Judge Biery did, after all, make one change; replacing all refernces to "government" with "Government."

speeding wouldn't justify the indictment. Claiming you have evidence about one crime isn't a free pass to invent another crime. Except, apparently, in Biery's courtroom.

And, by the way, there was no mention of the government's secret submission – the jury instructions and that "almost-script" from the missing four minutes. If those instructions cleared the government, and our argument was therefore meritless, why not say that in the opinion?

This was a hatchet job, through and through. My hands were shaking in anger, maybe fear, as I sat there, staring at the screen. I felt the helpless frustration bubbling up and launched a squish ball at the ceiling. The phone was ringing with high-priced lawyers, but I ignored them. I had to go home and tell Beth. Our last real opportunity to end this before trial was gone.

—⅃⅃ᴧ—

The toll of it all set in around 4 a.m. I jerked awake, mind racing around what had become of me and my company. The company had seen its legal costs jump, profits sink, and R&D pipeline go sideways. But for me, years of living in survival mode – years of putting the company first and me second – was catching up. I couldn't focus when I was around the few friends I had, and I'd lost some others along the way due to my prolonged truancy. My brothers and sisters didn't seem to understand what I was going through, and I was too protective of my aging father to let him in on it beyond surface explanations. I tried to lose myself in normalcy – mowing the lawn and running to lose weight ("you don't want to be the fat, slow guy in prison," I joked, nervously) – but there was an edge to it now. And now that our motions had failed, that edge would only get sharper until the final cut, either way, at trial.

In the back of my mind, I had always thought of this thing as a temporary distraction – something that would disappear. Even after four years, and even after the indictment, I thought the case would find some way to resolve itself. It wasn't just hope, either, it's what I believed would happen. The bosses at DOJ would step in, a judge would gut their case, somebody at FDA would go public exposing the whole thing as overblown nonsense – I don't know. But no longer could I continue to think that.

As I lay in bed and the dominoes in my mind fell, I started feeling queasy. *Was this for real, or was I just thinking myself into feeling sick?* "No, it's real," said my stomach. I started a controlled rush to the bathroom, my stomach confirming its intentions along the way. I reached the toilet, dropped to my knees and tossed the previous night's dinner. As dizziness set in and my vision narrowed, I knew from experience that I was about to faint. I needed to get all the way to the ground, but before I could choose between hitting the marble floor with my head and the porcelain target with what was left in my stomach, my body made the choice for me. I was out.

I came to with my head resting on the bathroom scale. As I opened my eyes and saw the pool of blood on the floor from my bloodied nose, two words looped in my mind.

"Bob, no."

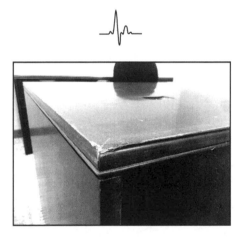

Bob Shibley used to work for us back when we were just a start-up. He came highly recommended by Gabe Veigh, a device entrepreneur I respected greatly. So after a quick interview, I hired Bob as our V.P. of operations. He was coming off of a mid-life crisis that saw him divorced and managing a bar in Vietnam, but Bob had since found a new wife, and our cushy relocation package lured him to Minneapolis to start the next chapter of his life.

But almost as soon as Bob started, it was clear he was in over his head. He didn't know what to do and couldn't do the things people were telling him he should be doing. One of our contractors, who had worked with Bob at a prior company, explained why. Bob was really just a purchasing manager – someone who sets terms and manages relationships with vendors – not someone who knows the business inside-out and sets up manufacturing systems. I called up Gabe. "I was afraid that might happen," he told me, explaining that he'd pushed Bob on me because he wanted to help him get back on his feet after returning from the Pacific Rim. Not helpful, Gabe – to me or Bob.

With nowhere to hide an unqualified senior-level employee, and work that needed to get done for the company to succeed, I had no choice but to fire Bob. And because I was still handling human resources at our fledging company, I'd have to do it personally. I slipped into his office on a Tuesday, explained to him that we needed to make a change, and presented our severance offer. Three months paid leave, even though he'd barely worked three months, and he could keep the relocation money and the Ford Excursion we'd given him. He shook my hand, packed up his things, and left that day.

Later that week, Bob called me. I was out of town, meeting potential investors for our next round of funding, but he told my assistant he wanted to set up a meeting. I planned to stop by the office after flying home on Sunday morning to catch up on some work, so I told him to drop by then.

I'd already put in a couple hours by 4 p.m. when I heard Bob rap on the front door. Being the only person around the building on Sunday, I opened the door and led him back to my office, unsure of what Bob wanted to discuss.

After some pleasantries, he began. "I'm financially in bad shape and I need to ask you for a favor."

"Okay," I responded, uncertain but polite.

"Will you give me an additional three months of severance pay?"

I felt my blood pressure rising. Bob hadn't lost anything by joining Vascular Solutions. I'd given him a shot and it didn't work out, and I'd offered him what we both knew was a generous severance package for a company in our position. "I can't do that, Bob," I replied, hiding my frustration as best I could. "We're a start-up, and three months' severance is more than fair."

"Okay," Bob said, as he stood up and put his right hand in the pocket of his winter jacket. There was a desk between us – and at 50, five feet nine inches tall and 160 pounds, Bob was not a physically intimidating guy. So I didn't think he was going to punch me. But then I watched, almost in slow motion, as he slid his hand from his pocket to reveal a handgun.

I gasped, pushed my desk chair back and pleaded, "Bob, no."

"Relax," he said dismissively. "I'm not going to hurt you." He turned around, put the barrel in his mouth, waited two long seconds, and pulled the trigger. I sat petrified, turning away only at the grating pop of the shot. It gave way to an unforgettable "smack," as Bob's head careened off the corner of my desk and settled on the floor. I averted my eyes from his body but heard a feint gurgle coming from in front of my desk. Then, nothing.

That was my first sleepless night at the company, and by far the worst. I replayed and replayed it. Why didn't I see this coming and stop it? What if I'd let my anger get to me and snapped at him? I couldn't stop thinking about the sobering words of the responding officer. "You're lucky he didn't shoot you first," he said. "They usually do that."

Beth rushed in, woken by the noise and now startled by my sliced nose and the bloody bathroom scene. "Are you okay?!"

"I'm okay," I assured her, patting the scale I'd landed on like a pillow. "I'm lucky."

CHAPTER 17

LUCK

December 2015 – 2 Months to Trial

I don't believe in luck.

Maybe that's what you'd expect to hear from the hard-ass corporate caricature some have made me out to be. But the truth is, I do believe in luck. Because good things happen on occasion, even when you don't have occasion to expect them. That had been my experience with launching a company, meeting my wife, Beth, and falling into the GuideLiner's success. And just when it looked like this rigged steeplechase might rip away my optimism – the singular quality that allowed me, in my mind, to tolerate the unpleasantries of business – we hit our first run of luck.

Oddly enough, it began by getting indicted again. The government brought in another grand jury and staged a do-over, returning what's called a superseding indictment. I'm not entirely sure why. It may have been an effort to clean up some loose language in the indictment we could've attacked on appeal, but I think it was more likely (conspiracy theory coming) a bid to whitewash the shenanigans they pulled with the first grand jury. *Look, these new guys indicted, too – forget about the misconduct the other grand jury saw!*

But even a pessimist could see the silver lining of the superseding indictment. The government dropped a third of their case – that dumb adulteration argument – which meant that we didn't have to waste the jury's attention dispelling Finley's lead-brained but complex theory about FDA's regulatory purview.

In an unrelated development, we got a new judge. After issuing his soul-crushing order, Judge Biery announced he was dropping the case. Incredibly, picking it up would be the one judge in the country we would've hand-picked, Royce C. Lamberth of the D.C. District Court, a jurist who described himself as "no rubber stamp for the government."

That wasn't the only reason we found the salty old judge so attractive. He was a veritable folk hero in the medical community, having authored a scathing opinion that FDA "exaggerates its overall place in the universe" when it took the position that off-label uses of drugs are unsafe until it evaluates them. We'd cited his opinion in our First Amendment motion to dismiss, and now we'd get the author himself for trial.

How'd we get so lucky? Well, Judge Lamberth had achieved "senior status," and with it the flexibility to travel around the country to hear cases, if he so pleased. A native San Antonian, Judge Lamberth had made a tradition of returning to his hometown in the winter to take cases, and now – a result of Finley's "I'm not ready yet" delay – Lamberth's schedule matched up with ours.

For us, it was perfect. Judge Lamberth would give us berth to show that FDA wasn't some infallible acronym – it was just a government office full of regular people. And in another break, we learned, incredibly, that one of those people had been hired directly from McDonald's.

Randolph Copeland was the middle-aged FDA reviewer who bungled our application to add the word "perforator" to our indications, and our private investigator had finally tracked him down. Copeland had no experience or background in medical devices, although he had held a number of government jobs, from substitute teacher to systems engineer for the National Missile Defense Program. But right before he came to the FDA in 2007 and was assigned to evaluate the range of clinical circumstances in which varicosities in the lower extremity could be associated with reflux in the great saphenous vein, he was managing the fry flow at the local Golden Arches. He had been in on some interesting discussions while he was at FDA, and said he'd be willing to testify for us.

But before we sat down with Copeland, another guy came out of the woodwork. "Howard," Tom Vitt rushed to say on a call out of the blue, "you won't believe the voicemail I just received from Eddie Pedregon." That didn't make sense. Why would "Fast" Eddie Pedregon, the guy who breathed life into DeSalle Bui's ship-launching complaint, be calling the lawyer who sued him and got him fired at Spectranetics?

"Are you sure it was Eddie?" I asked. Tom forwarded me the voicemail, and sure enough, it was.

Mr. Vitt, my name is Eddie Pedregon. I am a former employee of Vascular Solutions and I've been called in the case against Howard Root. I have some information that may help your client and I wish to speak to you about this, uh, as soon as possible. I was used in this case to get the indictment and it was based off a whistleblower's accusation in order to get financial gain from the company. Please give me a call. 915-***-****. I want to help, uh, your client.

The mysterious, guarded voicemail sounded like something out of the *The Big Lebowski*. I told Tom to call him back and see if he was for real, or if he just wanted a free rug, as it were. Tom did, and he said Eddie seemed genuine. "He says that DeSalle manipulated him and told him exactly what to say to the lawyer," Tom said. "Eddie would testify that he was instructed to not promote the Short Kit for perforator veins and that you didn't do anything wrong. He's upset that this has gone so far and that he helped start it."

It all sounded a little too good. Eddie wasn't as much of a scammer as DeSalle Bui, but he was, by this recent admission, someone who would help file a fraudulent lawsuit. If we were going to be able to use this, I wanted my lawyers to interview Eddie and smoke out any B.S. Luckily, Richter and another King & Spalding lawyer happened to be in San Antonio later that week to meet with Hirschhorn about jury selection. We arranged for Eddie to fly from El Paso to meet them, and in so doing, pried open a Pandora's box of nonsense and treachery.

According to a memo prepared by the private investigator we hired to be present, the interview started out normally. When asked why he reached out to the company, Eddie said "because I do the right thing." He explained that he was a "pawn in the game of DeSalle Bui," whom he believed was now in Belize living it up off the proceeds from the civil settlement.

What he had to say "would clear VSI," Eddie told our lawyers. He explained that VSI employees were trained never to promote for perforators, and that the supposed off-label promotion to a doctor in Amarillo, Texas, the nexus that allowed the case to be filed in the Western District, didn't happen. DeSalle gave Eddie's name to the government and told Eddie to say that he promoted the Short Kit for perforators at the instruction of his regional manager Shane Carlson. None of that was true, Eddie said. DeSalle was a "con man" who used him out of necessity because DeSalle never saw a perforator treated himself.

And that's where things took a strange turn. "I'm your star witness," Eddie said, followed by claiming that he'd been black-balled from the industry and wanted his job back at VSI. Our attorneys told him they obviously couldn't do that, frustrating the self-proclaimed "star witness." Pedregon got up, requested to speak with the private investigator alone, and led him outside the hotel meeting spot.

Once outside, Eddie said that his testimony "could go either way," and suggested that if "$1,000 or $600" showed up in an envelope, he wouldn't know where it came from.

You can't make this stuff up. After denying Eddie's, let's say, "request," the investigator informed our lawyers, who, obviously, told Eddie that nothing like that would ever happen. It was all we needed to hear, and it meant that we didn't have to worry about Eddie testifying against us. Plus, if they called Bui, we'd have an explosive, albeit unpredictable, answer.

$$\text{---}\bigwedge\hspace{-0.3em}\bigvee\hspace{-0.4em}\text{---}$$

They say you make your own luck. And, knowing that we'd need plenty of it with trial quickly approaching, we were in the final stages of the manufacturing process.

While the lawyers were rearranging our witness list, piecing together the exhibit list, and endlessly rewriting their cross-examination outlines, I was getting ready myself. I watched my taped testimony from the mock trial over and over again. *Keep your hands down. Don't look so smug on direct.* I bought a two-week supply of button-down shirts and a good shoe polish. If they weren't going to like me, it wouldn't be for a scuffed loafer.

As our preparations shifted into overdrive, Bud tried to jam up the gearbox with a last-minute settlement offer. Like the rest of his offers, though, it was essentially the same, if not worse.

This one involved the company pleading guilty to the misdemeanor mis-branding counts, in exchange for dropping the felony and stripping from the statement of facts all references to Medicare fraud, thus reducing the chance that HHS would ban the company from future business. What a bargain. But wait, there was more. The floated deal would also require the company to pay a multi-million dollar fine, adopt stifling compliance provisions, and "cooperate fully in the prosecution of Howard Root."

Bud also made me an offer – four years of probation and no jail time if I pled guilty to felony conspiracy to defraud the United States, a charge that would automatically ban me from the healthcare industry. In other words, forced retirement with an ankle monitor. We had four weeks over the holidays, until January 8, 2016, to decide.

My initial reaction to the deals echoed the response Paul O'Connell sent to the rest of our board: "Two words, and they're not 'Merry Christmas.'" But because I was conflicted out, the company's decision was not mine to make – it was Paul's and the board's other five independent directors. I wasn't worried about Paul, of course, but I was still concerned that some of the others could get weak-kneed at the last minute and take the deal. Thankfully, I didn't think the government had moved enough to make the directors flinch, and majority rules meant that four votes out of six would be needed to approve the settlement offer.

Richter excused himself and his trial team from the settlement discussions with Bud. "We need to keep our foot on the pedal here," he told me. Not only would the settlement courtship take up his team's time, he said, it would dull their fighting spirit. He suggested we bring in a ringer to negotiate with Bud, and King & Spalding had the perfect guy on their bench – Gary G. Grindler, the former Chief of Staff to Attorney General Eric Holder who once held Sally Yates' current job. If there was anyone the selectively-sycophantic Bud would swoon over, it was Grindler.

Under Richter's plan, Grindler would tease the best offer he could out of Bud and present it to our independent directors for a vote, while the rest of the team continued marching in formation toward battle. Let Bud waste his time chasing this dead end. I liked the clear, proactive plan, and Richter's sudden embrace of a black ops approach. "Activate him," I would've said if we were in a spy movie, but instead I probably said something less cool, like "sounds good." Same result; Grindler was on it.

While Grindler danced with Bud, we looked for ways to crystalize our complicated case for the jury. The government's theory that the CEO could be responsible for reading every one of these "perforator" trip reports was ridiculous; I just needed a way to get that across. I had access to sales rep reports covering over a quarter-million doctor visits during the time we were selling the Short Kit, but the jury would only see the 50 bad ones. After Bud showed them needle after needle after needle, those 50 reports would look like they were the whole haystack.

The solution was obvious. I present … The Tower of Trip Reports!

One year's worth of sales reps' trip reports, printed out, center-hole drilled, and tethered over an aluminum rod to a four-wheel dolly with an extendable handle – the only device I invented in 2015. Stacked up, they rose over Pauzé's head, and this was only one year's worth (out of seven)! By the time we got to present our case at trial, I figured, the jury would be bored drunk from weeks of repetitive testimony. So, if we could sober them up with a corny visual aid, I was all for it.

Meanwhile, Grindler and Bud were locked in an email flame war. Their last-minute negotiations started cordially, with Bud agreeing to transition to a "bland" statement of facts that he was "99% sure" would not include any fraud allegations against the company. But with Bud, the seasoned Grindler was now seeing, the shiftiness was endemic.

The proposed statement of facts Bud sent over on December 22 (my birthday) was about as bland as a Tabasco enema. *Happy Birthday!* "I must say that I was taken aback by the proposed wording in this document," Grindler responded. "It alleges knowing and intentional acts, explicitly asserts that the sales campaign was 'misleading,' and claims that VSI concealed the facts. You stated that you were 99% sure there would be no fraud language … Are you now saying otherwise?" Grindler continued by infantilizing Bud, writing, "My experience as a prosecutor is that the government frequently works with defense counsel on the allegations that will form the basis of a plea – it is not just a version of facts from the government's perspective." Grindler sent back a red-line cutting out the defamatory language.

Bud didn't budge, of course. "The counter-offer you sent in the form of edits to my proposed plea agreement … reflects a bare minimum admission of guilt by VSI, and signals an anemic level of cooperation from the company in the prosecution of Howard Root." He even lobbed back some of Grindler's condescension. "I'm confident that with the extensive prosecution experience you and your partners have, you will be able to move closer to my offer without more specifics from me. As we discussed early on, I'm preparing for trial, while you apparently are not."

This wasn't going anywhere, and Grindler was at his wits' end. The time had come to go to the board.

Our chairman, John Erb, convened a January 4 vote by phone. I called in to give my perspective and then dropped off the line when it was time for the independent portion. As I waited in my home office for the decision, my stomach felt like I'd swallowed a peach whole.

I knew that the board could wipe their hands clean of this whole saga right now if they wanted; all they had to do was cut me loose from the company I'd created. By doing that they'd eliminate the biggest risk to the company – exclusion from the U.S. healthcare industry – and preserve the jobs of its 550 employees. For now, at least, who knew how the company would do with my eager replacement Chad Kugler. As the time dragged on, my feeling of unease intensified. The hardest part about fighting the government, I was realizing, was just getting to the courtroom. Waiting by the phone as the minutes passed, I was tantalizingly close – yet so far.

The call came from Erb. "We're going to trial." Apparently after Grindler ran down the offer and its consequences, the board had only one substantive question, from Rich Kramp, the newest member. "Do we have to sign a false statement about Howard if it would help our shareholders financially?"

"No," our long-time corporate counsel from Dorsey responded, "Absolutely not."

"Okay, that makes it easy," Rich replied.

Marty Emerson, the board member who worried me the most, chimed in his instructions: "Tell Bud to go to hell."

And with that, the board unanimously sent me into battle. *Wish me luck.*

Step 3

TREATMENT

CHAPTER 18

THE RODEO COMES TO TOWN

6 Days to Trial

My arrival in San Antonio was greeted with rain. Another reminder that this wasn't a vacation, in case it wasn't obvious from the dreary beige wallpaper of the Springhill Suites (which we appropriately called "Camp Springhill"). I'd learn that nobody really comes to San Antonio to vacation. It's a place people end up that happens to offer a few vacation activities. Kind of like how I don't go to the airport for Ben & Jerry's, but it happens to be there. Or how I don't go to Ben & Jerry's for subpoenas.

For the next two months, we'd booked a block of 30 rooms at Camp Springhill. The rewards points would be massive – if I ever got a chance to use them. Are there prison upgrades in the Marriott network?

Our relative permanence in the hotel contrasted the weekly circus that rolled into town. Over the next month, our roommates would include Comic-Con, a pre-teen cheer competition (think moms with matching uniforms and dads with mullets), and THE RODEO, a big thing in San Antonio. It was like living in perpetual Halloween, to which we always showed up as "the Suits."

The Suits lived in the War Room. Camp Springhill had two conference rooms – one was the size of a baseball infield; the other a baseball dugout. With 14 attorneys and paralegals to stable, we had a Goldilocks problem and no middle bed. We chose the dugout to be our War Room, mainly because the hotel gave it to us for free, leaving the big room (worryingly dubbed "The Alamo Room") to be used for something the Comic-Con-ers called a "Tekken 2 Tournament." Under the unofficial law of trial, the Suits were only permitted to leave the War Room for two reasons: 1) Going to court and 2) Sleeping between the hours of 3 and 7 a.m. [Note: The second allowance was not necessarily applicable to junior associates and paralegals.]

When I arrived, our defense team was far from full strength. Only a skeleton crew had come down early to argue preliminary motions before Judge Lamberth, our white knight in a black robe.

Don't get fooled by their tame name; these "preliminary motions" can be bombshells that lay waste to one side's case. This is done through requests called "motions in limine," which are issue-specific gag orders that either side can request. It's a high-stakes legal shootout on the eve of trial, and we had a full clip loaded. Knowing that Judge Biery's last official day on the case was January 4, we waited until January 5 to start firing.

The other side only gets seven days to respond to a preliminary motion, and if the response isn't persuasive, they could lose and end up having to try their case with both hands tied behind their back. We had a dedicated team of specialists in D.C. led by Jeff Bucholtz writing our motions and cranking away rapid responses to those filed by the prosecutors, a luxury we knew the government couldn't match. Altogether we filed 225 pages (and hundreds more in exhibits), drawing 150 pages of response out of the government. We weren't just outworking them, though; I thought we had the better arguments. It was going to be fun watching Judge Royce "no rubber stamp for the government" Lamberth take a sledgehammer to the prosecutors' watermelon of a case.

Lamberth handed down his orders the day after I arrived. One by one, they were posted to the court's PACER website. DENIED. DENIED. DENIED. DENIED. The War Room was taking steady fire. As dust billowed from the smoldering rubble, Pauzé could only stare at the wall. Shaking his head slightly in disbelief, he muttered, "I thought he'd at least grant one."

It was a bad day, my second one in Texas. An ominous start to the Lamberth era, and a harsh reminder that we were on the prosecutors' turf. Not just geographically – it's the entire criminal justice system that is the prosecutors' turf. They decide whom to charge, what to charge, and when to charge. They were at home, and after our attempt to legally hobble them failed (again), they'd be playing at full strength. Maybe my luck had run out.

CHAPTER 19

FIVE YEARS, 12 PEERS

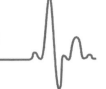

1 Day to Trial

T he security line was long. It was 7:45 on Monday morning, and I was stuck in a tail of over 100 potential jurors waiting to enter the John H. Wood Jr. United States Courthouse, which fittingly resembled a flying saucer boarding for lift-off. A month earlier, the San Antonio Express-News described the courthouse as "a crumbling relic of the 1968 World's Fair, plagued by mold, asbestos and contaminated water ... in such disrepair that it poses serious health and safety risks to the public." Once the gem of the HemisFair's U.S.A. Pavilion, it was now home to opossums and feral cats that had gnawed the electrical system to tassels.

After the '68 Fair – which lost over $48 million in today's dollars – the old Confluence Theater was converted into a federal courthouse. In the intervening half-century, it'd become clear that the design specs for displaying "the world's largest curvilinear motion picture screen" were not ideal for housing one of the nation's busiest courthouses.

For starters, it was an aggressively poor use of space. Like a 70-foot-tall bundt cake, the only useful portions of the courthouse were around the perimeter. All that empty middle space left the theoretically-large building cavernous, dark, and missing a few things. Comically, the judges shared the hallways and elevators with prisoners. Less comically, everyone shared a set of closet-sized bathrooms. The vermin problem lead to an eating moratorium on the ground floor, meaning we had to reserve a conference room on the top floor in which to safely gobble our sandwiches. The government, meanwhile, huddled with their lunchboxes by a cluster of chairs on the second floor landing designated "law enforcement only." What a perk.

The potential jurors around me looked in surprisingly good spirits, considering they were spending their Monday morning queuing to enter a massive concrete biohazard. They were mostly blue-collar types – not too many looked like they would be able to identify with a medical device executive from Minnesota. But I knew from our mock jury work that at least half of them would vote to acquit. We just had to figure out which half.

Once I made it past the courthouse's friendly-but-deliberate security team, I headed to Courtroom 2. This was traditionally the kingdom of Judge Biery, who had been auto-banished to the visitor's courtroom for the duration of our trial. But Courtroom 2 was still his, he reminded us. Just before Judge Lamberth kicked off jury selection, Judge Biery popped his head in; I could see he was wearing an open collared shirt and blue jeans – no robe. I could only assume he was wearing cowboy boots. "Don't get up," he ordered the handful of lawyers who recognized him outside of his superhero outfit. "I just want to let y'all know how much I regret not sitting in here with you for the next five weeks." His gardening-tanned smile belied the sentiment. Nothing like a life-appointed judge mocking something that will decide the fate of your freedom and life's work …

This is a good time to remind you that if Judge Biery didn't want this trial, he could've granted our motion to transfer venue. He could've had his empty courtroom all to himself, and we would've been back in Minneapolis, where the trial belonged. Instead, he kept the case as a housewarming gift for his buddy Lamberth. "At least the court reporter will be happy making a little extra money," Judge Biery quipped.[16] *Jackass* – the only word that came to mind as he ended his cameo by slinking back to chambers.

While the lawyers waited for Judge Lamberth to take the bench, I studied the 12-deep prosecution team: four prosecutors, three paralegals, two federal agents, an FDA lawyer, a witness coordinator, and a jury consultant. The prosecutors wore serious and important looks, seemingly avoiding eye contact with me, their pre-taxidermy trophy. But it was George Scavdis – the FDA investigating agent – whose curiousness my gaze couldn't shake.

Scavdis was a younger guy than I'd imagined when reading all of his interview memos. He just sat there at the prosecution table, hands raised to his bearded mouth, looking straight ahead as he mumbled to himself. I would notice this odd behavior – along with his multicolored, paneled shoes that may have been lifted from a bowling alley – throughout the trial. It wasn't until Scavdis finally took the stand, on the last day of the government's case, that I'd understand the flood of emotion buried beneath the mumbling. But that was still four weeks away.

CLAP CLAP. "All rise." Lamberth took the bench to tell us that 125 eligible jurors had shown up. They were being held in the basement jury assembly room, a space still recovering from a widespread flea infestation two months prior. According to the same newspaper article, when federal employees went in to repair flood damage, they came out of the basement "just covered in fleas."

---

[16]I'd learn that although the court reporters – whose work is a special form of magic – get a base salary, the real money comes from the rush transcript surcharge that big trials like ours pay. Biery never had those. Perhaps coincidentally, those trials would interfere with lunchtime basketball and afternoon gardening. Judge Biery's regular court reporter had just quit due to the lack of action in his court, and true to form, the visitor's courtroom remained overwhelmingly quiet throughout trial.

A hundred other potential jurors – perhaps regular San Antonio Express-News readers – had managed to get themselves removed from the jury pool by submitting written excuses. Most of these excuses were based around jobs or non-refundable cruises. I'm not sure why a trip on Royal Caribbean trumps civic duty, but it was good enough for Judge Lamberth, and in turn, good enough to save them from parasitic exposure.

Once Judge Lamberth finished with his juror status report, Bud rose, and in his syrupy-sweet-but-noticeably-artificial tone, said, "Your honor, I'd like to ask my own excuse."

"Denied," barked Judge Lamberth. "Oh, I'm sorry," the judge feigned with a chuckle. "I'm supposed to listen to the excuse before I deny it." Judge Lamberth, like most judges, has a sense of humor dulled by decades of captive audiences. I politely laughed and smiled along with the lawyers, while on the inside wondering if anyone in the courthouse was actually taking this matter seriously.

Bud laughed (for too long) and then continued, "I said earlier that my opening would be only 30 minutes, but when I timed it over the weekend, it's more like 40 minutes long."

"Okay," replied Judge Lamberth. Hold on – did Bud wait until the weekend before trial to practice his opening for the first time?

We'll get back to that, but now it was time for *voir dire*. That's the French legal name for jury selection, which is pronounced "vwuah deer" everywhere except Texas, where it's twanged up to "vorr dyer." Judge Lamberth summoned the jury pool from flea purgatory, and in a massive wave they overflowed the sparsely-furnished courtroom. Jurors here, jurors there, jurors everywhere – including, for first time, in the jury box.

It was my first time seeing how trial would really look, and my position at the defense table would be perfect. I was on the wall opposite the jury box, with the witness stand on my left, the lectern on my right, and the jurors in between. The action would all take place in front of me, but thankfully, far enough away that the jury couldn't see me sweat. To top it off, I'd already scoped out the tallest, most-amply-cushioned chair in the courtroom and branded it with a Post-it reading "Howard's Chair" so no one would steal it. What more could I need?

Having a comfortable chair turned out to be especially useful on my first day in court, which was a sleeper. More juror excuses. Doctor's appointments, babies, and sick parents seemed legitimate, but some were stretches. My favorite was a Verizon employee who dramatically announced, "No one does what I do at work." I imagined "America's #1 Network" crashing because she got stuck with jury duty.

A tedious morning was spiced up by the clerk delivering red meat to the defense table – the completed juror questionnaires. Hirschhorn was adamant about having a questionnaire that was one page and one page only. As part of our pre-trial motions last week, Judge Lamberth had chosen our one-page questionnaire over the government's six-page version, in what would go down as the only favorable pre-trial ruling we got. Favorable under-sold it, really; this thing was a gold mine. From the focus groups, we knew what type of jurors we were looking for, and the more we could learn about them, the easier we'd find them. Here are some of the questionaire's most probing questions, along with the illuminating answers they teased out:

Question #8	**What are your feelings and/or opinions of doctors and patients using medical devices for unapproved ("off-label") uses?**
Juror #11	**"Not safe!"**
Question #12b	**Name 3 people you admire or respect the least.**
Juror #40	**"1) Donald Trump, 2) Charlie Sheen, 3) ISIS"**

Question #13	What 3 words or adjectives would you use to describe yourself?
Juror #63	"I realize this is a serious question, but I am having a hard time answering it without the use of sarcasm. Maybe that's enough to answer the question right there."
Question #15b	Would you want to serve as a juror in this case?
Juror #81	"No. I am apathetic to corporate misconduct."

That one page gave us all we needed. So as the court's day wrapped up, Pauzé asked Judge Lamberth to make sure it would be all the government would get.

PAUZÉ: We'd ask that neither party do any electronic research on the jurors overnight. We're not going to do it, and we'd ask that neither does the other side.

JUDGE LAMBERTH: Agree.

BUD: Wouldn't occur to us.

JUDGE LAMBERTH (laughing): I don't know that I buy that one, but don't do it.

Judge Lamberth had the right instinct. Pauzé had already seen the government's jury consultant sitting in the rotunda on his computer, busying himself with frantic clicks. Since the jury questionnaire gave up jurors' names and ages, it would be easy to troll social media for valuable information. Who knows what the government had already dredged up, but we wanted to stop it right there.

That night, we huddled in Camp Springhill to pore over BBQ and the thick packet of questionnaires. Say what you will about jury consultants – "soothsayers" or "voodoo" or "expensive" – this Hirschhorn guy had jury picking down to a fascinating science. If you ever want to avoid jury duty, pay attention. Here's how it works:

Stage two of *voir dire* would see each side try to bait jurors into being struck *for cause*; that is, disqualified by the judge for being incapable of rendering an impartial verdict. If you can get a juror you don't like tossed for cause, you don't have to waste a precious preemptory challenge down the line. Between me and the company, we'd get ten of these "black balls" that we could use to strike any juror for any reason or no reason at all. The government would only get six – one of the few trial rules that favors the defendant.

It's in this *for cause* stage, before you get to the black-balling, that the juror questionnaire is a weapon. For example, 16 of the first 50 jurors in line answered question #8 (opinion on off-label treatment) in a way that showed prejudice. This had the effect of potentially tripling our strikes. But there's another layer to this. Our attorney could use those prejudicial answers as an opportunity to question the juror in an educational manner. *If the judge has told you that the law says it's legal for doctors to use a medical device off-label, is that something you could follow?* It's a win-win. If the juror disagrees, they'll be struck for cause. If they agree, we've got a promise from a potential juror. And as a bonus, we've just back-doored legal instructions to the rest of the jury pool, listening in the courtroom.

So what type of juror was Hirschhorn hunting? Above all else, to win, we'd need to convince the jury that the government was wrong. It wouldn't be easy, because the government usually gets it right. Or at least we'd like to think so. As one juror would explain the next day:

You see all of these things on the news about other cases. And people on these big cases, it seems like, most of the time, they are guilty and they know that they are. They are wasting the time of the judge and everybody else in order to try to prove an innocent verdict, when they know that they are not. So, now, can I ignore that part of my view? I am not real sure about that.

That'll get you struck. The jurors we were looking for were either distrustful of the government (hard-line conservatives, minorities), outside-the-box thinkers, or corporate-types who understood the realities of managing employees. At all costs, we wanted to avoid "rule followers," especially teachers and government employees. And we'd use occupation, self-description, and their list of least-admired people to cull them out.

After watching Hirschhorn analyze each juror that night, I was confident that we'd get a good jury. But I knew just one bad juror would be enough to block the unanimous not guilty verdict we'd need to win. For me and the company, a hung jury was almost as bad as a loss. It would mean another year of purgatory, likely followed by another trial. And I didn't know if our business could survive that. We were putting the ball in Hirschhorn's hands, and we needed him to pitch a perfect game. And yet, for some reason, I trusted him completely.

The next morning we were back in court, ready to pick a jury. As first chair, Pauzé would be our guy for *voir dire,* but shockingly, it was Assistant U.S. Attorney Christina Playton who stepped up for the government. Why not Bud, I wondered – the senior prosecutor from the office who talked such a big game about going to trial? "This is what happens when you don't do cases." Pauzé said, confirming my feeling that this was weird. "Sending Christina up to do juror strikes is an amateur mistake. This is where you build rapport with the judge."

If Bud was rotund and overly-polished, Christina Playton was his spindly, abrasive counterbalance. Playton, we had guessed, was brought onto the case recently to do the work Bud didn't want to do. The motions, the exhibit preparation, and now the jury selection. According to our local contacts, Playton had made a career out of doing the work others ducked. As a freshly-minted prosecutor, Playton had taken the immigration cases that no one wanted but that the Western District of Texas had in ample supply. Deportation, asylum, and visa cases; she tried them all without help, pushing a handcart packed with case files into the courtroom and rolling up her sleeves. Her tireless work earned Playton a promotion to the white-collar group, and now here she was, trying her first major case.

As Pauzé said, *voir dire* is a time to build rapport with the judge. But it's also a time to build rapport with the jury. Playton is not a naturally charismatic prosecutor, in part because a squeaky twinge in her voice too freely reveals her contempt. But she is intelligent and always assertive. In *voir dire*, that meant that even if she didn't know exactly why the juror should be struck, she knew it was her job to see to it that he was. Here's Playton with juror #60, who raised his hand when asked if he had specialized knowledge.

JUDGE LAMBERTH: Tell us about your specialized knowledge.

JUROR: Well, in 1977, I started as a research scientist for Baxter Labs. I went on to design medical devices and then to shepherd them through manufacturing preparation and regulatory approvals. I have written [applications for FDA clearance]. I am familiar with [cites the applicable federal regulations by number].

JUDGE LAMBERTH: And other than that ...?

[Captive laughter]

PLAYTON: Wow.

JUDGE LAMBERTH: Okay. Any reason you couldn't be fair and impartial in doing that—

JUROR: Oh, no. I don't think so. I've thought about it, actually. Will I try to insert my knowledge into the evidence? No, I wouldn't. I am just going to listen to the evidence.

PLAYTON: Your Honor, we would like to, based on juror number 60's close connection with the medical device industry [and specialized knowledge], we would like to [strike] for cause on that one.

JUDGE LAMBERTH: You're going to raise 60 [for cause]?

PLAYTON: Yes, your Honor. I know he said that he could be fair and impartial, but, I mean, this is a person who uniquely would identify with the defendant in terms of what he's done – for many years he did just what the defendant's company does. And for this reason we move to challenge him for cause.

God forbid anyone on the jury of my peers *identifies* with me. Also, "for many years he did just what the defendant's company does"? Sounds like he might be next on the government's hit-list ... quick, get him a subpoena! Playton's challenge for cause was denied, but juror #60 unfortunately didn't make the final jury pool because his randomly-assigned number was 10 spots too high.

It was now time for the grand finale of jury selection – preemptory challenges. Judge Lamberth called for each side's list of black-ball strikes, and we asked for a moment to finalize ours. Hirschhorn had each juror's vitals written on a 4x6 index card he cribbed with notes throughout questioning.

During the recess, he turned the defense table into a game of juror solitaire. *This one goes here. This one's gone. If these two are struck, then this guy might get in. Let's not have that. Go back to how it was.* As I stood at Hirschhorn's side, I only felt strongly about one potential juror.

Juror #1 – Daphne – she was the one I was most worried about. Throughout *voir dire*, the middle-aged African-American woman refused to crack a smile. She looked straight ahead, sometimes at me, with a furrowed brow that said, "I'm confused as to why you're so evil." In addition, she worked as a building manager, putting her into the "rule follower" category we were desperately trying to avoid. I alerted Hirschhorn. "Don't worry about her," he snapped, still hypnotized by his cards. "African-American women are good for us, and I don't see any problems with her." I backed away and let him work, still not 100% convinced.

Two minutes later, there was only one move left on Hirschhorn's board. Our last strike was either going to be on Daphne or Michael (juror #7). Michael was a network engineer who listed his three most respected people as Elon Musk, his wife, and himself (in that order). The three people he respected the least were Donald Trump, Donald Rumsfeld, and Donald Glover. I doubt he liked Donald Duck much, either. He described himself as "analytical, nerdy, and logical," all deducible from his other answers. This was a guy who, while weird, I thought would be on our side. But for some reason I didn't understand, Hirschhorn hated Michael. I thought about it, reminded myself why I'd brought Hirschhorn here, and deferred to his judgment. Plus, I was sure the prosecutors would strike Michael anyway. *Turn in the card.*

Judge Lamberth knocked out the strikes, and we were left with our jury: The twelve who made the cut were jurors number 1, 4, 6, 9, 11, 13, 17, 21, 22, 23, 26, and 30.

Every juror the government struck was college educated, an obvious effort to get as far away from a jury of my peers as they could. And there were no double strikes, meaning the government didn't strike Michael after all. We could've had him. I was already second-guessing myself and Hirschhorn.

But to my shock, the prosecutors let in Stephen, the only juror wearing a necktie. I was sure they were going to strike the 54-year-old white guy with a management degree. He loved Ronald Reagan, Ted Cruz, and Rush Limbaugh. The kicker? He answered question 15a ("anything else that you feel is important for the judge and the attorneys to know about you?") by saying he was an Eagle Scout. Hey – I was an Eagle Scout! Troop 107, St. Anthony Village, May 1977. But the prosecutors didn't know that. And if in his mid-50s Stephen was still listing having collected those 21 merit badges as a defining achievement, I knew he would be my ace in the hole – if I could somehow work my scouting past into my testimony.

On the other hand, Daphne wound up making the jury, along with two others jurors I was suspicious of – Rebecca and Christine. Neither went to college, both had been victims of crimes against their homes, and both had ties to FBI agents. Not exactly model jurors for us, based on our mock trial analysis. When asked her opinion of off-label use, Rebecca had responded "Not safe!" *Oof.* And when asked for three people she admired the least, she said "Thieves, liars, and cheats." At least she didn't say "misbranders." Christine seemed problematic, too, saying off-label uses "should not be used," and that she "strongly agreed" that companies and individuals charged with crimes were most likely guilty. Hirschhorn had left both of them in because he thought they would go along with the crowd, but to me that seemed risky and speculative at best.

After 56 months, the fate of this criminal investigation would not come down to the prosecutors, some DOJ bureaucrat, or even the judge. It would come down to 12 people. Seven women, five men. And only one chance to tell them my story.

CHAPTER 20

OPENING MOVES

Day 1 of Trial

JUDGE LAMBERTH: At this time I'll ask the government to proceed with your opening statement.

Here it was. The proverbial moment we'd all been waiting for, but none in the room longer than me. The opening statements. The moment where all the guesses, all the anticipation, and all the planning about what the trial would or wouldn't be about goes out the window.

In openings, each side promises the jury what they'll show during trial and what it means. The idea is to build the jurors a mental cupboard – a sturdy one – in hopes that they stack the cans of evidence they'll receive in yours, not the other side's. For this reason, the opening statements were the best opportunity for both sides to win votes. "In the opening, you're playing to 12 jurors," Hirschhorn told me. "By closing, you're only playing to two or three."

The government was looking to serve the jury a round of cold Bud in their opening, going with the grizzled veteran and his hometown charm. By now Bud had been on this case for three years. Three years to think about what he would say. Three years to comb the pre-trial interviews, grand jury transcripts, and company emails for source material to tell the perfect crime story.

Pauzé would counter with the company's first words. And because there were two defendants, we would get two openings. But in an unorthodox move suggested by Hirschhorn, I opted for Lundquist to "reserve" my opening until after the government finished calling their last witness. And my delayed opening would be unanswered by the government, allowing our defense, mid-trial, to give the jurors a one-sided refresher. That meant this afternoon was the main event – Bud vs. Pauzé – in front of 12 jurors, 4 alternates,

20 attorneys, 1 yawny judge, and a courtroom gallery full of VSI employees.

I brought the employees down to show the jury that it wasn't some company logo on trial here, it was people. People with faces and families, packing our side of the gallery and contrasting the few lonely souls on the government's side. I even tried to showcase the cultural diversity of our employees. It was a gimmick, yes, but Hirschhorn told me to suck it up. I told these employees why I chose them, and maybe they appreciated the honesty, even if San Antonio wasn't their first choice for a coerced-vacation destination.

I looked at the gallery. Friends, colleagues, Beth. Every single person in the gallery had helped the company get to where it was today: strong enough to give the government a real fight. I found comfort in that – our shared past and current hopes. *Bring it on, Bud. Let's see what you've got.*

BUD: Ladies and gentlemen of the jury, good afternoon ... We're all required to follow the law, everyone in this courtroom. But the grand jury in San Antonio has indicted these defendants – Vascular Solutions, Inc. and Howard Root – for violating the law ...

Howard Root and VSI knew about the law. But Howard Root and VSI decided not to follow the law because it would make it more difficult for them to earn money.

Okay, not a bad start. That grand jury was tricked, but the jurors didn't know that yet. Was this a set-up for that "choices" theme that Pauzé torched me with in the mock jury? God, I hoped not.

The actions of Howard Root and VSI have brought us here today. The defendant sold a medical device that they knew based on their own testing could cause deep vein thrombosis, or DVT.

But every type of varicose vein treatment "could cause deep vein thrombosis." That can't be the reason we were here today.

[DVT is] a blood clot in the deep vein in the leg. In very rare cases that blood clot can break loose. It can travel to the heart or the lungs causing serious damage, sometimes even death. But that's rare. And we want to be very clear about something: We have no evidence, and we'll show you no evidence, that anybody died from using this device.

What? If this was "very rare" and Bud would show the jury "no evidence that

anybody died from using this device," that still didn't explain why we were
here today.

**Because the defendants couldn't prove that this device was safe
enough for use in human beings.**

Wrong – and that's not even a contested point. The FDA cleared all our
Vari-Lase products 12 separate times "for use in human beings." Even the
indictment acknowledged that.

**What device are we talking about? Well, it's that device right there
[pointing to Vari-Lase console on table]. It's a device that burns varicose veins utilizing laser energy ...**

It burns them! Now that did sound dangerous. Of course, no doctor would
say that, because they're not children hovering over an ant with a magnifying
glass. Doctors would say "ablate," "treat," or "occlude" to describe sealing
varicose veins with laser. But if you wanted to scare the jury about these crazy-
doctors-and-their-lasers, saying the word burn a few times might work. Or,
if you're Bud Paulissen, you might say it 26 times in a 40-minute opening.

Okay Bud, seriously. Tell us why we're here today. Lamberth is falling
asleep.[17]

**The defendant sold their device for treating and burning perforator
veins for seven years without FDA permission. Why? When you hear
the evidence, you'll know it's about money.**

It's about money? Weird thing for Bud to say, knowing that the Short Kit made
up just 0.1% of our total sales.

Sitting next to me, Pauzé started scribbling on his notepad, practically drooling at the opening Bud was giving him. As Bud droned on, an in-
tense-looking Tim Finley rose, Frankensteined his way to the podium, and
slapped down a note. Five minutes later he did it again. *Why was Finley passing notes?* They'd had years to work on this opening, and there was nothing to
respond to, because we hadn't said a word yet!

---

[17]He really was. Judge Lamberth had this thing where he'd recline back in his chair to an angle that hid
his eyes and then just suspend himself there, rather precariously, for five or ten minutes. When I saw him
jerk back to consciousness, I realized what was going on.

Next, Finley switched to playing ring girl, distracting the jury by holding up cards indicating how much time Bud had left … in an opening statement that had no time limit. This was kinda bad so far. What else did Bud have?

Defendant Howard Root is a lawyer …

That was at least true.

… He and VSI didn't want to get caught selling their kit for perforators without FDA clearance, so they had a cover story. "Short vein segment" is a word swap, and it's code for perforators. Sure, you can use it to describe other veins too. That's sort of part of the cover story. That's why it works.

No, that's not how a code word works. If "short vein segments" means lots of veins including perforator veins, that's not a "cover story," that's a category. It would be like saying "car" is a code word for "Lexus."

The defendants found out about [the DVTs in the clinical study] in late 2008. They buried it. They never publicly disclosed [it]. They never told the FDA. [Howard Root] knew about the 14 percent major blood clots. He buried that study result.

I buried it? Bud was making this too easy. Those DVTs, which three doctors all found to be harmless and clinically insignificant, were reported to both the FDA and NIH on publicly-available websites that Bud had seen. I know, because the website print-outs were on Bud's exhibit list.

At this point Finley started waving around a card indicating that Bud's unlimited time was up. I braced myself for Bud's grand finale.

Ladies and gentlemen, when you've heard all the evidence, you've seen the company emails, the company records, you've heard the testimony of former and current employees, we will ask you to hold VSI and Howard Root accountable for breaking the law. We'll ask you to find the defendants guilty of conspiracy to defraud the FDA, guilty of conspiracy to distribute misbranded medical devices in interstate commerce, and guilty of actually shipping misbranded medical devices from Minnesota to Austin, Texas.

That was it? Bud asked the jurors to find that we broke the law? I was expecting a big emotional appeal from the hotshot Texas prosecutor – *what happened?* And by the way, Bud didn't even explain what misbranding was.

Two local attorneys, both former federal prosecutors, told me afterward it was the worst opening they'd ever observed. It was almost insulting. After all the huffing and puffing during the five-year investigation, when the time came, Bud couldn't blow down a dandelion.

Maybe these guys weren't ready after all.

—∿—

Now it was Pauzé's turn. He strutted up to his personal podium, about two inches shorter than the government's adjacent one,[18] and gripped its sides. Strap in, everybody ...

> **Now, as you might imagine, folks, I've got a little bit of a lengthy presentation for you. I'm going to get to that in a minute. But there are a few things that the government said that just can't wait.**

Scripted "spontaneous" audible! And he made it appear even more impromptu than he did in the practice runs. *Tell us, Mike, what can't wait?*

> **Folks, the government told you that the FDA clearance for the Vari-Lase device did not – did not – cover the treatment of perforator veins. Ladies and gentlemen, that is simply not true. You are going to hear from witness after witness that the FDA signed off on the treatment of varicose veins. That means all varicose veins. And it includes perforator veins. And not just once, folks. The FDA signed off on Vari-Lase for the treatment of perforator veins a dozen times between 2003 and 2011.**

No crime here, people. He had to get that out there early. *But wait, was Pauzé saying that Bud lied to the jury?* Surely an Assistant U.S. Attorney would not.

> **The government suggested – no, he said. He said that VSI "buried" – I think was the word, and I think I heard it three times – buried these results and hid it from FDA and doctors. Ladies and gentlemen, far from hiding these results, VSI put them on FDA's own database**

---

[18] Days prior, Chrisina Playton worked herself into a huff as one of our paralegals dragged Pauzé's personal podium into the courtroom. "Who told you that you could do this? ... We only use one podium in this courtroom! ... There won't be enough room!" she protested. There was.

... This is FDA's *own database* [shows screenshot of website on the courtroom monitors]. The company filed the results on FDA's own database almost eight years ago. They didn't *bury* it.

VSI posted the results on not just one but two government websites. And if that wasn't enough, folks, if it wasn't enough to put it on FDA's own website and [NIH's] own website, VSI sent an email that you will see ... telling every single salesperson across the country about these results. They didn't *bury* it.

Pauzé stopped and snapped to the next page in his binder, staring down Bud in disgust. Just a few feet away, Bud, in the foreground of the jury, snarled back. The jury was riveted, staring at Bud, as Mike held for a dramatic pause, or should I say, pausé. The judge's young law clerk, who had been nodding at Bud throughout his opening, now wore a quizzical look on his face. Pauzé continued, now in a gentler voice.

Folks, the evidence in this trial will tell you about a company and a man who followed the law. The evidence will tell you about a medical device that has helped many and it has harmed none ... And, folks, the evidence will tell you about a federal government agency that made mistake, after mistake, after mistake.

Mistakes – what kind of mistakes?

The [FDA application] was assigned to an FDA reviewer by the name of Randolph Copeland. Mr. Copeland had been at FDA for about a month at this time ... And I don't mean to be critical of him personally, right, this is not his fault. But when he picked up VSI's file, he had almost no experience reviewing medical devices. In fact, folks, just a month before picking up VSI's complicated laser device file, you will learn that Mr. Copeland was managing a local McDonald's.

Boom. The government didn't know about that one until now, evidenced by the pinched look on Finley's face. The jury sat in stunned silence, trying to make sense of the Mickey D's-to-FDA career path. But the white-collar D.C. lawyer Pauzé had to be careful here; he didn't want the jury to think he was talking down to them about blue-collar jobs.

Now, folks, I used to work at a fast food place – it was called Penguin Point – so I'm not being critical of Mr. Copeland. But the last thing

that running a fast food restaurant prepares you for is evaluating highly technical laser medical devices.

See! The lawyer with the French name was just a regular guy. And that regular guy was about to take a big bite out of Bud's ham sandwich.

Folks, I want you to consider the government's conspiracy theory. The government's conspiracy theory is that in 2007 VSI and Howard Root began a multi-year intentional conspiracy to hide the marketing of Vari-Lase for perforators. Yet the first thing that they did was file a notification with FDA saying "We intend to market Vari-Lase for perforators."

Well that doesn't make sense. *Why would someone do that?*

The government's conspiracy theory says that VSI did this to make money. Right, you heard that. VSI did this to make money. Yet the charges focus on the Short Kit, which was 0.1% of the company's sales. More than two-thirds of the sales representatives didn't sell a single one of these Short Kits. Folks, for the few sales representatives that actually sold one of these Short Kits, you know how much money they made on average? Twelve dollars a week. Twelve dollars a week. The government's conspiracy theory is based on $12 a week.

That's less than a Penguin Point paycheck! Point made, now it was time for Pauzé to wrap it all up and hit that mistake theme again.

Ladies and gentlemen, as much evidence as I've discussed … there's a whole lot more you're going to hear when it's our turn to call witnesses. More about the safety of Vari-Lase. More about a device that has helped many and harmed none. More about how the government made mistake after mistake after mistake. And by the end of this trial you will see that on November 13th, 2014, the government made the gravest mistake of all. It brought federal criminal charges against a company and a man who are innocent.

Pauzé stopped, scanned over a jury seemingly craving more, and stepped down. Later, I spoke with those same two former prosecutors. It was the best opening they'd ever heard.

CHAPTER 21

HIJACKED

Trial Day 2

The opening curtain had been drawn – now it was time for the prosecutors to start their show. And since they controlled which witnesses they'd call, they controlled the storyline. They could roll out their case topic by topic, slowly building to a climax that "proved" I was guilty; or they could unload their conclusions early and let the evidence pile on. Our goal was just to survive. If we could make it through three weeks of government witnesses without them landing a knockout blow, it'd be a victory. If we could somehow come out even, I knew we'd be in great shape when I took the stand as our last witness.

Each witness is like a playing card whose value lies in what they'll say. Through pre-trial interviews of over 100 potential witnesses, the prosecutors had a chance to see nearly every card face-up. But winning at trial is about playing the right cards, and doing so in the right order. Three days before trial, Bud showed his hand, sending us a list of the 20 witnesses he planned to call at trial, in order.

As soon as we got Bud's list, the lawyers had it copied onto the War Room whiteboard. We huddled around to make sense of it. *No one from Austin Heart? How could they prove their misdemeanor charges? No DeSalle. Why Reuning first? What were they going for here?*

They were obviously sandwiching our sales reps between former employees, but that didn't tell me much about what their overall plan was, or whether it was any good.

And even if it was, so what? One thing you learn from running a company is that there's a difference between a good plan and a good job. Let's see if they could execute.

JUDGE LAMBERTH: Good morning, ladies and gentlemen. The government may call your first witness.

BUD: Thank you, Your Honor. The United States calls Frederick Reuning.

The courtroom doors opened and in walked our former V.P. of marketing, Fred Reuning, looking like a middle-aged IT guy. The marshal escorted him down the courtroom aisle and through the waist-high saloon doors. Something about that walk could make anyone look guilty, even Fred, a guy who gave off more of a victim vibe.

I wondered what I'd look like when it came time for my walk. Surely I'd handle it better than Fred, who looked lost in the belly of the courtroom, unsure if he'd ever make it up to the witness stand. Finley rescued his #1 witness, awkwardly ushering him around Pauzé's podium, past the jury, and to the stand. Shaky start.

Bud stood up to handle the questioning, no doubt eager to bounce back after his opening statement landed with a thud. Maybe he was better in a more interactive setting, I thought. And then he led off with the same clunky phrasing that had littered the grand jury transcripts.

BUD: Did you work at Vascular Solutions at some point?

FRED: Yes.

BUD: What type of business do you know Vascular Solutions to be in?

We didn't start out so hot, either. Richter was anxious to get his feet wet, and since he would cross-examine Fred, any objections were his to make. After the focus group debacle, I honestly didn't know what to expect. Here was our first objection of the trial – Richter trying to stop the government from showing the jury a VSI org chart.

BUD: Your Honor, move for admission of Government's Exhibit D-1.

JUDGE LAMBERTH: Without objection?

RICHTER: Your Honor, we do object to the admission. Testified to –

JUDGE LAMBERTH: Overruled. It is received.

Yikes. It seemed everybody on stage had early jitters, and that certainly included Fred, a man who was jumpy by nature. About 10 minutes in, Fred began choking mid-answer. Bud suggested Fred pour himself a glass of water from the stand's shiny steel pitcher. Fred's hands shook as he cautiously tilted the pitcher lower and lower and lower, but nothing came out. It was empty. A perfect metaphor.

I expected things from Fred. He was ostensibly capable, but he didn't always deliver. In 2008, three years after hiring him to run the marketing department, I reduced his role to managing only the Vari-Lase marketing because nothing was getting done. Sensing where this was going, Fred decided to leave the company in 2009 for the sweeter pastures of his previous job at Nestlé, saying to me, "Momma didn't raise no fool." I didn't answer.

Who knew which Fred was going to show up today: Fred or "FRED 2.0" (the honest-to-goodness name of his new one-man consulting business). On one hand, Fred had thrown the company way under the bus in a written admission he signed under oath. But on the other, he'd backed away from some of the statements in that admission during pre-trial interviews with Richter, citing government pressure as the reason he made them.

Once Fred found some water, it became clear that Bud was going to make this witness – and perhaps this whole trial – all about me. And Fred was well-prepped to play along.

BUD: In what sense was [working at VSI] tough?

FRED: Mr. Root is a very demanding boss.

BUD: Was he involved in any kind of mandate about eating on the company property?

FRED: Yes. There was one time when we had an ant infestation of some sort, and then an email came out that [there would be] no more eating at your desk. You could only eat in the company lunchroom.

Lunch in the lunchroom – *the horror!* It was irrelevant, of course, but it was the kind of stuff that might make a bad first impression with the jury, based on what I'd seen in the mock trials.

Bud moved on, and he seemed to be coming down with an acute case of doc vomit. In quick succession, he introduced field trip reports and board reports and design documents and sales meetings slides and study data and device labeling and more sales meetings slides. The jurors visibly struggled to keep pace. Most of the time, Bud didn't even ask Fred more than one question about the content of the document he labored to introduce. "Do you recognize this email? ... Did you receive it? ... Does it relate to your duties at Vascular Solutions?" And then Bud moved on to the next one.

Even if Bud was collecting small points by banking documents in evidence (guaranteeing that they would ultimately go back to the jury room), he was missing the big picture. This was his first witness. A juror might logically assume that it would be his best witness. I did. And maybe Fred was, but instead of grandstanding when he reached a supposedly incriminating point, Bud just lingered in silence for a bit too long before moving on to the next document, which was usually completely unrelated to the one he'd just shown. After an hour of this paper-shuffling, I looked around to see if it was resonating. Just as I thought. The jurors' eyes had completely glossed over, and my attorneys looked more confused than concerned.

This was good, because some of the documents getting lost in the shuffle looked pretty bad for us. Take, for instance, the email Fred sent to the entire sales force in March 2008. It read:

"Deborah [Schmalz, our V.P. of regulatory] and I have had a number of questions lately about the treatment of perforator veins and reimbursement. Based on the questions, I felt a quick summary of the situation was in order. First and foremost, we do not have an indication for the treatment of perforator veins. As long as there is no approved

clearance for perforator treatment by the FDA, it is not possible to submit a claim to Medicare for treatment of a perforator vein."

It was a jackpot email for the government. Here they had someone who was presumably knowledgeable – the V.P. of marketing, Fred – telling the entire sales force that perforators were not FDA-cleared and, for that reason, doctors couldn't get reimbursed by insurance for treating them.

Fred didn't know anything about regulatory matters or insurance coverage, and he was completely wrong in his analysis of both. But that didn't matter. Here was the foundation of the government's entire conspiracy theory, conveniently rolled into one email. This email had to be the reason Fred was witness #1.

So what did Bud do with it? Bud had Fred read the thing cover to cover (not just the highlights I picked out above), including the exculpatory and irrelevant sections. Okay, maybe this was the beginning of a long walk around the block Bud was going to go on with this email. As Richter once explained to me, there's an old prosecutor trick that when you get to the key evidence – say the knife in a stickup – you don't just ask about it once. You ask, "What color was the knife?" "How far was the knife from your neck?" "What was the look on his face when he held up that knife and threatened you?"

Here's the full list of questions Bud came up with for his jackpot email:

"Would Howard Root have been copied on the field employees' U.S. email chain?"

"Were you operating under the assumption as expressed here that the treatment or ablation of perforator veins with the Vari-Lase console and kit was not subject and eligible for reimbursement by Medicare?"

"Did anyone at VSI, including Mr. Root, approach you after this email went out and say 'Fred Reuning, you're just wrong'?"

That was it. Then Bud moved on to the next document in his pile of 33(!), one that was wholly unrelated to the email he'd just shown. And then he ended his direct examination of Fred.

─⎯⋀ⱽ⎯─

Enter Richter. He strutted to the podium in a pair of thousand-dollar Lucchese boots, a hold-over from his cowboy days as the U.S. Attorney for the Western District of Oklahoma. At six feet two inches tall, he wasn't wearing them for the extra height, more for the charm of a lawyer in gator boots, I guess. His first question was a softball.

RICHTER: Good afternoon, Mr. Reuning. How are you?

FRED: Good. Thanks.

Richter rushed the question, seemingly anxious to get to what he had planned, but still respectful of Southern decency. What was he so excited to serve up? The jury's first taste of government strong-arming.

Richter took Fred back to October 2013 and asked him about a one-page letter he received from Bud. It informed Fred that he was the target of an ongoing criminal investigation by four federal agencies that had "uncovered evidence indicating that [Fred] committed several federal crimes related to the marketing and sale of Vari-Lase." Bud's letter concluded, "If I do not hear from you or your attorney soon, we will present your case to the grand jury."

RICHTER: And you understood that this meant that these folks over here [pointing to the prosecution table] were threatening you with federal crimes?

FRED: Correct.

The jurors craned their necks toward Bud and Finley, no more than 10 feet from the edge of the jury box. Bud sat there, ruby-faced, statued to his chair. Richter continued.

RICHTER: And certainly that scared you, right?

FRED: Yes.

RICHTER: You were very scared?

FRED: Yes.

RICHTER: Got a wife and family?

FRED: Yes.

All of a sudden, Richter had gone from Bud's dry, document-torture into something personal, snappy, and emotional. And he was just getting started.

> **RICHTER: And you didn't think you'd done anything wrong at that time, did you?**

> **FRED: Correct. I didn't think I had done anything wrong.**

> **RICHTER: In fact, at no point in time prior to the government starting to accuse you had you ever thought you had been involved in any criminal activity?**

> **FRED: That is actually a correct statement.**

The government's pressure on witness #1 didn't stop with the target letter. Bud and Finley also waved a draft indictment in front of Fred with his name, as the sole defendant, in capital letters. It was an unsubtle reminder – *Hey buddy, all we have to do is file this. Better play ball.* It was truly that simple; since Fred's draft indictment only alleged misdemeanors, the prosecutors wouldn't even need to call a grand jury to torpedo his life. All this to intimidate a guy who comes off as frumpy and harmless. The contrast between the threats and the man was striking.

> **RICHTER: You understood the full weight of the consequences that could come from those charges?**

> **FRED: Yes.**

> **RICHTER: But you also believed those charges were false?**

> **FRED: Yes.**

> **RICHTER: You didn't want to be charged?**

> **FRED: No, I didn't want to be charged.**

> **RICHTER: You didn't want your career to be ruined?**

> **FRED: No, I didn't want my career ruined.**

Richter had a real way with the obvious questions, this way of making them just uncertain enough to be interesting.

> **RICHTER: And your wife is a pretty important person, isn't she, besides being your wife?**

FRED: Yes. Yes.

RICHTER: Currently the chairperson of the Hennepin County Commission?

FRED: Correct.

RICHTER: Largest county in Minnesota?

FRED: Yes.

RICHTER: So being the chairperson, that's a pretty powerful position?

FRED: Yes.

RICHTER: Tough for an elected official's husband to be charged with a crime, would you say?

Fred looked like he was about to have a panic attack. Maybe he did – I couldn't really tell from the other side of the courtroom. He rocked back in his chair, collected himself, and squeezed out an extended blink before answering.

FRED: Yes.

Richter had momentum, but he still had a lot of work to do with a frightened and unpredictable witness. The biggest minefield to navigate? That admission Fred had signed under oath. Here are some of its worst parts:

"I knew that Vari-Lase devices were not approved to treat perforator veins. This was common knowledge at VSI."

"Management at the company, including the CEO Howard Root, knew about and encouraged the sales force's efforts to sell Vari-Lase products for unapproved perforator use."

"By using the term 'short vein,' VSI concealed that it was selling the Short Kit for unapproved perforator use."

On the surface, it looked like an iron-clad condemnation of me and the company. But Richter didn't have to scratch too far beneath Fred's admission to reveal what it really was – a way out. A way out of that draft indictment getting filed and a way out of a grueling two-day "interview" with Bud and Finley in San Antonio.

RICHTER: Isn't it the case that when that interview began, the first two-plus hours did not involve asking you any questions whatsoever, did it?

FRED: No.

RICHTER: It involved simply Mr. Finley telling you in no uncertain terms what he thought about the case, right?

FRED: Correct.

RICHTER: His theories about the case?

FRED: Yes.

For a jury that had already taken in a heavy dose of the saccharine Bud, this next one would hit home.

RICHTER: Fair to say that the tone that Mr. Paulissen used in asking you questions here in the courtroom was very different than the tone that Mr. Finley was using with you in that interview?

FRED: Yes.

RICHTER: How would you describe the tone that Mr. Finley used?

FRED: More aggressive and wanting to make his point.

RICHTER: Were there times over those two days of interview where you had to take a break because of the arguing going back and forth?

FRED: Yes.

Several jurors swiveled their heads back and forth between the witness and the prosecution table. Others stayed locked on Bud and Finley.

RICHTER: Were there times where the prosecutors tried to put words in your mouth?

FRED: Yes.

RICHTER: And did there come a time during this two-day interview session in which they made it clear that the target letter might go away if you signed a statement?

FRED: Yes.

RICHTER: And on the – on the second day of your interview, the prosecutors prepared a statement, right?

FRED: Correct.

RICHTER: They wrote it?

FRED: Correct.

This wasn't an employee who came forward to report criminal activity in his former company. This was an employee who was pointedly threatened with criminal charges, then conscripted into endorsing Bud's trial outline to avoid the government following through on those threats. It was government browbeating, pure and simple.

Next, a few more questions about that knife, Mr. Reuning.

RICHTER: And when we got together, did I spend two-plus hours telling you what I thought about the case?

FRED: No.

RICHTER: Did I act like the bad cop and Mr. Lundquist act like the good cop?

FRED: No.

Now Richter was just having fun. Grandstanding in the way Bud hadn't, scoring points in the shadow trials of likeability and credibility. *That's nice, John, but get back to the big picture.*

RICHTER: Now, before meeting with the government, you thought you were innocent?

FRED: That's correct.

RICHTER: Before meeting with the government, you never thought Howard Root had done anything wrong?

FRED: Correct.

RICHTER: And you didn't think Vascular Solutions, VSI, had ever done anything wrong?

FRED: Correct.

RICHTER: Didn't think you or anyone else was a member of a conspiracy?

FRED (Dismissively): No.

By now everybody in the courtroom knew it – Fred had been hijacked. Richter had taken the government's #1 witness and made him our #1 witness. This was a different lawyer than I'd seen in the mock trials. Prepared, charismatic, and not afraid to deviate from the script in the Southern twang he'd suddenly adopted. With each "yes" answer, his confidence grew. And at one point during Fred's cross, Richter drew out an incredible 48 straight "yes" answers.

But now it was time to see how far that confidence could take him.

RICHTER: So it's safe to say, Mr. Reuning, the Defendant's Exhibit 368A [a screenshot showing VSI's disclosure of clinical study DVTs to FDA] debunks any accusation that VSI was trying to "bury" the results of DVTs in the RELIEVE study?

FRED: If you're saying we were very transparent when we started reporting them as soon as we knew about something, absolutely the company did that.

RICHTER: And transparency is certainly the opposite of burying something, right?

FRED: Yes.

Richter was leaping off cliffs, and Fred was happy to stand at the bottom and catch him. *Debunks?* Time to wrap this up before the wind blew and Fred started back-tracking.

RICHTER: Mr. Reuning, during your entire time at Vascular Solutions did you ever think that you were involved in a conspiracy?

FRED: No.

RICHTER: Did you have any meetings with Mr. Root or others at the company that you planned to commit crimes?

FRED: No.

RICHTER: No further questions.

Richter was done with Fred, but the defense wasn't. Next up, the jury would get their first helping of John Lundquist. Because Lundquist represented me, his main job would be to separate me from the money-grubbing jackass the prosecutors were painting me as. And a little Minnesota-accented humor would help move the ball in the right direction.

> **LUNDQUIST: Would it be fair to say that it was Mr. Root's philosophy and the company policy to get stuff right?**
>
> **FRED: Yes.**
>
> **LUNDQUIST: And that comes to compliance?**
>
> **FRED: Yes.**
>
> **LUNDQUIST: And it comes to ant infestation, too, doesn't it?**
>
> **FRED: Yep, it does.**
>
> **LUNDQUIST: He does NOT-LIKE-ANTS. Is that clear?**
>
> **FRED (laughing): Absolutely true.**

The jury erupted in laughter. There's a low bar for court jokes, but it was a good sign, nonetheless. Lundquist had introduced himself as likable, while laughing off the government's "Howard controls everything, down to where you eat your sandwich" narrative. And who likes ants anyway?

After Lundquist filled some gaps in Richter's cross-examination, he was finished with Fred. But at trial, whoever calls the witness gets the last word. This is called re-direct, or rebuttal. Questioning on rebuttal is supposed to be restricted to the topics covered on cross, but we'd find that was more of a theoretical rule in Lamberth's court.

Rebuttal was a chance for Bud to salvage his first witness and re-stress the points he should've hit harder in direct. The key to doing both, of course, was Fred's written admission. Bud went right after it.

> **BUD: Mr. Reuning, just a few questions.**
>
> **FRED: Sure.**
>
> **BUD: When you came to my office, Tim Finley and I interviewed with you. You were there with your lawyer [Dan Scott], correct?**

FRED: Correct.

BUD: He is a former Federal Public Defender for Minnesota?

FRED: You'll have to ask him what his résumé is.

Suddenly Fred was pushing back, answering dismissively in a tone that flashed years of pent up anger toward Bud and his colleagues. It was out of character for Fred, but understandable given the emotional epiphany he'd had on cross. He was done being the government's puppet, a sea change Bud must have felt. Bud needed to be careful now; that was FRED 3.0 up there.

BUD: Okay. Did Mr. Scott allow you to perjure yourself in my office?

FRED: I don't think so.

BUD: Okay. So you signed that statement under penalties of perjury, correct?

FRED: Correct. Yeah.

Not real subtle there. Bud was saying *not so fast* – reminding Fred that this wasn't over, implicitly threatening him with perjury charges for switching his story on the stand. Fred had a tightrope to walk, and Bud was going to try to push him off, one way or another.

BUD: Did you tell the truth when you signed the statement?

FRED: I believe I did. I don't have the statement to know what I said anymore.

Bud paused. This time not for dramatic effect, but to think. If a witness gets on the stand and contradicts something they'd previously said, a lawyer may use a "prior inconsistent statement" to show that he's not telling the truth. But smartly, Richter hadn't gotten Fred to disavow the statement itself – just to say that the prosecutors wrote it and argued with him when he wanted to make changes. *Should I pull it out and impeach him?* You could see Bud's wheels spinning, unsure of what to do. He repeated the question to buy himself more time.

BUD: Okay. But you believe you did [tell the truth]?

FRED: Yes.

> BUD: And when you testified on direct examination when I was asking you questions today before this jury, did you tell the truth to the best of your ability?

> FRED: Best of my ability.

Bud leaned over the podium, looking like the word "impeach" was at the tip of his tongue, and then he moved on. He just moved on. To his big finish with his #1 witness – quibbling over how long that interview in San Antonio *really* lasted.

> BUD: Okay. And we met about 1:00 in the afternoon on the first day and broke up about 5:00 that afternoon, didn't we?

> FRED: That's my memory, yes.

> BUD (turning serious): I'm sorry. You do agree with that?

> FRED: Yes, I agree with you.

Bud was getting testy, and this was just his first witness.

> BUD: And we met the next morning about 8:30 or 9:00 and broke up around noon. Is that about right?

> FRED: We took a break for lunch.

> BUD: Okay. And then what time did you leave my office?

> FRED: We came back, reviewed the statement and I think I left mid-afternoon. I can't remember precisely.

> BUD: So this is a day-and-a-half at the most, maybe a full day?

> FRED: Correct.

> BUD: Not two days?

> FRED: Not two days, yes.

Wow, *game changer.* One-and-a-half days, not two. All Bud was doing was reminding the jury how long it took to pound that admission out of poor Fred. Alright, Bud, last question.

> BUD: And the documents we discussed here in front of this jury this morning on your direct were all created long before you met in my

office, correct?

FRED: Yes, they were.

BUD: All right. Thank you. Nothing further.

And with that, the government's first witness stepped down. We were elated. That night in the War Room, Pauzé half-seriously suggested we send the government a settlement offer: *Drop the charges now and we won't sue for malicious prosecution.* We never sent it over, but behind the joke was the truth of how brutal Bud's first two days were, for both him and the government's credibility.

I floated to sleep that night. The first two days of trial had gone well. Shockingly well. Surely it couldn't be this easy, could it?

CHAPTER 22

EXPERTS

Trial Day 3

Another government document dump. They'd tried to jam us up with 15,000 pages of new material in the week before trial (never mind that the final discovery deadline had months since passed) and, as soon as their first witness left the stand, Finley handed over another mystery disc. This one, though, was different. While the other brink-of-trial productions were transparent efforts to bury new documents among ones we'd seen before, this was an entirely novel set, seemingly designed to draw our attention.

In addition to the emails and interview memos we were used to getting, the prosecutors gave us a dozen videos. They were shaky, raw footage of … something. One showed guys in lab coats poking at a vein with a pair of forceps. Another showed digital readouts of high-tech thermometers. But the money shot showed a laser fiber pushed into what looked like a vein on a napkin. As the laser fired, voices in the background began counting, "one, two, three, four … " then POOF, the vein went up in smoke! The billowing continued for three seconds, at which point a German-accented Donald Trump impersonator weighed in with his scientific opinion: "Vow … it's yuge."

I sat in a corner of the tiny War Room as the lawyers pored over the accompanying emails, trying to make sense of this government-funded science fair project. They revealed that we were looking at a pig vein, or as the emails dressed it up, a "porcine sample." The "experiment," to use the term loosely, was hastily conceived and scheduled for January 26, 2016, at FDA's office in Silver Spring, MD. The prosecutors had been on the case for almost five years, but they waited until *six days before trial* to stage this laughable exhibition they'd use to try to put me in prison.

But the experiment never happened. At least not on January 26th. When we traced a FedEx tracking number at the bottom of an email, we discovered that the government tried to overnight their pig veins from California on Monday, January 25th. But they didn't arrive first-thing the next day as planned. That's because the weekend before, a record blizzard dropped two feet of snow across Maryland, throwing a wrench in the prosecutors' pig probe plans.

Instead of reaching FDA's offices, the dead bio-matter spent Tuesday decomposing in an unrefrigerated FedEx facility in D.C. The government's new expert witness – a doctor named Dr. Robert E. Lee (who proudly, astonishingly uses his middle initial) – didn't think it was a big deal. In an email to the prosecution team, Dr. Lee rendered his clinical opinion with great precision, saying, "as long as they stay cool it should hopefully be OK. Even left out in cooler on a snowbank it should hold it for another day." A snowbank. That was his plan. Shockingly, none of the prosecutors objected to the Confederate Doctor's email. A senior lawyer from FDA, however, suggested maybe the shipment should be re-routed to her house, where she could keep it in her refrigerator. But the pig veins never made it there either, meaning her husband didn't have to worry about frying up some mistaken bacon for breakfast.

But there was more in the government's production than just German-narrated pig-flame videos. They'd also sent us a series of horrifying slides marked as government exhibits. One included graphic photos of oversized, cherry-red blood clots on gauze pads.

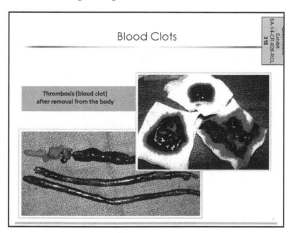

A reverse Google image search showed that the photos appeared to have been lifted from a 2011 presentation at a Turkish medical conference, and they were completely unrelated to our Vari-Lase product and varicose veins.

Next was another Google-ripped government exhibit of a guy with a purple leg next to a guy with an ulcer-blackened leg, supposedly to show what might happen years after a patient got a DVT. But again, this image had nothing to do with Vari-Lase or varicose veins.

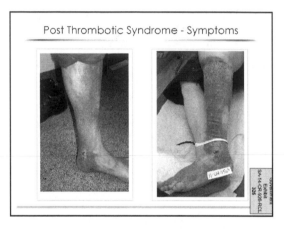

And then, everybody's favorite: a drawing of leg vein anatomy, in crayon.

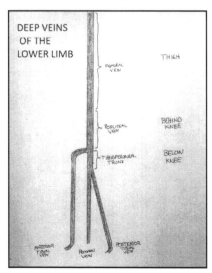

We searched on Google for "crayon drawing of over-simplified venous anatomy" but couldn't find anything. Pauzé stuck the childish art on the War Room fridge where it belonged. That was good for a laugh, but seriously, were they planning on using this stuff in court?

The clinical nature of the data dump made us worry that Dr. Lee, listed as witness #5, might show up ahead of schedule. Richter emailed Bud that night and asked if his witness order had changed. It had not, Bud replied. But we didn't trust Bud, so Richter had a team of lawyers spend the night preparing to go to battle with Robert E. Lee.

Here's what the scene looked like as Judge Lamberth settled into his seat at 8:35 a.m. the next morning in court.

> PAUZÉ: Your Honor, the government walked over to me this morning at 8:25 and informed us that they were not going to call [their next scheduled witness]. Instead, they were going to call witness 18, a doctor from Connecticut. Obviously, the government had to fly in the doctor. They had to make arrangements, I am sure they met with him, and made a decision to call him. They let us know this morning at 8:30.

That explained why, 10 minutes earlier, I had seen Finley wander over to the defense table, and shortly thereafter, Pauzé leap out of his seat. I couldn't hear it, but here's how it was later reported to me:

> FINLEY: Mike, there's been a change of plans. Next we're going to be calling Dr. Duncan Belcher.
>
> PAUZÉ (springing to his feet): How long have you known?
>
> FINLEY: Calm down, Mi—
>
> PAUZÉ: No, Tim. How long have you known? Did you know last night?

Finley appeared flustered by Pauzé's high-speed, venom-laced assault. Lawyers from each side filled in as reinforcements behind their guy, like a baseball brawl where the dugouts empty.

FINLEY: We –

PAUZÉ: Why didn't you tell us last night, when you knew?

PLAYTON: It was very late …

PAUZÉ: Too late?!

MARSHAL: All rise.

The door to chambers swung open and, with it, decorum was restored.

Judge Lamberth looked annoyed by Finley's witness substitution surprise, but not enough to stop him. Instead, the judge issued a flaccid warning to both sides. "At the end of each day, then, tell me what the plan is for the next day on the record; I don't want any of this nonsense."

When Pauzé got done shaking his head, he struck back. To allow more time to prepare for our cross-examination of Dr. Belcher, Pauzé dragged out his cross-exam of witness #2, Kip Theno. That blocked Dr. Belcher from taking the stand until the afternoon, meaning his direct exam would take up the rest of the day, and we'd have the overnight break to prepare a cross-exam of a witness for which we had no outline, exhibit binder, or prepped examiner in the courtroom.

If ever there were a gentler man than Fred, it was Dr. Duncan Belcher. After the excruciating long cross of Theno finally finished, Dr. Belcher stepped into the courtroom in wrinkled khakis and an outsized Oxford, his head leading his body by a half-step in raptor-like fashion.

Dr. Belcher introduced himself so quickly it drew a rebuke from the court reporter. This seemingly only increased the doctor's nervousness. It was Christina Playton asking the questions this time, making the first few minutes a sonically painful amalgam of screech on her end and speed on his. After they both settled in, it was clear Dr. Belcher had been flown down on late notice to tell one story.

DR. BELCHER: The first time I heard about perforator treatment using a laser was from Glen Holden [VSI's sales rep].

PLAYTON: Prior to that, had you considered using a laser on a perforator?

DR. BELCHER: No. It had not really occurred to me.

According to Dr. Belcher, Glen said that VSI had a "perforator kit" coming out. But later, when our Short Kit was launched, Glen returned and announced that the company was "calling it" the "Short Kit." The government was selling this as "VSI rep approaches an uninterested doctor about treating perforators, then promotes it using a code word." It was this story, Bud & Co. must have believed, that was going to turn the tide after a choppy first two days of trial.

By the time 3:30 rolled around and Judge Lamberth called it a day, Playton had yet to finish her direct of Dr. Belcher. As planned, we'd get the night to polish our cross, and they wouldn't see it coming.

That's because, while the Constitution required the government to turn over notes from their pre-trial interviews, the defense had no obligation to do the same.[19] And that summer we'd sent a team of attorneys up to Connecticut to interview Dr. Belcher. They loved the guy. In fact, if it weren't for his story about Glen turning him on to perforators, Dr. Belcher would've been on our witness list. The best part of the meeting, my lawyers said, was when they showed Dr. Belcher our FDA indications and asked if it covered perforators. He studied it, shrugged, and shot back casually, "Yeah, works for me."

Funding my lawyers' trip to Connecticut paid off when the next morning Richter hijacked his second witness. Richter asked Dr. Belcher about his 11 years of experience with Vari-Lase, and he responded that he'd had "nothing but good outcomes" with VSI's "high-quality" device and found it "safe and effective." Dr. Belcher proceeded to tell the jury that "short vein segments" are a real thing, and he treats them. The DVT risk, he explained, was "completely hypothetical" and something he'd "never seen." He went so far as to agree with Richter that telling someone (as Bud told the jury in his opening) that the device showed a 14% DVT rate "would be misleading" because it would "incorrectly give the listener the impression that this was a real problem." And as for the FDA indications, the big question for the entire trial, Dr. Belcher

---

[19] The Supreme Court has ruled that the government's disclosure of material tending to impeach the character or testimony of prosecution witnesses is mandated by the Constitution. If an analogous obligation applied to defendants (it doesn't), the government could just list every possible witness, sit back, and force the defense to release possibly-self-incriminating material. That would defeat the purpose of the Fifth Amendment.

agreed that treating perforator veins was covered under all three parts of the Vari-Lase indications.

As Dr. Belcher's cross-exam continued, I realized that by not including him on our witness list, we'd baited the government into calling him, which allowed us to get into our story weeks earlier than we would've been able to if we'd called him as our witness. Unintentional, but oh so successful.

Richter was now on a roll, scoring bonus points by 1) using the word "groin," 2) gesturing to his groin, and 3) getting the witness to say "groin." This and a few chuckle-headed questions about whether "size matters" added a surreal fog to the cross. There are few settings – very few settings, let's say – outside a courtroom where John Richter could give a medical lecture and have it endorsed point-by-point by a Yale-trained interventional radiologist. But today it happened, and Dr. Belcher seemed as pleasantly surprised by it as I was.

As *Dr.* Richter paced around the courtroom, tall in his cowboy boots and clearly feeling his oats, he pivoted back to the government's pressure tactics. Keep in mind, again, that Dr. Belcher was one of the government's witnesses.

> **RICHTER: Now, let me direct your attention back to October 23rd of 2014, when Agent Scavdis came a calling?**
>
> **DR. BELCHER: Uh-huh.**
>
> **RICHTER: During that call, he insinuated, did he not, that claims you made might be Medicare fraud?**
>
> **DR. BELCHER: He insinuated that billing for perforators would be Medicare fraud.**
>
> **RICHTER: When he said that, you certainly found that concerning, didn't you?**
>
> **DR. BELCHER: That would be concerning.**
>
> **RICHTER: You certainly don't think that you've ever engaged in Medicare fraud?**
>
> **DR. BELCHER: No.**

RICHTER: And fair to say that if you ever want to scare a doctor, just accuse them of or insinuate them of committing Medicare fraud, right?

DR. BELCHER: Yes.

RICHTER: No further questions, Your Honor.

Richter wasn't fishing there. Down to the word "insinuated," we knew what Dr. Belcher would say, because it's what he told our lawyers during that interview in Connecticut.

On re-direct, Playton did her best to rehabilitate her witness, but as would happen numerous times throughout trial, it backfired.

PLAYTON: Did you think it was scary, that conversation [with FDA Agent Scavdis], or concerning? How would you characterize it?

DR. BELCHER: It was just – I wasn't sure what he was investigating immediately … And then as we started to talk, he said something to the tune of we could either talk on the phone or he could subpoena me down to San Antonio and we could meet in person.

Whoa! We didn't know that one was coming, and Playton just walked right into it. Once more the jurors jerked their heads to the prosecution table, focused now on Scavdis, he who constantly stroked his bearded chin. The "phone or San Antone" revelation was a gem that underscored our powerful, preexisting narrative. These guys were threatening everybody – even doctors.

After Dr. Belcher's appearance, the prosecutors had called three witnesses, and we'd flipped two of them. Maybe Bud & Co. would wise up and start asking witnesses what they thought about the case, instead of just telling them what the government thought. Or maybe they wouldn't.

CHAPTER 23

EXPERTS: PART TWO

Trial Day 5

Strutting to the stand was the government's only FDA witness, Neil Ogden, a 25-year veteran of the agency who looked it. It's not that he was old and wrinkled, just that he exuded that look of a "government man" from the '50s. He wore a boxy suit and an unexpressive face, his silver hair slicked to the side. A prototype bureaucrat, the ultimate stiff-looking middle manager from Washington, D.C.

Ogden was the Branch Chief for General Surgery Devices who signed off on all 12 of our FDA clearances, as well as the guy who supervised the response to our failed effort to add "perforator" to our label. He was here to testify that we didn't have clearance to market for perforators, knew we didn't have the clearance, and behaved like we did. The prosecutors didn't want Ogden to lose the jury with FDA inside baseball or droning regulatory lessons. All they needed Ogden to do was endorse their chronology and get off the stand. And at this, the suddenly-smooth-sounding Tim Finley was successful.

After Ogden introduced himself, that is.

FINLEY: Will you please introduce yourself to the jury?

OGDEN: So my name is Neil Ogden, Neil Raymond Painter Ogden. I got four names when I was a kid, so I like to use them.

Crickets. The jury looked at Ogden like he was a weirdo, and rightly so, after an introduction like that.

But Finley quickly moved on and got his story in. As Ogden remembered, in 2007 we sent his team an application to add the word "perforator" to the indications that covered all 80 versions of our Vari-Lase procedure kits. FDA asked for safety data to support the language change, but we didn't finish our study in time to respond. So in March 2008, after the statutorily-prescribed time limit had run, FDA sent us a letter withdrawing our application. It included a boilerplate warning: "If you market the device without FDA clearance/approval, you will be in violation of the [law]." This was a big point for the government, and Finley didn't hopscotch over it like his partner Bud had done with Fred. Instead, he twisted the knife, while simultaneously anticipating our response that the FDA warning was a mistake.

> **FINLEY: So the FDA instructed the company not to sell the device [for perforators]?**
>
> **OGDEN: Correct.**
>
> **FINLEY: So VSI did not object or disagree with any of these letters?**
>
> **OGDEN: No.**
>
> **FINLEY: Anything from VSI that the FDA has received stating, "We disagree with you because you already gave us permission to distribute this for perforators"?**

Finley loved this question-form. Did anyone ever say to you [insert extremely specific communication]? The answer was never "yes," of course, but the question itself was a way of sneaking in Finley's own testimony on what a reasonable person would've done. It was an impermissibly leading question, but we were quickly learning that Judge Lamberth wasn't exactly a stickler for the Rules of Evidence.

> **OGDEN: No, there's no such communication.**
>
> **FINLEY: Anything from VSI stating that it didn't intend to comply with these letters because you were wrong?**
>
> **OGDEN: No.**

FINLEY: Now, if VSI did not agree with your decision, did they have the right to appeal it and go above your head to the next highest level of FDA?

OGDEN: Yes, they did.

FINLEY: Did they do that?

OGDEN: They did not.

Point made – the perforator application died because we failed to give FDA safety data, and we never challenged FDA's letter saying we couldn't market for perforators. As he did each time before moving on to a new section of his outline, Finley halted, drew a box on his notepad around the questions he'd just asked, and scratched a big "X" through it. And then he moved to the next step in our supposed plot, with an intense look, as always, in his eyes.

FINLEY: To your knowledge, did VSI ever tell the FDA that it launched the [Short Kit] with the same design and model numbers as [their] Perforator Kit, with a different name?

OGDEN: No.

The government's courtroom assistant put a series of side-by-side comparisons up on the courtroom monitors – the same ones Richter wanted back at our mock trial. The proposed labeling for the "Perforator Kit" on one side, the Short Kit's actual packaging on the other. Next slide. The proposed instructions for use for our "Perforator Kit" (which talk about treating "perforators") on one side, the Short Kit's actual instructions for use (which talk about treating "short vein segments") on the other. Finley was scoring real points, and doing it all in a tone of modulated calm that seemed designed to inoculate himself against our tales of intimidation. But then he choked.

FINLEY: If VSI used the term "short vein segment" to hide the fact that it was – whoa. Just pardon me a second. I think I just lost my voice.

OGDEN: It's the pollen.

FINLEY: Yeah. Thank you. Excuse me. May it please the Court – I'll put this in my mouth and try to continue again.

Finley pulled a lozenge from his pocket, unwrapped it, and pitched it into his mouth. He desperately tumbled it around a few times, and then continued his examination – pausing intermittently to deposit grotesque noises into the podium mic.

> **FINLEY: So the question was [chomp chomp chomp] … if VSI had used the term "short vein segment" [chomp chomp] … to hide the fact that it was [chomp] … distributing devices for perforator use [chomp chomp chomp] … would you consider that deceptive?**
>
> **OGDEN: Yes.**
>
> **FINLEY. If VSI did that, would it interfere with your ability to do your job?**

Lost in Finley's mouth distraction was an important government argument. By naming the device "Short Kit" and saying it was used for "short vein segments," the government claimed we were hiding the fact that the device was actually intended to be used for perforators, and was therefore illegally misbranded.

This argument is important, but it also is bogus. FDA's job is to regulate what companies say about their medical devices, not what they think. Finley was saying, "We know what you intended to market the Short Kit for … even if that's not what you were marketing it for." Dr. Belcher already said there was a real market for non-perforator short vein segments, so for FDA to say we couldn't sell it for that market – that, instead, we must be selling it for perforators – would be a textbook example of FDA stepping outside "its place in the universe," to quote Judge Lamberth. And yet, here was Neil Ogden, an agency lifer, lost in space.

> **OGDEN: If companies are hiding their intentions, how can we actually adequately assess what they want to do and how they wanted to do it? It makes our job extremely difficult.**
>
> **FINLEY: And if they had done that, would they have kept you from evaluating the safety and effectiveness evidence that you had requested?**
>
> **LUNDQUIST: Argumentative, Your Honor, and hypothetical.**
>
> **JUDGE LAMBERTH: Overruled.**

OGDEN: Yes, they would have.

FINLEY: Thank you, Mr. Ogden. No further questions.

At under an hour, it was the government's quickest and most effective direct examination yet. Finley had strung together a misleading story, but tightly. Now it was up to Pauzé to unwind it.

Pauzé had spent the last six months preparing to take down Neil Raymond Painter Ogden. Hell, by the time Ogden hit the stand, I would've been comfortable hiring Pauzé as a regulatory expert. He'd put in the time – tediously analyzing the 13 FDA applications we'd filed for Vari-Lase, competitors' filings, and the intra-FDA memos the government gave us in discovery. He grafted all of this against a mental road map of the statutes cross-citing to statutes citing to regulations, unlocking how those actual legal requirements interplayed with FDA's non-binding guidance and the facts of our criminal case.

While Pauzé had been prepping, Ogden had been in San Antonio "enjoying the Texas sunshine, checking out some sights, River Walk, the King William historic district, some missions" and even doing "2 more miles on the jogger treadmill" at night, according to an email the prosecutors gave us after Trial Day 2. Between his sightseeing and jogging, Ogden managed to "read old [FDA] applications" on Vari-Lase and then "head over to Bob Miller's Bar-B-Q for lunch." Sounded like he was having a lovely time, but N.R.P.O.'s vacation was about to end.

Over a two-day marathon cross, Pauzé would put Ogden's preparation and stamina to the test. *The FDA made mistake after mistake in this case.* That was the theme Pauzé promised in his opening argument – which the prosecution team sent to Ogden to review.[20] Now it was time for Pauzé to deliver

---

[20]The government turned over an email showing that the FDA attorney assigned to this case (Beth Weinman, the same one who wanted the pig veins shipped to her house) emailed Ogden the transcript of Pauzé's opening statement to prepare for his testimony, a violation of court rules that require fact witnesses to be sequestered before testifying.

on those promises, against a witness who knew (or at least thought he knew) what was coming. Pauzé's first question posed the thesis.

PAUZÉ: Mr. Ogden, does FDA ever get it wrong?

OGDEN: We work very hard not to.

PAUZÉ: I know. But do you ever get it wrong?

OGDEN: There have been instances, yes, where FDA has gotten things wrong.

Pauzé then walked Ogden through our perforator application. Why it wasn't assigned to a more experienced reviewer. How it instead ended up on the desk of new hire Randolph Copeland – he of immediately-prior McDonald's employment. How even though our V.P. of regulatory assumed the word "perforator" would be added without a hassle, she got a surprise invite for a conference call to discuss "deficiencies" in the application. On that call was Mr. Copeland and also Mr. Ogden. Or as Ogden remembers it …

PAUZÉ: There was a telephone call with VSI and FDA, correct?

OGDEN: I don't recall.

PAUZÉ: Okay. Well, you participated in that telephone call, didn't you?

OGDEN: I don't recall.

PAUZÉ: You don't recall participating in a telephone call in September 26th, 2007, with the folks from VSI?

OGDEN: No.

According to FDA's own notes, Ogden was there. And on that call, Copeland backed down from a number of supposed deficiencies he'd flagged in our application, admitting that he didn't realize Vari-Lase had already been cleared by FDA and on the market for years. But Copeland persisted with one request: that we provide performance data showing Vari-Lase could treat perforators. FDA, Copeland said, required the same of our competitor VNUS before they were allowed to add "perforator" to their indications.

Ogden testified that this was consistent with his understanding – that FDA did require clinical data of VNUS. Ogden even sent an email to his colleagues saying that "our friends at VNUS" sent in data showing an impressive 90% closure, saying "I'm ready to sign off" and adding, "our clinician says no worries for this one."

And then Pauzé put that VNUS data in front of Ogden. It showed that VNUS' "success" was based on tracking only 10 of the 97 patients in the study.

> **PAUZÉ: So you have no idea what happened to 90 percent of the veins that were treated?**
>
> **OGDEN: Not from [what VNUS submitted]. Nope.**
>
> **PAUZÉ: FDA is not going to rely on a clinical trial when you have 10 percent follow-up with the patients, right, Mr. Ogden?**

It was a tricky question for Ogden. On one hand, it's preposterous to give any weight to clinical data with 10% follow-up. That's like a teacher giving a student an A on a 100-question test after looking at only 10 answers and nine happened to be right. With a sample size like that, the data was functionally worthless. But if you read FDA's emails about that VNUS application, it looked like the agency actually did give it weight. So Ogden had two choices: say FDA considered the data and make their operation look foolish (but in so doing help the prosecution), or say FDA didn't consider the data, protecting its reputation (but helping our defense).

> **OGDEN: Correct [FDA would not rely on a trial with 10 percent follow-up].**
>
> **PAUZÉ: Okay. And when you suggested to Agent Scavdis [in an interview] in August of 2011 that FDA relied on it, that was a mistake, right?**
>
> **OGDEN: So VNUS had a number of applications. This was just one of them.**
>
> **PAUZÉ: But this is the one that you were discussing with Agent Scavdis, correct?**
>
> **OGDEN: I believe so, yeah.**
>
> **PAUZÉ: Okay. So that was a mistake?**
>
> **OGDEN: Yes.**

Mistake #1 confirmed. On to Mistake #2: the data Copeland and Ogden asked for on that conference call was illogical. Copeland said that to satisfy FDA's need for safety data on perforators, we could either do a clinical study on perforator treatment in humans or treatment of the great saphenous vein (not perforators) in sheep. We were asking for specific clearance to market Vari-Lase for the treatment of perforators, and FDA was asking for safety data on a vein that was already listed in our label, and for some reason sheep data would suffice.

> **PAUZÉ: Okay. So ... [it] would be unusual to request clinical data for a specific indication that had already been cleared. Would you agree?**

> **OGDEN: I agree, yes.**

> **PAUZÉ: Okay. So was that a mistake?**

> **OGDEN: Yes.**

Mistake #2 confirmed. Pauzé next pried into an opening Ogden had left him on direct, when he said that "short vein segments" was a VSI-invented term. Ogden said the same thing during one of the first interviews for the case in August 2011, and since then it had been adopted as a tenet of the government's case. According to Ogden, "short vein" was a code word with no meaning. But in reality, FDA was quite familiar with the term. In fact, two years before VSI's perforator application, VNUS had successfully changed its labeling to add the treatment of "shorter vessels including perforators."

> **PAUZÉ: So you knew two years before you looked at the VSI application that other companies were using the phrase "shorter veins" to describe veins that would include perforators, correct?**

> **OGDEN: Well, it says "shorter vessels."**

> **PAUZÉ: Is there a difference between vessels and veins, Mr. Ogden?**

> **OOGDEN: The words are different.**

> **PAUZÉ: You have a degree in biomedical engineering?**

> **OGDEN: The words are different.**

> **PAUZÉ: Do you think that there's any difference between "vein" and "vessel?"**

OGDEN: Probably not.

PAUZÉ: Probably not. Okay. So you'll agree with me, then, that shorter vessels means shorter veins, right?

OGDEN: Yes.

Mistake #3, check. After landing three big shots, Pauzé down-shifted to a walk through of every one of our FDA applications, a painfully-deliberate exercise that drained the remainder of the afternoon. Unbeknownst to Ogden, it was an elaborate setup for the fireworks Pauzé had planned for the next day. As 3:30 mercifully hit, the jury departed and the lawyers filed out of the courtroom, ready to begin another night of preparations. That is, all except Bud.

I know this because our team's star paralegal, Sara Brescia, caught Bud rifling through the witness binder we'd given Ogden to refer to on the defense stand. In it were all the documents Pauzé planned to show Ogden, including those slotted for the next day's fireworks display. Make no mistake, this was valuable intel for a scrambling team of prosecutors with an unprepared witness.

When paralegal Sara told Bud, "I don't think you're supposed to be doing that," Bud kept on flipping and mumbled something about finding that "one document." Luckily, Lundquist's junior partner, Kevin Riach, was still hanging around the nearly-abandoned courtroom to call out Bud's inappropriate behavior and wrestle the binder from his sticky fingers. The prosecutors were worried, that's for sure. They had reason to be – their regulatory case was trash, and Pauzé had put in the prep time to sift through it.

The next day Ogden served as pallbearer for the government's case. What looked like the world's most boring cross-examination Monday afternoon was, it turned out, only a lengthy embalming. Pauzé continued Tuesday morning by dragging Ogden through the rest of the FDA applications, but now he was asking the questions that mattered.

PAUZÉ: So [VSI's] indication that was cleared here in July of 2005 covers varicose veins, correct?

OGDEN: Yes.

PAUZÉ: They could be perforator veins, correct?

OGDEN: Could be interpreted that way.

The jury didn't react, but the answer was a show-stopper. The government's only FDA witness just testified that we were cleared to market for varicose veins, including perforators. My eyes lit up. And then he said it again.

PAUZÉ: All right. And if we go to the third page, this lists the indication that was cleared; is that right?

OGDEN: Correct.

PAUZÉ: Also it refers to varicose veins, correct?

OGDEN: Yes.

PAUZÉ: And perforator veins, correct?

OGDEN: It could, yes.

Stunning. Perhaps realizing that he had just buried the government's "hand picked" case, Ogden tried his best to stop the funeral.

OGDEN: But nowhere in the indication does it say "perforator veins."

… which allowed Pauzé to slap his hand for trying.

PAUZÉ: You'd agree with me that perforator veins can be varicose, right, Mr. Ogden?

OGDEN: Yes.

PAUZÉ: And the clearance says "varicose veins," correct?

OGDEN: Correct.

Done. But still that damn computer-generated form letter withdrawing our perforator application was standing. Not for long.

PAUZÉ: Now, [the withdrawal] letter didn't affect any of the existing clearances up to this point that we've discussed, correct?

OGDEN: Correct.

PAUZÉ: Including the clearance with respect to the treatment of varicose veins, correct?

OGDEN: Correct.

PAUZÉ: Varicose veins includes great saphenous veins, correct?

OGDEN: Correct.

PAUZÉ: Short saphenous veins, correct?

OGDEN: It could.

PAUZÉ: And perforator veins, correct?

OGDEN: It could.

As far as I could tell, the only reason Pauzé didn't drop the mic at that moment was that it was affixed to the podium. After two days of coaxing Ogden to lower the government's off-label case into the grave, the only thing left to do was to shovel some dirt on top of it.

PAUZÉ: Now, Mr. Ogden, is it fair to say that over the last couple of days you've been surprised by some of the things that you've seen?

OGDEN: No.

PAUZÉ: You haven't been surprised by anything you've seen?

OGDEN: No.

PAUZÉ: Okay. [But] you testified that FDA doesn't always get it right, correct?

OGDEN: Correct.

PAUZÉ: Okay. And you agree with me that FDA didn't get everything right in this case, correct?

OGDEN: Which case?

PAUZÉ: What we've been talking about over the last two days.

Oh, that case. As an FDA Branch Chief, Ogden was used to being the one asking all the questions. Now answering questions as a sworn witness, he was indecisive and grabbed wildly at anything that might buy him a few more seconds or a clean path to the nearest exit. But at this point, even the prosecutors couldn't save him.

PAUZÉ: Mr. Ogden, you would agree that you made some mistakes along the way, correct?

FINLEY: Your Honor, he's testified –

JUDGE LAMBERTH: Sustained.

PAUZÉ: Mr. Ogden, I've got – I've got no further questions. Thank you.

It was beautiful to watch. Finley objected that his only FDA witness had testified so voluminously to the agency's mistakes in this case that saying "yes" again would be cumulative and unnecessary. Sometimes, folks, you don't ask the questions for the answers.

Pauzé had succeeded in mowing down the government's FDA expert, but its physician expert, Dr. Robert E. Lee, continued to lie in the weeds. Dr. Lee was originally slotted in just behind Ogden, as witness #5. But when Ogden left the stand, it wasn't Dr. Lee who stepped up. Nor did Dr. Lee testify as witness #6, or #7, or #8. Juggling the witness order, it seemed, was becoming the prosecutors' favorite pastime. And Christina Playton was Babe Ruth.

Here are some highlights, all in open court:

Trial Day 3

PLAYTON: We will continue with Dr. Belcher. We know that for sure. After that, we will do Ms. Schmalz, Mr. Arnone . . . . And I need to verify, Your Honor, that all of these people are here. I think they are.

> **PAUZÉ: Neil Ogden and Dr. Lee are FDA employees, so –**
>
> **PLAYTON: Yes. They are here.**

He was indeed "here." At Camp Springhill, to be exact. Even though we told the prosecutors where we were staying and told them not to put any of their witnesses up at our hotel, each morning began with our legal team watching Dr. Lee plow through handfuls of double chocolate mini-muffins at the Camp Springhill breakfast buffet.

Trial Day 4

> **PLAYTON: For what we have next week, Your Honor? It may not be exactly in this order, but we believe Mr. Arnone, Mr. Ogden, Lee, and McIff.**

Trial Day 5

> **JUDGE LAMBERTH: Yeah. Okay. You're still going with Lee and McIff next?**
>
> **PAULISSEN: Your Honor, we need to get an out-of-town witness on and off the stand tomorrow.**
>
> **FINLEY: [So] DeVito – because of his schedule change – [then] McIff and Lee.**

Trial Day 6

> **PLAYTON: Your Honor, I had informed defense that Dr. Lee, who was kind of coming up, got sick. So we're just pulling him out for right now until he's feeling well enough.**

By now they weren't fooling anyone. One member of our up-at-all-hours legal team, in fact, saw Dr. Lee walk into Camp Springhill at 9:30 the previous night, presumably from a late dinner or prep session. Too sick to testify in federal court the next day, though.

By now, Pauzé could only mock the elaborate Dr. Lee charade.

Trial Day 7

> **PAUZÉ: May I inquire as to the health of the good doctor, Lee?**

FINLEY: I hear he's better. We have another doctor who we want to get out of here, so we'll put her in there next.

Trial Day 8

JUDGE LAMBERTH: All right. So then we're looking at Tuesday just having Lee and Arnone and Valls?

PLAYTON: We're not calling Arnone, Your Honor.

JUDGE LAMBERTH: You're not calling Arnone. Okay.

PLAYTON: No, Your Honor.

JUDGE LAMBERTH: All right. So we're looking at Lee and Christian and Valls.

PLAYTON: Those are the remaining witnesses, and Agent Scavdis. I think this weekend our plan is to go over everything and see if there's any – anywhere we can cut. And if so, what. So we'll have a better idea. But that's –

Righhttttt ...

Trial Day 9

JUDGE LAMBERTH: And then all that remains is Dr. Lee?

FINLEY: Your Honor, we are going to make a decision this weekend over whether we need to call Dr. Lee.

CHAPTER 24

THE TRUTH

Trial Day 6

I n the 1998 film *A Civil Action*, two lawyers sit in a courtroom hallway, waiting for a jury verdict.

> **Robert Duvall: What's your take?**
>
> **John Travolta: They'll see the truth.**
>
> **Robert Duvall: The truth? I thought we were talking about a court of law. Come on, you've been around long enough to know that a courtroom isn't a place to look for the truth.**

Rare as it was, my case could come down to the truth. And our First Amendment motions were about protecting our right to it.

Those motions were denied by Judge Biery, but they weren't a total failure, as they forced the government to claim they weren't trying to punish truthful speech. This assertion laid the groundwork for a game-changing jury instruction that Judge Lamberth delivered spontaneously at the outset of jury selection.

> **I want to say one thing now, and that is, the [law] does not prohibit truthful, nonmisleading off-label promotion. In other words, if the promotion is truthful and not misleading, it is not a crime.**

It was a huge break, in line with the state of the law, but unexpected in its timing and clarity. Throughout the investigation, the government envisioned this case being about how our reps were talking to doctors about perforators. Now, thanks to Judge Lamberth, not only did the prosecutors have to show that our clearance didn't cover perforators (somehow overcoming their own

FDA witness' admissions that it did), but they'd also have to show that what our reps said about perforators was false or misleading. To no witness was Lamberth's truth instruction more applicable than Danny McIff.

The doors opened and our former sales rep from Utah swaggered in, head high. He was barrel-chested and buzz-cut, no doubt wearing his best suit. This wasn't the "poor piece of roadkill" Bud had sold him as during plea negotiations. Today, Danny McIff – the only man who agreed to plead guilty in connection with this case – was the government's star witness.

McIff was the face the government would put to the crime. Here was a guy who was out there every day, visiting doctors, carrying a Vascular Solutions bag. They would show McIff was recommending that doctors treat perforators with laser, training them on how to do it, and then teaching his fellow sales reps how to replicate his "success." All under the nose of management, he'd say. The entire conspiracy in one meaty-faced witness.

McIff took the stand like the happiest admitted criminal I'd ever seen. On prompt, he introduced himself. His radio voice boomed as he enunciated each consonant, eyes trained on the jury box. McIff was well-prepared, just as his regional manager, Kip Theno (witness #2), had been days before.

Theno – a grandiose[21] regional manager – had admitted to sitting for "six or seven" pre-trial meetings with the prosecutors, each lasting up to five hours. During those sessions, they devised a script for what he'd say at trial. Theno's

---

[21]Our lawyers held an ongoing contest to find Theno's most pretentious yet meaningless sales phrase in his emails. "Laser is the lexicon of our society" could not be topped.

job was to point the finger at McIff (his former subordinate), setting up pins that McIff would knock down onto himself by admitting guilt. With McIff's admission, the doctrine of *respondiat superior* (Latin for "if an employee does something bad the company is responsible") would kick in, rendering the company, and me as its "responsible corporate officer," automatically guilty.

And early in his questioning by prosecutor Charles Biro (A.K.A. Doogie Howser, J.D.), things were going according to plan.

> **BIRO: How is your relationship with Mr. Root?**
>
> **MCIFF: It was always friendly.**
>
> **BIRO: Has that changed at all?**
>
> **MCIFF: No.**
>
> **BIRO: How do you feel generally about your time at Vascular Solutions?**
>
> **MCIFF: They took care – they treated me well. They gave me a job, let me succeed in it, took care of me.**

This established a key premise. McIff wasn't some disgruntled former employee – he was a contrite young man who liked his job but was led to do illegal things and was now taking responsibility for his actions. Premise accepted, it was time to get to the juicy part of the story.

> **BIRO: Now, did you leave Vascular Solutions voluntarily?**
>
> **MCIFF: No, I did not.**
>
> **BIRO: And how did it come that you left Vascular Solutions?**
>
> **MCIFF: I was terminated on a phone call with Howard Root in August of 2011.**
>
> **BIRO: And how is it that you came to be terminated?**

I'll take this one, Danny.

—∿—

Why I Fired Danny McIff: A Timeline

February 18, 2008 – Unbeknownst to me and without obtaining the required approval, our Western regional manager Kip Theno tells his sales rep McIff to give a presentation on perforator treatment at an upcoming regional sales meeting. McIff creates two clinically-focused documents for his talk – a Word document called "Tips for Treating Perforators" and a PowerPoint, "TREATING PERFORATOR VEINS!!!" He presents them to 12 VSI sales employees at a Holiday Inn in Burbank, California.

June 30, 2011 – While working through an airport ice-cream cone, I learn that VSI is being served with a subpoena asking for the "Tips for Treating Perforators" and "TREATING PERFORATOR VEINS!!!" by name.

July 1, 2011 – Our general counsel emails every employee in the company and orders them to retain all documents relevant to Vari-Lase and perforators so the company can respond to a subpoena. Notably, the fact that the subpoena was sent by criminal prosecutors isn't mentioned because we don't want to cause pandemonium while we figure out what it's about.

July 12, 2011 – Several sales reps – including McIff – are asked to turn in their laptops at the sales meeting in Minneapolis. Forensic analysis of McIff's shows that a few days before the meeting, he deleted both documents.

July 14 – 22, 2011 – McIff lies to our newly-retained criminal defense attorney Bill Michael during four separate conversations about deleting the documents, finally admitting what he did in the last one.

August 25, 2011 – I fire McIff for repeatedly lying about deleting the documents.

A few weeks after I fired him, McIff called me and said he had a job offer with a competitor, one that he needed to support his family. Like all of our sales reps, McIff made a commitment not to work for any of our competitors immediately after leaving VSI. But because of his financial situation and because he called to ask permission before he took the new job (unlike DeSalle and Eddie), I granted him a release. He took the job and wrote me an email thanking me five separate times in one paragraph. Pauzé had shown the email in his opening, explaining, "That's what Howard Root did to Danny McIff."

Prosecutor Charles Biro hoped to take the sting out of our anticipated cross-exam by telling a rosy version of "what the government had done to Danny McIff." That story began nearly two years after Danny left VSI, when a one-page letter showed up at his door.

BIRO: Did you receive a target letter at some point?

MCIFF: Yes, I did.

BIRO: Generally what did the target letter say?

MCIFF: That I was a target in a federal investigation regarding the Short Kit. And that I was being potentially charged with multiple different charges.

BIRO: Which charges do you remember?

MCIFF: Obstruction of justice, mail fraud, wire fraud, the selling of misbranded medical devices.

The letter listed seven different federal statutes that Finley (the signatory) had "reason to believe" McIff had violated. One was obstruction of justice stemming from his deletion of those computer documents, a crime that carried a 20-year prison sentence. This was the prosecutors "throwing the book" at McIff, and the letter said he had 14 days to respond. If not, they'd go to a grand jury and have him indicted. Not surprisingly, McIff chose to respond, and ultimately to "cooperate" with the prosecutors.

BIRO: Did you enter a plea agreement regarding the charges that were listed in the target letter?

MCIFF: Yes.

BIRO: And which charges does the plea agreement cover?

MCIFF: It covers the selling of misbranded medical devices.

BIRO: And is that a felony or a misdemeanor?

MCIFF: A misdemeanor.

BIRO: Now, has the United States provided the plea agreement in exchange for anything other than completely truthful testimony?

MCIFF: No, sir.

BIRO: And are you prepared to give completely truthful testimony today?

MCIFF: Absolutely prepared to.

It was a credibility boost for the government in front of a jury that didn't know the backstory. All they knew was that the government accused this guy of being a criminal, and here he was admitting to criminal charges. It was no coincidence that the misbranding charge the government had him eat was the same one the company and I were facing. So under the government's gambit, if the jury took McIff at his word that he was guilty of misbranding, the government would have their conviction of the company and me.

In addition to the guilt-by-association angle, talking about McIff's plea allowed Biro to back-door testimony about how misbranding is only a misdemeanor – something a lawyer couldn't say in opening or closing or in the jury instructions. *Don't worry, jurors, it's just a little misdemeanor – look how cheerful this guy from Utah looks about it!* Of course, we were prohibited from telling the jury that little misdemeanor would imperil the company's existence and end my career, plus result in prison time.

Part of McIff's deal with the government, signed and turned over to us only a few days before trial, was that he would testify "against VSI and Howard Root." In the deal's factual recitations, Danny claimed to have told me about his involvement in activities he was now admitting were illegal. This was a reference to one email, an email the government trotted out so often we had to give it a name: the "Bright Tip Email."

Sent in 2007, before the Short Kit was even conceived and before the government alleged the conspiracy had even started, the Bright Tip Email described McIff's visit to a vein clinic in Utah. Not just any vein clinic, though, a prominent one that Danny's father, Dr. Bruce McIff, just so happened to have co-founded. During the visit, Danny showed another doctor at the clinic our new Bright Tip laser fiber (which had a special tip that "glows" under ultrasound) and later emailed a summary of the interaction to me and Theno. Biro had Danny read the whole thing.

"**Dr. Black used the Bright Tip this morning. The case went very well and, like everyone previous, the fiber is very easily seen from the ultrasound and makes positioning easier and fast, certainly far superior to anything a bare-tip fiber can show. We treated a left greater saphenous vein of a 75-year-old male.**"

That was from the first paragraph. Hopefully by now you've gathered that the great saphenous vein is not a perforator, but if not, *the GSV is not a perforator.* Then, three paragraphs into the six-paragraph email came the only part that mattered, as far as the government was concerned.

"**Dr. Black was quite impressed with the product and is very excited to use it with perforator cases. One of the biggest obstacles with perforator cases is seeing where your laser fiber is within the vein. The product will alleviate that problem tenfold.**"

Biro was practically wetting himself in anticipation to ask the next question.

BIRO: And then what did Mr. Root do with your email?

MCIFF: Mr. Root forwarded my email out to all the field employees for Vascular Solutions, all the sales reps, clinical specialists, et cetera.

BIRO: And what did he write?

MCIFF: "I know it's getting to be old news, but here's another great Bright Tip case, this time from Salt Lake City at one of Diomed's largest U.S. customers. Thanks, Danny. And congratulations on the great result. Howard."

It was literally *the only* email I ever sent to the sales force that contained the word "perforator." But even in this email, as McIff himself admitted, I wasn't talking about perforators at all.

BIRO: Now, do you know if Mr. Root was responding to the paragraph of your email which discusses the possibility of using the product with perforator cases?

MCIFF: No. I believe Howard was responding to the successful outcome of the case.

That's the only logical way to read the email. I said "congratulations on the great result" and the only result described was Dr. Black treating a patient's

GSV. In the years leading up to trial, I wracked my brain to remember whether I'd even seen that reference to perforators in the Bright Tip Email, and I still honestly don't know. I do know, however, that at the time I cared nothing about perforator veins. And I also know that it's always been 100% legal for a doctor to treat perforators, so forwarding along a doctor's interest in doing so was absolutely legal.

But the prosecutors had a case to make, and they had to push forward with whatever scraps of "evidence" they could cobble together, in a bid to tie me to their perforator conspiracy theory.

BIRO: Did Mr. Root include any caution about the perforator mention that you included in your original email?

MCIFF: No, he did not.

That must've been my plan the whole time. Wait for a rep to email me about a doctor's hypothetical future use of laser on perforators, then forward that around to the entire sales force without mentioning it, to retain plausible deniability. Ridiculous.

If the Bright Tip Email was the cornerstone of the government's conspiracy, the rest of the bricks were trip reports. And Biro was about to lob a truckfull at my head. Biro read the exhibit numbers of each McIff trip report he said evidenced illegal promotion: 59, 66, 67, 68, 69, 70, 73, 105, 118, 119, 232, 233, 234, 235, 236, 237, 238, 239, 240, 241, and 242.

BIRO: Take a second to familiarize yourself with those.

It was a stunt, of course. McIff couldn't read 21 trip reports in 20 minutes, much less 20 seconds, but it didn't matter. Biro then had McIff walk through each of the entries, hoping to bury the company in an avalanche of perforator references. Here was the worst:

"I'm pushing perforators heavily with both of them, and we are going to line up a two-day perforator party here in mid-November, and we're going to train, study and treat. It will be excellent."

But instead of turning this trip report itself into a prosecutorial perforator party, Biro just moved on to the next one. It was a tactical gaffe from a junior prosecutor anxiously racing to check off the next question on his outline.

BIRO: Now, Mr. McIff, did anyone ever discipline you or critique you or criticize you for the field trip reports we just looked at?

MCIFF: No, nobody did.

A few days earlier, McIff's supervisor, Theno, testified that he saw that McIff was promoting for perforators, but didn't stop it. Why? Because, he said, bosses like me in the home office also had access to the trip reports, and he never heard anything negative back, so he assumed we were okay with it. That turned the entire idea of his job managing 12 sales reps on its head, and ignored what he'd heard me say many times – not to promote for perforators until the word was on our label. But it allowed Theno to wriggle himself off the hook.

Up on cross-exam was Rob (don't call me Ben) Hur, himself a recent addition to King & Spalding's trial squad. Rob had been drafting motions and sitting in the gallery at the start of trial, but at the advice of Hirschhorn that "the jury's gonna get bored hearing the same two lawyers all trial," we plugged Hur in to shoulder part of the witness load as the government's case grinded on. Unlike Pauzé and Richter, I'd never seen Hur speak in any sort of formal legal capacity, so I had a few reservations. But he had the pedigree – Stanford Law turned Supreme Court law clerk turned federal prosecutor – and more important, Pauzé vouched for him. So here was Hur, a boyish 40, getting called up to the podium for his first trial experience in private practice. Go get 'em, kid.

Hur started off by introducing himself to McIff. But in reality, he was introducing himself to the jury. The Korean-American Hur had a resonant voice that rivaled McIff's soothing baritone, and a bed-side manner that made you think he was talking to a friend on the stand. Hur, however, made it clear that appearances were not reality.

HUR: I noticed Mr. Biro called you "Danny" several times, but we're not on a first name-basis yet, are we?

MCIFF: You're welcome to call me "Danny."

HUR: Okay. But we haven't spoken before today, have we?

MCIFF: No.

It was an old defense lawyer stand-by. *We've never spoken, but you're good friends with the government, aren't you?* It was a line that had appeared in nearly every legendary cross-exam, but it was still fresh to this jury. I noticed they'd perked up a bit when Rob took the podium, wondering who this new guy with the spiky hair was. And while he still had their attention, Rob got right to the most important issue – the truth.

HUR: You liked your job?

MCIFF: Yeah, very much so.

HUR: You liked it very much. And the parts you enjoyed about it were visiting doctors?

MCIFF: Yes.

HUR: Day in, day out, you were talking to them about high quality-products. The doctors agreed that they were high quality-products?

MCIFF: Yes.

HUR: And they were using them to help patients?

MCIFF: Yes.

HUR: And you weren't lying to these doctors, were you?

MCIFF: No.

HUR: Okay. You weren't trying to mislead these doctors, were you, Mr. McIff?

MCIFF: No, I was not.

By the time McIff could finish answering one question, the next one was already flying back at him. It kept the jury on their toes, but it also took away the precious thought-time McIff would need to push back or reverse course. Softball question, softball question, softball question, then BANG! – McIff "admitted" he'd always told doctors the truth. McIff didn't know it, but two minutes into his cross, he'd already kneecapped the government's entire case.

But McIff needed to be careful. It was a fine line he was walking. One condition of his plea agreement was that he wouldn't deny his guilt in court, and if he contradicted the recitations of his plea agreement, he could see his "no jail time" clause disappear and those obstruction of justice charges resurface. Rob knew that McIff couldn't totally come on board for the defense, but perhaps instead of running him over with our speedboat, we could toss him a lifeline and tow him alongside to safety. Hur did exactly that. What McIff thought "back then" became the lifeline, a safe way for him to contradict his plea today without breaching his plea agreement.

> **HUR: But back then – and, again, we're transporting ourselves back in time to when you're [on vacation with your family] in Santa Barbara before you get this document preservation notice [from VSI]. At that time you didn't think you'd done anything wrong, did you?**
>
> **MCIFF: No, I did not.**
>
> **HUR: You didn't think you'd violated company policy?**
>
> **MCIFF: By selling perforators?**
>
> **HUR: By [doing] anything.**
>
> **MCIFF: No.**
>
> **HUR: And you certainly didn't think you'd broken any federal laws, did you?**
>
> **MCIFF: No, I did not think that.**

Hur was leading the witness with a light touch and a sympathetic tone. At the same time he was putting the jurors in Danny's well-polished shoes, he was eroding the credibility that Biro had built up on direct. But now it was time to knock out the pillars of Biro's examination, those trip reports.

> **HUR: Mr. Biro asked you about some trip reports. And I want to ask you some questions about the very same reports that he asked you about. Okay?**
>
> **MCIFF: Okay.**
>
> **HUR: [Please look at government exhibits] 59, 66, 67, 68, 69, 70, 73, 105, 119, 232, 233, 234, 235, 236,237, 238, 239, 240, 241, 242.**

In any of the visits to doctors that were documented in those trip reports, did you lie to doctors?

MCIFF: No, I did not.

HUR: In any of the trip reports that I just called out did you say anything misleading to those doctors?

MCIFF: No. I was very open.

HUR: That's all the questions I have for you about those trip reports.

Rob dismissively flicked to the next page of his outline, neutralizing Biro's perforator avalanche. He rolled on, keeping his cross-hairs laser-focused on what Judge Lamberth said mattered – the truth.

HUR: Mr. Biro asked you a number of questions about presentations, [including] "Tips for Treating Perforator Veins." In any of those presentations did you lie?

MCIFF: No.

HUR: In any of those presentations was there anything untruthful in there?

MCIFF: No.

HUR: In any of those presentations was there anything misleading in there?

MCIFF: No.

HUR: That's all the questions I have about those documents.

I snuck a peek at the jury – they were getting it. In 15 minutes, Rob had conquered the key sections of a cross we once imagined lasting days. And now came the really good stuff. In the setup, we learned that McIff told doctors the truth, created only truthful presentation materials, and never believed he'd violated the law or company policy while at Vascular Solutions. Yet McIff had been told by the prosecutors he violated multiple laws. And he was now risking his career and reputation by agreeing to plead guilty to a criminal charge. Something didn't add up.

HUR: Now, just to be exact about this, you've signed on the dotted line of a plea agreement; is that right?

MCIFF: Yes, sir.

HUR: Okay. But you haven't actually entered that plea?

MCIFF: No, I have not.

HUR: And that means you haven't stood there in court, looked the judge in the eye and said "I'm guilty of this crime" – is that right?

You could see the wheels turning in Danny's head. *Maybe I don't have to take the deal.*

HUR: Okay. So when you were negotiating with the government about this plea agreement, did they tell you that giving perfectly truthful speech to doctors is not a crime? They didn't tell you that, did they?

MCIFF: No.

HUR: And that's all you were doing all those years, right?

MCIFF: That was what I thought I was doing, yes.

If that's not illegal, then maybe I can fight this thing. Maybe I can avoid the shame of being the convict son of a prominent Mormon family. Maybe I can keep my career.

HUR: And during [your plea] discussions, obstruction of justice figured pretty prominently in these discussions, right?

MCIFF: Yes, it did.

HUR: Okay. And the government told you, "You can sign on the dotted line here [and plead guilty to misbranding], or you can face a potential obstruction of justice charge with a 20-year max?"

MCIFF: That is correct.

HUR: That was the choice they posed to you, right?

McIff nodded as the jurors scooted to the edges of their green leather seats. The absurdity of it all was striking me freshly – threatening to put somebody in jail for 20 years for dragging a few computer documents into the trash bin, all to boost their leverage over me in negotiations. It was diabolical, really.

> **HUR: Now, when they were posing that quote-unquote "choice" to you, did they tell you that their investigation wasn't actually obstructed at all? These documents that you deleted, they had those documents. They have had them since 2011 when the company and Howard Root recovered these documents and turned them over to the government. Did they tell you that?**
>
> **MCIFF: We didn't get into that, no.**
>
> **HUR: You didn't get into that. Would you have liked to have known that before you signed on the dotted line?**
>
> **MCIFF: Sure.**

I looked over at the prosecutors. They, like the rest of the courtroom, were frozen in the moment. The tension was that visceral type, the type that makes you want something to happen. Rob Hur had dimmed the government's star witness, and now, with a final burst of questions, he invited Danny to implode completely.

> **HUR: So let's look at this choice that the government gave you. On the one hand, an obstruction of justice charge with a 20-year max and it's going to deprive you of your liberty, potentially, and your livelihood, right? So that's one choice that you have.**
>
> **And on the other hand you can sign on the dotted line with a plea agreement that guarantees you no jail time, right? And the government told you they were going to put in a good word with the Department of Health and Human Services [so you wouldn't be excluded from working in the healthcare industry], didn't they?**
>
> **All you have to do is testify against the company and against Howard Root. Those are the choices that were given to you, right?**
>
> **MCIFF: That was the agreement.**
>
> **HUR: Pretty easy choice – wasn't it, Mr. McIff?**
>
> **MCIFF: Yes, it was.**
>
> **HUR: That's all the questions I have.**

CHAPTER 25

PLAYING DIRTY

Trial Day 7

The government was a wounded bear. Now they'd charge at us with all they had; we expected that. We just didn't expect the judge to do the same.

Judge Lamberth must've been wondering what the hell was happening. He hadn't seen an acquittal in his courtroom in over a decade, a statistic I thankfully learned only after my verdict. Yet here were these brash defense lawyers flipping witnesses like pancakes. On top of that, the prosecutors didn't really seem to know what they were doing. That dud of an opening Bud laid down, for instance. Or Finley, when he asked Bud for permission to hand the witness a document. Hint: you ask the guy in the robe!

FINLEY: May I take it up, Mr. Paulissen?

BUD: It's *the Court* we ask.

JUDGE LAMBERTH: Yes ...

Maybe Judge Lamberth didn't understand that we were supposed to be winning. Maybe he saw a company led by a former lawyer that he thought played fast and loose and now wanted off on a technicality. I don't know. But at some point, Judge Lamberth decided to pitch his tent in the government's camp. The exact moment the Prosecutor Lamberth era began will never be known, but here are three theories as to why it began, ranked in order of likelihood.

3. The Johns (Richter and Lundquist) refuse to stand while addressing the Court.

Despite a pre-trial warning from the court clerk that attorneys must stand while addressing the bench (and a second one following their noncompliance), the Johns continued to remain seated while making their rather frequent objections. This one seems too petty.

2. A VSI employee refers to the Honorable Judge Royce C. Lamberth as "Jabba the Hutt" in the stairwell within earshot of his law clerk.

This comment is obviously not ideal, even if the resemblance to the Tatooine crime lord is. Still, I doubt that's a conversation the young clerk would want to have with his ornery boss. Struck for lack of Lamberth knowledge.

1. Former VSI V.P. of regulatory does lunchtime-180 on crucial testimony.

On day four of trial, Deborah Schmalz hesitantly testified that when she told me in 2007 that we should file an FDA application to add "perforator" to the label, that advice was based on "the law." The government liked that, because if she thought the law required additional clearance before selling for perforators, and we went to market without it, they had their conspiracy. And then we broke for lunch. As soon as court resumed, Schmalz spontaneously announced that she'd "like to correct one response [she] gave right before the break." For the next 10 minutes, she tried to explain that she considered both the law and the non-law guidance (FDA's recommendation). Essentially, she was saying we didn't have to submit an application to market for perforators, but FDA would probably prefer that we did. Finley tried to pull her away from that whole guidance thing and back to the law. Judge Lamberth was displeased throughout.

> **FINLEY: Was it or was it not required by law? I believe your answer before lunch was "yes." Is it no longer possible for you to answer that question "yes" or "no"?**
>
> **SCHMALZ: I don't believe it's possible to answer that question "yes" or "no." What I'm trying to say is that you take all of these things into account when trying to decide.**
>
> **JUDGE LAMBERTH: The question was what you thought *at the time*, not today or not what you thought before lunch. His question was, "What did you think at the time that you made the submission?" That was his question.**

Judge Lamberth straightened up in his chair to bring his wrath down on Schmalz. The witness box sits like a lowered sidecar to the judge's bench, matching the power dynamics of this encounter. It was the first time Judge

Lamberth had questioned a witness during the trial, and it was about to be the first time Schmalz had been berated by a federal judge.

SCHMALZ: Can you repeat the question, please?

JUDGE LAMBERTH: I just did. Did you not understand me?

SCHMALZ: At the time my decision to submit the [FDA application] took into account the law *and also* the guidance documents that FDA had issued.

JUDGE LAMBERTH: I give up.

I think Judge Lamberth figured we got to Schmalz over lunch. We didn't so much as say a word to her, but I could see how a witness-tainting theory could conveniently explain both Schmalz's backtracking and Fred Reuning's earlier flipping. We were paying their lawyer bills, after all (as Minnesota law requires). Plus, we'd met with them and their lawyers multiple times for pre-trial interviews. And when the prosecutors asked to do the same, many of the witnesses asked for immunity and refused to sit for private prep sessions.

This apparently raised another red flag for Judge Lamberth. Why, if witness after witness was saying they hadn't done anything wrong, did so many of them require immunity before testifying? In the drug cases Lamberth was used to seeing in D.C. District Court, immunity agreements were most often reserved for gang members snitching on their co-conspirators. But here, no one was snitching, even those who had immunity.

Immunity is a courtship. The prosecutor asks a witness to testify (either at trial or before a grand jury), and the witness plays hard to get by invoking their Fifth Amendment right against self-incrimination. *I don't want to testify, because if I do I might incriminate myself.* So to take that excuse off the table, the prosecutors go to a judge and get an order saying "you have to testify, but you can't be prosecuted for anything you say (unless you lie)."

The number of steps it takes to get to an immunity agreement makes them relatively rare, yet in our case witness after witness was strolling in with immunity. The reason for this was obvious. The prosecutors were acting irrationally: yelling, making unpredictable threats, and building a case under a theory that seemed dubious at best. The witnesses' lawyers realized this quickly, in part because there were only two of them. So when Jon Hopeman and *The Best Defense Lawyer Nobody Has Heard Of,* Dan Scott, picked up on the prosecutors' game, they started demanding immunity for their clients. But again, Judge Lamberth didn't know the backstory. All he knew was that it was frustrating to watch a web of seemingly self-confessed-criminals spin a successful tale of innocence.

The tinderbox lit when Bob Lehoullier, our easily-rattled sales rep from Maine, finished testifying. Or so he thought. Lehoullier had stammered through vacillating admissions and excuses, made mostly-indecipherable by his thick, Bostony accent. Growing weary, and with little to show for their examination, the prosecutors gave up. And that's when Judge Lamberth tagged in.

> **JUDGE LAMBERTH: Let's see counsel at the bench. [To Lehoullier] Can you step down and stand right over by [the jury box]?**

Conference with attorneys at bench:

> **JUDGE LAMBERTH: I understand this guy can be led anywhere, but it is offensive to me that he thinks that he did nothing wrong. Then why did he insist on immunity? I can ask those questions or the government can ask them, but I think it cries out for some understanding – if he did nothing wrong – why he wanted immunity. So if you want to object to that, you can.**

Offensive? I agree. It is offensive that a judge would assume the only reason a witness would demand immunity is because he is guilty. It's also offensive that a judge who's been on the bench for over 30 years and eight days of this trial couldn't see how scary these prosecutors' tactics were. But this wasn't *Judge* Lamberth, it was now *Prosecutor* Lamberth. Thankfully, Biro still couldn't frame a question to save his life.

> **BIRO: Mr. Lehoullier, I would like to ask one additional question. When we first started yesterday, I talked to you about when you had requested an order granting you immunity and I believe yesterday and today you basically testified that you didn't believe you had done anything wrong. Is that your testimony?**
>
> **LEHOULLIER: Yes.**

BIRO: Could you explain to the jury why you don't believe you did anything wrong, but you asked for immunity before you would testify in court in front of a grand jury?

Lehoullier took this as an invitation to launch into a comprehensive defense of Bob Lehoullier, at about triple Perry Mason's speed and a third of his clarity. "Doctors talked to me first about treating perforators and it was covered by the label," were the arguments he was going for, I think. But he didn't answer the question, so Biro tried again.

BIRO: And so why did that make you request immunity?

LEHOULLIER: I think just – I wanted to make sure I would come up and tell the truth without any harm to myself.

BIRO: …Okay. Thank you.

Biro gave up, and I don't blame him. It's difficult trying to pin down an elusive legal ninja like Bob Lehoullier. Not everybody's cut out for it, and apparently Biro wasn't. Thankfully, Lamberth had had enough of Lehoullier as well, and he was excused to return to Maine.

But this failed foray into cracking the immunity riddle didn't dull Lamberth's resolve. And a few days later, he decided he'd handle the questioning himself. But this time, he ran into a more coherent witness – our sales rep from Virginia, Anthony Ramiro.

JUDGE LAMBERTH: Can you explain what the reason was why you insisted on immunity before you would talk?

RAMIRO: I feel like I've not done anything wrong here.

JUDGE LAMBERTH: Then why did you need immunity?

RAMIRO: It's kind of like insurance. You might not need it, but it's nice to have it.

Bravo. Clear, concise, believable. The jurors nodded in agreement. Ramiro had just closed his biggest sale ever for VSI.

When Lamberth wasn't painting our witnesses as reluctant criminals, the judge took to hitting his new favorite punching bag, John Richter. Richter, you see, was the defense's secret weapon. After successfully slipping Dr. Belcher into the lineup on the third day of trial, the prosecutors were getting even bolder with their game of Three-Card Witness Monte. Almost every day, another mystery witness appeared, each with reportedly-pressing travel plans.

Counteracting this was Richter, a man with a supernatural talent for filling dead air. It's maybe something you develop when you charge over $1,000 an hour. His long-windedness had infuriated me on conference calls, but it was considerably more endearing when you could cheer for it. By going into human rain delay mode when the government had a surprise witness in the on-deck circle, Richter gave us enough time for our paralegals to organize the binders and Pauzé to plot the next witness' undoing.

Lamberth, however, didn't appreciate the technique. Here's what happened when Richter tried to launch into a new, tangential line of questioning with a witness he'd already taken too long with:

JUDGE LAMBERTH: If we're going to start another area, we're going to take our morning break.

RICHTER: Okay.

JUDGE LAMBERTH: I thought you were going to end someday. [Walks off.]

BAILIFF: All rise.

After Richter proceeded to carry his cross-exam through the next break, Lamberth growled off the record, "I've heard of a filibuster in Congress, but I'd never seen one in court, 'til today." It had the words of a good-natured joke, but not the tone.

Meanwhile, the government was basking in its favored son status, even if Judge Lamberth didn't know who they all were. After Biro wrapped up a plodding exam in which he lured a witness into saying there was no legitimate market for the treatment of "short vein segments" that VSI could have been legitimately pursuing, Pauzé moved to introduce an extraordinary email Finley sent us in discovery. Written by Biro and sent to the entire prosecution team, it read: "[T]here is a legitimate market for 'shorter vein segments' that VSI could have been legitimately pursuing." Judge Lamberth studied it, looked up, and asked …

JUDGE LAMBERTH: Who is "Charles Bro?"

Biro rose from his seat, pushed up his glasses with his index finger, and raised his hand. "That is me, Your Honor." Judge Lamberth pretended like he knew the name of the attorney who'd held the podium for the last two hours. "Oh, *Bro*? Oh, *Biro*. I see. I couldn't read it. Okay." *Bro* – who was, despite his youthful appearance and high-pitched voice, not wearing suspenders and a spinning bowtie – explained that this was his privileged work product that was never intended for us to receive.

Bro demanded it back. Pauzé, though, wasn't quite ready for that – holding his position at the podium and waving the email around like a bully who'd just ripped the waistband from Biro's underwear. "We received lots of emails to the prosecution team, so if there is a claim as to work product on this, this is news to us, Judge," Pauzé said patiently.

Bro was pissed. By now he'd developed a serious case of "crazy eyes" and was shaking in anger – either at Pauzé's delighted crassness or for being exposed by his colleague Finley's sloppy document handling.

Bro snapped. "That's mine – give it back!" Pauzé sidestepped away from the podium, and Biro lunged at him. "Gimme that!" He snatched the printout and attempted to regain his composure by flattening out his trial-wrinkled suit. We still had electronic copies of the email, of course, but after all that drama, Judge Lamberth still wouldn't let the jury see it.

Then there was the *McCopeland* scandal. As we did with every potential witness, we asked the prosecutors for any interview notes they had on Copeland, our FDA reviewer. Finley said they hadn't interviewed him, but curiously added that Copeland "did not have any relevant knowledge beyond what is reflected on FDA records." Which, of course, is the type of thing you could only find out from an interview. Then, two days before trial, Pauzé asked Finley again. This time Finley changed his story and now divulged that FDA Special Agent Scavdis had called Copeland, but that it wasn't a "real interview" – they merely discussed when they might be able to speak again.

Not believing Finley's story, we brought Copeland down to San Antonio mid-trial for an interview of our own to see if we'd want to call him in our defense. Copeland had a lot to say. He said there was a heated internal disagreement within FDA as to whether VSI needed to submit study data in order to put the word "perforator" in the label. The laser expert in the group said "no," but another employee said "yes" and eventually won out. FDA Agent Scavdis knew all this, Copeland said, because he told him so during their phone interview. It was a shameless violation of the government's Brady duty to disclose exculpatory evidence to defense counsel, but at this point, it was only half-way shocking.

The Basu memo, though, was all-the-way shocking. In it, Sankar Basu, an experienced FDA reviewer assigned to evaluate our next FDA application for another version of the Vari-Lase procedure kit, determined that treating perforators and treating the GSV were "substantially equivalent" uses. Therefore, he recommended, the word "perforator" could be added to our indications automatically. The Basu memo never left FDA's campus, though, until the government turned it over to us in discovery.

Naturally, the prosecutors tried to keep it from the jury. Neil Raymond Painter Ogden didn't actually sign it, they said – it was merely signed "for NRO" on his behalf. For some reason, that was enough for Judge Lamberth to block us from bringing it up with Ogden. Later, Finley tried to get it excluded altogether by saying this was just an internal memo; it never went outside the FDA. Lamberth bought that reasoning too, saying, "If it didn't go outside of the agency, it's not going to the jury."

Pauzé's face melted away from his body when he heard Judge Lamberth block the jury from ever seeing the Basu memo. This was supposed to be Pauzé's smoking gun – the document that proved just how unjust this conviction campaign was. Lamberth's decision to block it was so unsupportable it probably rose to "abuse of discretion," meaning it could have been used to overturn a conviction on appeal. That was, if Pauzé could get his objection on the record …

PAUZÉ: Okay. Well, I'd just like to make a record, Your Honor.

JUDGE LAMBERTH: Okay.

PAUZÉ: So the conclusion in the internal memo is that the indication that's requested is the same.

JUDGE LAMBERTH: I understand.

PAUZÉ: Is –

JUDGE LAMBERTH: I read it. I read it. I saw it.

PAUZÉ: And counsel indicated it was a cut-and-paste error, Your Honor. It's not a cut-and-paste error.

JUDGE LAMBERTH: It doesn't matter.

PAUZÉ: No, I know, Your Honor. May I just make a record?

JUDGE LAMBERTH: I'll try to sit back.

PAUZÉ: I appreciate it.

Pauzé began again as Lamberth swatted away the microphone and reclined in his lifetime-appointed La-Z-Boy. When Pauzé finished laying out a measured and passionate argument as to why the Court couldn't keep this crucial document from the jury, Judge Lamberth rocked back to the microphone, casually.

JUDGE LAMBERTH: All right. That's rejected.

Not denied, not overruled. *Rejected.* Not even a legal term, really. Pauzé was crestfallen. All those thoughts that this would be *our judge* – the one guy with the power to see through the FDA's overreaching, self-important beadledom were officially extinguished. All the work we'd done to prepare for this case, and all the success we'd had early in trial. It was all being systematically undone by unhinged prosecutors and a judge with his thumb on the scales of justice.

CHAPTER 26

13 HOURS AS A SLEEP-DEPRIVED ASSOCIATE

Trial Day 8

T his memorandum summarizes the eighth day in trial for King & Spalding junior associate Stephen Saltarelli, my co-writer, referenced earlier in this book as "some lawyer I've never heard of."

To: Howard Root
From: Stephen Saltarelli

6:50 a.m. – Alarm goes off. Hit snooze.

7:00 a.m. – Alarm. Snooze.

7:10 a.m. – Debate relative merits of showering and making a third run at snooze button. Choose shower.

7:12 a.m. – Become hypnotized by warmth of shower, creeping fatigue. Catch self in mid-pass-out lean.

7:26 a.m. – Inhale Camp Springhill sausage patty for 14th consecutive day.

7:42 a.m. – Walk to court. Maximize exposure to sun in attempt to counterbalance 23.5 hours spent indoors each day.

7:54 a.m. – Stand in line to enter concrete Rolo of a courthouse. Advised by VSI employee counsel J. Hopeman that grey suit doesn't match brown shoes.

8:38 a.m. – Take the Hot Seat.[22]

8:49 a.m. – Yawn as B. Lehoullier returns to the stand for second day of cross.

8:52 a.m. – Hear word "perferahtahhh" on loop, courtesy of B. Lehoullier's New England drawl. Yawn again.

9:10 a.m. – Fall asleep in federal court.

Explanation of Attorney Sleepiness

Night before:

12:05 a.m. – Review 94-page PDF produced hours earlier by government re: surprise witness Dr. Asbjornsen. Document completely scrambled, evident by fax page-stamps.

12:07 a.m. – Rearrange pages vis-à-vis page number on fax stamp. Discover 15 pages missing, replaced by 15 duplicates of other pages in the PDF sent by government (*e.g.* two page 1's, zero page 2's).

12:17 a.m. – R. Hur inquires. Email to prosecution team:

> **Upon properly ordering the documents you produced earlier tonight, we have determined that the documents omit 15 of the 94 pages provided to the government. While the document includes a total of 94 pages, 15 of those pages are duplicates. Please provide the missing materials immediately.**

---

[22]The Hot Seat is the right-most chair immediately behind the defense table. Duties while in the Hot Seat include but are not limited to: passing notes to the real lawyers, passing tissues to sniffly lawyers, locating documents for the real lawyers to use on cross, ensuring government attorneys receive a copy of each document shown to the witness on cross.

12:37 a.m. – Reply from lanky government paralegal R. McAuliffe to R. Hur: "Counsel, The document we sent earlier tonight is an exact copy of the PDF file that was produced to Agent Scavdis from [Dr. Asbjornsen]." Attorneys trade looks of suspicion in War Room.

1:22 a.m. – Following Van Halen air-drum session, J. Richter announces that Dr. Lee cross outline resembles fecal matter.

1:48 a.m. – J. Richter shakes head, laments that "Dr. Lee outline needs so much work … so much good work," spikes designer glasses on keyboard. Seismic event registers 6.3 on the Richter scale.

1:50 a.m. – J. Richter announces that he "Can't be doing this," citing speaking role in court next day. Assigns Mormon-looking patsy P. Cooch [identified elsewhere as M. Culkin] to finish the outline. J. Richter departs room in tense silence. P. Cooch – having officially been "Richtered" – appears on verge of tears and/or transforming into vampire.

2:15 a.m. – Consume refrigerated fried chicken; assist now-raccoon-eyed P. Cooch's effort to repurpose sections of old, 60-page Dr. Lee outline into new, 56-page outline.

2:57 a.m. – Give up. Leave P. Cooch to ascend into vampiredom alongside nocturnal paralegal J. Rennert, rearranger of trial binders to reflect allegedly new outline.

3:40 a.m. – Contemplate cruelty of conk out cunctation coupled with exhaustion.

4:00 a.m. – 6:50 a.m. – Host light nightmares re: documents missing from Dr. Lee binder.

9:11 a.m. – Reawaken as head snaps forward, rebounds. M. Pauzé walking witness through series of boilerplate compliance questions. Pinch arm to retain consciousness, determine technique overrated.

9:18 a.m. – M. Pauzé calls out Defense Exhibit 1408-T, turns to corresponding tab in binder. B. Lehoullier turns to 1408-T in his binder. Dig in Banker's Box, search for folder labeled 1408-T. Got it. Rise, pace twice toward prosecution, hand document to C. Biro. Straighten tie. *Good job.*

9:19 a.m. – M. Pauzé employs 1408-T to counter argument that after VSI received subpoena, reps began referring to perforators in trip reports as "short vein segments" to conceal perforator pitches. B. Lehoullier reads aloud 1408-T. Exhibit shows him writing "perforator" twice in a trip report submitted *after* the subpoena.

> **PAUZÉ: So you didn't stop using the word "perforator" just because you heard that there was an investigation, correct?**

> **LEHOULLIER: Correct.**

9:21 a.m. – M. Pauzé flips to next tab in his binder; calls out 1408-U. Look for manila folder labeled 1408-U. Located. Calmly stride to C. Biro, place document on desk. Note his failure to say "thank you" this time. Remind self re: still doing good job. Retake Hot Seat; avoid eye contact with jury.

> **PAUZÉ: Let's look at Defense 1408-U. Do you recognize that, Mr. Lehoullier?**

> **LEHOULLIER: Yes.**

9:22 a.m. – M. Pauzé scans for another example of Lehoullier using "perforator" in trip report post-dating subpoena. Prepare gloating facial expression for the jury; notice M. Pauzé's hesitation. Experience horror as M. Pauzé looks back and mouths, "Where is it?!" M. Pauzé asks question to buy time.

> **PAUZÉ: Okay. Is this another field trip report?**

> **LEHOULLIER: Yes.**

9:23 a.m. – Frantically scan document. Confirm that it post-dates subpoena – should be the one. Review entry referencing irrelevant doctor visit. Another irrelevant one. Find entry discussing Vari-Lase. But description says "short vein segment." What?! Determine there must be another entry in here. Irrelevant. Irrelevant. Flip page. Separate entry says "short vein segment" too. *Ohhhh fuck.* Realize I have introduced government-friendly document on cross. *Bad job.*

9:24 a.m. – Picture witness being beheaded with document, own firing. Pointlessly wonder how wrong exhibit number made its way into outline. Field second emergency look from M. Pauzé, counter with look of motionless terror. M. Pauzé receives message. Glance at prosecution table, observe C. Biro reading 1408-*Uh-Oh*. M. Pauzé commences emergency evacuation (paraphrased).

> **Let's take a look at your grand jury testimony. No, actually, let's look at the other one. You testified twice, right? Let's put that up on the projector. Oh, Judge, you won't let me? No big deal, let's just read some of it. Look over here. Not over there.**

9:26 a.m. – Look back at C. Biro. Exhibit 1408-U no longer in his hand. Momentarily take up religion, pray 1408-U stays out of C. Biro's dainty hands on re-direct.

9:27 a.m. – Sit paralyzed in fear-shame as C. Biro begins re-direct. Slide eyes around courtroom, searching for hints of impending crucifixion. *Is that it in his hand?* Close eyes, feel throat swell as C. Biro unsheaths first document.

> **BIRO: Good morning, Mr. Lehoullier.**

> **LEHOULLIER: Good morning.**

> **BIRO: Defendants just showed you …**

Brace for imminent public flogging.

> **BIRO: … what was previously marked and entered into evidence as Government Exhibit 4.**

9:28 a.m. – *Government Exhibit 4?!* Not the trip report! Blood pressure restored to sub-ischemic levels.

9:32 a.m. – Three-hundred seconds of torture end without junior associate ruin. Wonder why C. Biro didn't show it. Calculate likelihood M. Pauzé's diversion worked. Permanently take up religion, enroll in Church of Pauzé.

9:36 a.m. – B. Lehoullier, least coherent government witness, steps down. Figure remainder of day should proceed smoothly. Pre-trial interview memos suggest government calling Maine "Phlebologist" Dr. Asbjornsen to tell single contained story about denial of insurance pre-authorization for perforator treatment. Plan to return to hotel for mid-day nap after this witness, whilst remainder of team remains in court.

9:37 a.m. – Dr. Asbjornsen tip-toes to witness stand, resembling jolly librarian in muumuu. Not wearing Birkenstocks on feet, but doing so in spirit.

9:38 a.m. – T. Finley rises to handle direct, dropping Hot Seat occupant to fourth place in King & Spalding Fantasy Prosecutor League.

9:46 a.m. – Realize defense team is in midst of government ambush – Dr. Asbjornsen being used as disguised expert witness.

> **FINLEY: Are you familiar with the Society of Interventional Radiologists' recommendation about when it is appropriate to use a laser to treat a perforator?**
>
> **DR. ASBJORNSEN: I am pretty sure [they] recommend [only] treating perforators when patients have ulcers or very debilitating, very life-limiting aspects of this disease.**

9:47 a.m. – Fume at government asking non-expert witness about collective opinion of third-party academic group whose individual members could only testify as experts. Write note to defense table flagging this as "expert testimony *inception*." Tear it up before passing. R. Hur, covering Dr. Asbjornsen on one-day notice, attempts to stop madness.

> **HUR: Your Honor, this testimony appears to be straying well within the territory of expert witness opinion testimony. Dr. Asbjornsen was not noticed as an expert.**
>
> **FINLEY: Your Honor, I have about 70 pages of transcript where Mr. Richter opened the door and asked all of these medical questions on all of these subjects.**
>
> **HUR: Your Honor, that is completely irrelevant as to the proper scope of this testimony. She has not been noticed.**
>
> **...**
>
> **JUDGE LAMBERTH: The objection is sustained.**

9:53 a.m. – Finley disregards ruling, returns to well.

> **FINLEY: Have you had a chance to review the full [RELIEVE] study results?**
>
> **DR. ASBJORNSEN: Yes, I have.**

FINLEY: And when did you do that?

DR. ASBJORNSEN: Last night.

9:54 a.m. – Dr. Asbjornsen admits she didn't even read entire document, provides curious explanation.

DR. ASBJORNSEN: I think I said I couldn't read [part of it]. The font was too small.

9:58 a.m. – Anxiety grows at defense table. Notes descend on Hot Seat at breakneck speed. *Need DVT disclosure to FDA.* Email paralegal waiting upstairs by printer. *Are the medical textbooks in the courtroom?* No. Text associate to retrieve them from hotel War Room. *She said paid Dr. consultants = biased. Who does she consult for?* Fire up the Google. Pine for calm pre-nap Hot Seat experience I anticipated.

10:12 a.m. – T. Finley attempts to introduce repulsive photo of oversized blood clots. R. Hur successfully argues it's irrelevant, returns to the defense table, crumples it into ball, throws it on courtroom floor. H. Root picks it up, smooths it out, places in binder labelled "Book."

10:20 a.m. – Morning break. Abscond to second floor bathroom. Engage faucet to wash hands, recall it being rocket-powered too late. Absorb wave of water bank-shotting off sink onto J. Hopeman-assessed mismatched suit. Hurriedly disengage faucet. Pat dry mismatched suit. Nod sheepishly at C. Biro, who enters wondering what the hell is going on.

10:49 a.m. – More objections. Question whether T. Finley ever attended law school.

FINLEY: Are you able to tell your patients about [studies on perforators] if the company doesn't give you the information you asked for?

HUR: Same objection, Your Honor.

JUDGE LAMBERTH: Sustained.

FINLEY: I'd like to ask you to try to do something. Try to step out of your doctor role.

HUR: Objection, Your Honor.

JUDGE LAMBERTH: Sustained.

FINLEY: [Continues metaphysical line of questioning.]

JUDGE LAMBERTH: No. That objection is sustained.

FINLEY: Was it leading? All right. I'll ask another question.

JUDGE LAMBERTH: You want to come to the bench, I'll tell you what it is.

FINLEY: I'll move on. I'm not sure I want to hear the answer.

11:08 a.m. – R. Hur moves to rebut testimony that independent vascular surgeons who analyzed RELIEVE study were "biased" because they were paid for their work.

HUR: Unfortunately doctors have busy practices. And those that are qualified enough to really bring the judgment that's required, it's tough to get part of their time, isn't it?

DR. ASBJORNSEN: Tough, but not impossible.

HUR: *But not impossible.* Fair enough. Have you ever served on a clinical events committee?

DR. ASBJORNSEN: I'm part of an advisory board ... which is a paid position.

HUR: Okay. So what's the name of the company?

DR. ASBJORNSEN: Varithena.

HUR: So it sounds like Mr. Finley might say that you're not providing your honest or unbiased opinion to Varithena.

DR. ASBJORNSEN: I am probably not because I'm being paid by them to help them figure out if their product is good. So I'm trying to figure that out by working with them.

HUR: Right ... ?

DR. ASBJORNSEN: So it is a biased opinion.

11:09 a.m. – *Curveball!* R. Hur bemoans witness' willingness to belly-flop onto own sword for no reason.

12:03 p.m. – Lunchtime. On way out of courtroom, T. Finley comforts Dr. Asbjornsen with hand on her back, as if to say "you're doing great." Confirm with former federal prosecutors that this is way sketchy. Note on social level that it was awkwardly executed.

12:05 p.m. – Select mystery sandwich from upstairs conference room. Demolish it before noticing onions, which are bad. Pawn off partners' exhibit requests on paralegals.

12:52 p.m. – R. Hur resumes cross. Morning adrenaline fades, roast beef and covert onion sub settles, sleepiness returns. Disguise yawn as cough.

12:55 p.m. – Dr. Asbjornsen continues stonewalling R. Hur, answering 80% of questions with "That's what it says." R. Hur gives up, retires to the defense table, passes back final note: "I hate her."

1:12 p.m. – Dr. Asbjornsen feeling loose again on re-direct.

> **FINLEY: Mr. Hur made reference to the fact that there was –**

> **DR. ASBJORNSEN: Who is Mr. Hur?**

> **FINLEY: Mr. Hur. He was the gentleman who cross-examined you.**

R. Hur waves to stand, inciting uncontrollable witness giggle fit.

> **DR. ASBJORNSEN: I'm sorry. I'm sorry. Yes ... I can't even remember his name.**

1:24 p.m. – Dr. Asbjornsen steps down, just as jury appears to be catching up on sleep. Speaking of which ...

1:42 p.m. – Arrive at hotel. Turn off lights, collapse into bed. Investigate why stupid red light on BlackBerry is blinking. Open message ...

> **Richter needs you to be working on the Dr. Lee outline.**

CHAPTER 27

PARADE OF IGNORANCE

Trial Day 9

The song played on repeat in my hotel room. It was an annoying work habit I had, but I could get away with it tonight because Beth was back in Minnesota. This time, though, as I trudged through a backlog of emails and sales reports, I wasn't getting the trance effect I usually got from looping a song 30 times straight. Natalie Prass' opening lyrics kept drawing me in. My partial hearing loss made it tough to pinpoint the words, so I Googled it.

> **I don't feel much**
> **Afraid I don't feel anything at all**
> **In the name of love**
> **I keep close but I am gone.**

That's how I felt about VSI now, I realized. I was still keeping close to our business, our products, and our team's mission – to develop new medical devices to improve patient lives. It was something I truly loved, but it wasn't worth prison. Or even the fear of prison, for that matter. And each time the song kicked back to the beginning, those words caught me again – "but I am gone." I tried to keep pushing through my work – like I'd done every day since the indictment hit 14 months ago – but I realized I was gone, checked out, at least for the night.

I left the hotel in search of ice cream. Eyes peeled, I walked alone in the residual warmth of San Antonio's darkness. It felt nice to chart a path without structure, to just meander along the crushed-stone walkways of the cheesy Riverwalk. Groups of tourists were all around me, but one congregation across the river stood out. As I neared the local Coyote Ugly franchise, I saw a young man, hands cuffed behind his lower-back, being talked at by a trio of cops.

When I'd come across a similar scene in the past, I'd think, "I wonder what that guy did." Now I was wondering when his arraignment would be, what kind of lawyer he'd get, and about the strain it would put on his family. His journey through the criminal justice system was just beginning, while mine was nearing its end. Everyone around could see he was accused of a crime, but could anyone guess that I was days away from a possible felony conviction and prison sentence?

Bud got to try this case out of his San Antonio home, yes, but he still had to justify the luxury. That meant tying the charges to the Western District of Texas, which meant poring over sales records and trip reports to find a local Short Kit sale. They found one in Austin, just an hour-and-a half up I-35. A clinic called Austin Heart purchased three Short Kits and a console from VSI back in 2010, sales that were now each charged as a separate misdemeanor count. Despite all the focus on Connecticut and Maine and Utah, all eight of the substantive charges in this case (four against the company and the same four against me) would come down to what happened between our sales rep and a doctor in Austin. If even one of those eight charges stuck, I'd be out of my company, out of a career, and in prison.

Our rep in Austin was Chris Harrelson, an amiable guy who once worked in a cardiac cath lab with Dr. Matthew Selmon, the cardiologist who went on to head the vein practice at Austin Heart. When Harrelson started working at Vascular Solutions, he paid Dr. Selmon a visit and found out that Austin Heart was building a new vein center and shopping for equipment to stock it. Decent lead.

The prosecutors claimed Harrelson won that business by illegally promoting Vari-Lase for perforators to Dr. Selmon. But Dr. Selmon wasn't on their witness list. And there was a good reason for that – the same reason they had to scramble and bring in Dr. Asbjornsen from Maine at the last minute.

You see, the government interviewed Dr. Selmon, and based on the interview notes they turned over to us, it didn't go well. Dr. Selmon reportedly said that 1) he was the one who brought up perforators; 2) Harrelson's salesmanship had nothing to do with Austin Heart buying a VSI laser console;

and 3) in his experience, treating perforators with laser was safe and effective. With Dr. Selmon now "unavailable" owing to his unhelpful memory and experience, Harrelson was the government's only shot at getting convictions on those eight misdemeanor charges.

From our perspective, Harrelson, a former paramedic and X-ray tech, was a chance to showcase our knowledgeable, clinically-focused sales force. Unfortunately, things started a little rough on that front. First, Harrelson didn't know how much money he made.

> **PLAYTON: So it's somewhere between $100,000 to $200,000? But you don't have any idea where it falls in between there?**

> **HARRELSON: I do not know the exact number of what I made.**

> **JUDGE LAMBERTH: That wasn't what she asked you. Listen to her question and answer that again.**

> **PLAYTON: How do you budget if you don't know how much money you make?**

> **HARRELSON: My wife pays the bills online.**

> **PLAYTON: Okay. So you think that you make about $150,000, approximately?**

> **HARRELSON: Approximately.**

> **PLAYTON: Okay.**

> **JUDGE LAMBERTH: Is that so difficult?**

> **HARRELSON: No.**

Once she got through that roadblock, Playton played her hand according to the book. The same playbook the prosecutors used whenever one of our sales reps was on the stand: *Ask the basic stuff first, save the bombshells for re-direct.*

They ran that play because it worked. We wouldn't get the chance to respond to whatever topics the government saved for re-direct. Technically re-direct should be limited to the scope of cross, with sandbagging prohibited, but like many other rules of evidence, Judge Lamberth saw this one as more of a suggestion.

We suspected there was one specific bombshell waiting for Harrelson on re-direct. On direct, Playton kept coming back to a binder Harrelson gave Dr. Selmon. It was the standard glossy fare we gave to doctors thinking about starting a vein practice. Nothing exciting – it described the procedure, gave general background on billing, and had sample advertisements clinics might use. But that binder, the one Harrelson dropped off with Dr. Selmon, was on the prosecution table for a reason.

Inside its front pocket was a series of loose-leaf brochures for various VSI products. On the bottom of the back of one of those brochures for the Vari-Lase procedure kit was a paragraph of fine print. It said:

> *The Vari-Lase Procedure Kit is indicated for the treatment of varicose veins and varicosities in the lower extremity that are associated with superficial venous incompetency and reflux in the Great Saphenous Vein, Short Saphenous Vein* **and perforator and tributary veins.**

At the very bottom it said, in bold, "For international use only." Somehow, the international brochure, correctly stating that we were approved to treat perforators by name in Europe, had made its way into a U.S. doctor's binder. Who messed up? Harrelson? One of the interns I hired to send literature out to the reps? It didn't matter, because in the eyes of the law, every employee acts for the company, and I was responsible for all of it. It might as well have come from my desk, stapled to a picture of me holding it up and smiling. There's almost no chance anyone meant to give Dr. Selmon the international brochure, but that also didn't matter. Misbranding is a strict liability crime, meaning that intent isn't a prerequisite for guilt. And there's almost no chance anyone from Austin Heart actually read this brochure, much less the fine print, much less relied on it, but that didn't matter, either.

We knew that the brochure was in the binder on the prosecution table, but we didn't know for sure whether *they* knew. Until Playton gave it away on direct.

PLAYTON: And were those materials that are in the front pocket, were they contained inside that binder when you gave it to them?

She moved on without mentioning the brochure, but the exchange made it almost certain that she'd swoop back for the kill on re-direct. She was, in essence, betting on us not having seen the brochure. It left us no choice but to raise the issue ourselves. And since Richter was handling the witness, the discussion would be of the casual, long-windup variety.

> **RICHTER: And so, obviously, we are not in Europe, right?**
>
> **HARRELSON: No, sir.**
>
> **[7 questions later]**
>
> **RICHTER: Did you discuss the fact that you were giving him an international brochure [with Dr. Selmon]?**
>
> **HARRELSON: I did not. I wouldn't have given him an international brochure. It may have been sent to my home by mistake, because, like I said, I grabbed from my bin of brochures, saw the front cover, [and it] looked like the same as the U.S. ones we have.**

The self-inflicted wound minimized the blood-letting. Playton could still have some fun waving around the brochure on re-direct, but Richter bringing it up on cross meant Harrelson's jaw wouldn't catch a right hook.

Playton came out hot on re-direct, riffing on one of the prosecutors' favorite subjects – capitalism. On cross, Richter had asked Harrelson to talk about how our medical devices are used to save patients' lives. Re-direct would be Playton's chance to show it was really *all about the money*. As she launched into re-direct, her feathery beauty pageant mannerisms turned as sharp as her tone.

> **PLAYTON: VSI doesn't make a penny no matter how many patients it helps unless it sells medical devices, correct?**
>
> **HARRELSON: That's correct.**
>
> **PLAYTON: VSI is not a charity?**
>
> **HARRELSON: No.**
>
> **PLAYTON: It's a for-profit corporation?**
>
> **HARRELSON: That's correct.**
>
> **PLAYTON: VSI, the defendant, doesn't pay you $191,000 a year to help your [doctor] friends out, does it?**
>
> **HARRELSON: No.**

To hear Playton tell it, the corruption of the medical practice went deeper than just the sales reps. It went to the heart of the industry, to those complicit in the institutionalized graft, the doctors.

> **PLAYTON: But if your folks went out and were saying to the doc, "There is this thing you can do, and it will put a nice car in your garage. Just buy this console and not only start treating veins – you may be treating veins now – but add perforators."**

Christina Playton viewed herself as the one who was speaking the truth, staying up late at night to write examinations exposing the crooked doctors and their servile cadre of sales reps. The thing is, though, Playton was doing so from the house she shared with her husband, Michael Albrecht, M.D., a surgeon who specializes in hernia repair. Unfortunately, it's impossible to tell from Google Maps how nice the cars are in their spacious 4-car garage attached to their lovely San Antonio compound.

$$-\!\!\!\bigwedge\!\!\!\!\bigvee\!\!\!\!-$$

Survival was the order of the day when the government called a sales rep like Harrelson. Survive in order to score points where it really mattered – the doctors, regulatory experts, and our witnesses. This week we were in full defensive mode, trying to survive an onslaught of salesmen. In addition to Bob Lehoullier, they'd already put up two other VSI sales guys from New York, neither of whom were great for us.

Name: John DeVito
Position: Sales rep
Worst Trip Report: "[The doctor wants] to see perforators done. Have scheduled [training] and will push hard after that."
Worst Grand Jury Testimony: "It could be seen as devious," in reference to an email asking a fellow rep to "text me what they call them then" after being told that doctors in Massachusetts couldn't bill insurers for perforator treatment.
Weirdest Moment: This epic Bud Paulissen re-direct, concerning the "devious" reimbursement email above:

> **BUD: What's the date on this email between you and Glen Holden?**

DEVITO: October 18, 2011. He states "you can't bill for perforators, not approved."

BUD: So this is six months after you received the lengthy email [saying Medicare "probably" won't pay for perforator treatment], correct?

DEVITO: No.

[Bud continues talking]

DEVITO: No. It's four years.

BUD: In 2011, okay. *Four years* later Glen Holden gives you a two-line response, *doesn't he?*

DEVITO: Correct.

BUD: No further questions.

Name: Dick Steitzer
Position: Eastern regional manager
Worst Trip Report: "I know his years and years of calling on this doctor will pay off when he finally does perf cases with them."
Worst Grand Jury Testimony: "I would say that everybody in my region sold or tried to sell the Short Kit or inquired about it somehow with perforators."
Weirdest Moment: Lamberth's interruption with erroneous lesson on First Amendment law.

PAUZÉ: Okay. And you understood that it was entirely appropriate to give information to doctors who were looking for information with respect to perforators, correct?

STEITZER: Correct.

JUDGE LAMBERTH: If they ask?

STEITZER: Yes.

JUDGE LAMBERTH: If you volunteered, it's different, right?

STEITZER: If I volunteered – if I volunteered –

JUDGE LAMBERTH: If you start talking about it yourself, then you're promoting it, right?

STEITZER: Right.

JUDGE LAMBERTH: That's the distinction?[23]

STEITZER: Right.

These sales reps were killing us. As long as a sales rep was on the stand, the prosecutors could forget (and make the jury forget) about their case's glaring defect – that our FDA clearance covered perforators. All that these sales reps knew was that we told them not to promote for perforators. So that's all the prosecutors could squeeze out of them, before showing them that some did it anyway. Sure, each rep would admit on cross that they didn't know the law and hadn't carefully read the indications, but that was defensive. The show the prosecutors put on with our sales reps was calculated to leave you feeling that talking about perforators was illegal, full stop.

When the sales reps were on the stand, Finley could present the case he thought he had when he showed up to that first meeting in Minneapolis in 2013. It's the case he and Bud still were acting like they had, even to the point of ignoring the case they actually needed to make, one based on false or misleading information. I shuttered to think where we'd be if they'd put these sales reps up as their first five witnesses. How many jurors would we have lost before we even got a chance to score our first point?

The sales rep testimony forced me to realize the risk of the position I'd held since 1997. We have over 100 employees in the field selling our medical devices. If even one of them says one word about a product that's outside its indications – even if I told them not to say that word and even though the doctor can legally use it for that word – I could literally end up in prison. Prison. And worst of all is that computers and iPhones guaranteed that the sales reps' emails and trip reports would live forever. Even a bumbling prosecutor like Biro could arrange a few emails to make it look like an epidemic. I'm only 55, and I always pictured myself running VSI until I was well past 65. But seriously, does unprotected risk of incarceration sound like a job perk you'd want?

$$\dashv\!\!\wedge\!\!\wedge$$

---

[23]That's not the distinction.

I could feel momentum leaking the government's way. But to keep it heading into Presidents' Day weekend, they'd need to get something good out of Shane Carlson, the last Friday witness to take the stand.

Shane was a dangerously agreeable regional manager who'd supervised both McIff (after Theno) and Harrelson (during the courting of Austin Heart). Shane followed closely behind the bailiff as he made his way into court, baby-faced and looking uncomfortable in a slightly-tight suit. The jury didn't know it yet, but this was the poster boy for government witness tainting.

Shane was one of the first, and most mistreated, government witnesses. His first interview was punctuated by Lauren Hash Bell's angry outburst, caused by Shane denying that we told our sales reps to promote for perforators. He was thereafter warned he needed to come back for a second interview to "fix" his statements, or risk being indicted for perjury. To cap it off, "fire Shane Carlson" was subsequently listed as a term in every settlement proposal we received.

Sanely, Hopeman got his client immunity before that second "fixer" interview. But when Shane arrived, it didn't seem like much of an interview at all. More of a performance that began with a riddle. Shane's earlier statements seemed "incomplete and incorrect," Bud said, before Finley chimed in to say he didn't think Shane had "deliberately" lied. The next 46 minutes were an education for Shane. Bud and Finley explained their case, document by document. "The cat was out of the bag," Finley said. Shane "would be practically alone" if he chose to deny that VSI was breaking the law, Bud added. To back up that claim, they read Shane the secret grand jury testimony of Carrie Powers and Dick Steitzer, a clear violation of the law.

By the end of the interview, Shane Carlson rolled, as most anyone would've. He agreed to sign an admission under oath that claimed, among other things, that Vari-Lase products "were not approved for the treatment of perforator veins" and that "Medicare generally did not pay for procedures involving unapproved devices." I could tell the statement was written by the prosecutors, because Carlson didn't have any regulatory or reimbursement knowledge himself.

On Friday, as the mellow wakeboarding enthusiast Carlson settled into the stand beside the judge, Bud re-took the podium for his second straight witness. The senior prosecutor had been benched for days after a disastrous start, but this Friday was his. Seemingly, it was the resurrection of Bud, and this time, he was examining a witness he'd personally threatened. Up until now, the prosecutors' strategy had been to assign one of the clean hands (Playton or Biro) to examine the witnesses Bud and Tim beat up before trial. But now there was a sense of urgency. They needed Carlson to hold the line on his written statement in a way that Reuning hadn't, and evidently Bud wasn't going to outsource the job this time.

And this time, Bud didn't look at all interested in the soft touch tact he and Finley had employed thus far at trial.

BUD: Okay. Now, you've met with counsel for your employer and for Mr. Root prior to your testimony here today, haven't you?

SHANE: I have.

BUD: Let me guess. Two times?

SHANE: Yes, sir.

BUD: For about two hours each?

SHANE: Approximately, yes.

Guessing answers – that was a new one. But Bud was wrong. Carlson's meetings with our lawyers were actually longer, about four hours each. Carlson was just agreeing with Bud to be agreeable, judging by the deer-in-headlights look on his face. Later, Bud circled back to ask Carlson to see if he could recall whether the meetings were in fact longer, and Shane said they were. Cue Bully Bud berating Shane for agreeing with Mind-Reader Bud.

BUD: Okay. Why did you think that you ought to tell us it was a couple of two-hour sessions instead of a couple of half days?

SHANE: Just … I was listening to you –

BUD: Okay. I didn't mean to – I didn't mean to force you to say that.

No, of course Bud wouldn't *force* him to say anything. But now, Bud wanted to know more about those privileged meetings with VSI's lawyers, and he was willing to pry to find out.

BUD: Did you discuss some of the things that your testimony would cover?

SHANE: Yes, sir.

BUD: Okay. Did they discuss with you the fact that you're not a regulatory expert?

SHANE: Yes.

BUD: Okay. Did they discuss with you what the indication was for the Short Kit?

It looked like Bud was just getting started, but Richter had already had enough. He burst from his chair with a befuddled look.

RICHTER: Your Honor, may we approach?

JUDGE LAMBERTH: [Grunts, summons lawyers to the bench]

RICHTER: The way these questions are being asked, they potentially call for privileged information, right? He's more than capable of asking questions about what the actual facts are.

BUD: Judge, I'm just trying to bring to light these cryptic cross-examinations that all the current employees have gone through. Two meetings for two hours. Not a regulatory expert. The perforator vein happens to be a surface vein.

JUDGE LAMBERTH: The objection's overruled.

BUD: Thank you, Your Honor.

Bud won, but he strangely moved on anyway, to a topic he *knew* our defense lawyers had talked plenty about in those pre-trial meetings: Shane's first meeting with the prosecutors, way back in August 2012.

> **BUD: So I set the scene. A lot of lawyers in the room when you were at the U.S. Attorney's office in Minneapolis [for your first interview], correct?**
>
> **SHANE: Yes, sir.**
>
> **BUD: Everybody's wearing a suit or court attire, in the case of [prosecutor] Lauren [Hash] Bell, something appropriate for court ... But you're wearing a polo shirt. Do you remember that?**
>
> **SHANE: Yes, sir.**

What!?

> **BUD: Okay. I'm not criticizing that. I'm just trying to refresh your recollection.**
>
> **SHANE: Right.**

No, I'm not criticizing you, it's just that you were wearing something inappropriate that you bought from an outlet. And somehow it only got more distasteful.

> **BUD: So in 2012, when you were approached to be interviewed by the Feds in Minneapolis, you were anxious because you knew you'd been promoting with the intent that these consoles and kits be used for perforator treatment, correct?**
>
> **SHANE: Anxious? Yes, I was very anxious.**
>
> **BUD: Okay. No kidding, what degree of anxiety did you have? What was it? How did you feel about that?**
>
> **SHANE: Very high.**
>
> **BUD: Very high anxiety?**

Bud was strangely excited by this, in that cartoony, mustachioed-British-aristocrat way. *Anxious? Really??? Do tell!* All because Shane's nerves helped Bud paint the picture he wanted, one of a guy who was scared because he violated the law and then lied about it to the Feds. But Shane wasn't exactly buying the narrative.

BUD: Here you are in a room with three federal lawyers, a federal agent, [and] two more lawyers on [videoconference]. High anxiety. You misled them about what you had done, didn't you?

SHANE: Not intentionally.

BUD: Well, let's break that down. You were highly anxious about being busted for what you'd done, for selling these things for an unapproved use, correct?

SHANE: It was more [what] my reps that had done – or that had the information.

BUD: Okay. So you were anxious because you felt like the people who reported to you had promoted this for inappropriate use, correct?

SHANE: That was the appearance, yes.

That was the *appearance*. Exactly. The *appearance* was that the government must know what they're talking about. If they say perforators are off-label, they must really be. If they say your reps promoted it off-label, they must really have. And if they threaten to get you fired or charged with perjury, they really might.

BUD: That led you to be anxious, because you knew you had misled the investigators by saying, "I told Danny McIff at least five times, stop doing it. Stop marketing for perforators."

Shane had admitted in his second interview that this statement was untrue. Maybe he did lie to them during that first interview. Or maybe they led him into an untruth. I don't know. But everyone in the courtroom had just seen that the latter was possible, when Bud led Shane into saying the defense interviews lasted only two hours each. Either way, the prosecutors were overplaying their hand, because I'd bet my boat against a bagel that even if he did lie, squeezing out a few more bucks for his region's scant Short Kit sales wasn't the reason.

By getting Shane to agree that he had misled the prosecutors, they had banked another way to prove their catch-all concealment conspiracy, the amorphous felony that was quickly becoming the government's targeted charge. They claimed in the indictment that Shane lied in order to hide an ongoing conspiracy from them. In fact, Shane's "lie" was one of the "overt acts" in their charged conspiracy. After threats that he'd be charged with perjury, and threats that he'd be fired – finally, the prosecutors got what they wanted: a sheet of paper with Shane's signature at the bottom. And Bud wasn't about to let Shane back away from it now.

Over Lundquist's objection, Bud read it line by line. When he reached something controversial, he tried to guard against future slippage. Or, as I called it, Richter-proofing.

> **BUD: Now, have you had a revelation about perforator treatment since [you signed this statement in] October of 2014?**
>
> **SHANE: "A revelation"?**
>
> **BUD: The revelation being, do you think the indication still does not cover perforator treatment, or do you think it does?**
>
> **SHANE: Oh, I don't think the indication's changed.**

Friday afternoon ended with a lot more of that. Bud didn't finish his crawl through Carlson's statement, but he'd made his point. Our employee said, under penalty of perjury, that the company broke the law. That was all that mattered, really, because that's what the jury would remember heading into the long weekend. They'd have three days to play back the government's surge, and the prosecutors would have three days to bask in the resurrection of Bud.

Hard work and incompetent prosecutors helped us dominate the first week-and-a-half, but a few bad days to end the second left a nervous taste in my mouth. Even if they couldn't get their unanimous conviction, I was worried they could at least get one or two jurors to hold out for a hung jury. The result would be less climactic, but equally disastrous – we'd have to begin trial prep all over again. I thought back to that guy handcuffed outside Coyote Ugly. Maybe he was ahead of me in this march through the criminal justice system after all.

CHAPTER 28

OPERATION BIG SECRET

Second Weekend of Trial

Saturday morning on frozen Lake Minnetonka. For the first time in weeks, I woke up in my own bed, eager for a return to normalcy. It was Presidents' Day weekend, and trial wouldn't pick up again until Tuesday. In the meantime, I had Saturday penciled in for couch lounging, Sunday for catching up on paperwork, and Monday for masquerading around the office as though I were still running a business. Vascular Solutions, unlike the federal government, would be working on Washington's birthday.

By Saturday afternoon, my plan was blown. As had happened many times over the last five years, an email pulled me back into the trenches. This one was from Mike Pauzé: Ghostwriter at Law. After his pitch-perfect opening on behalf of the company, I asked Pauzé to draft Lundquist's opening. Because we elected to defer *my* opening statement until after the government called its last witness, Lundquist's speech would be a mid-trial undefended chance to score points with the jurors, who wouldn't hear a response from Bud & Co. until weeks later at closing. It was, in hockey parlance, an "empty net." Lundquist graciously relinquished the pen to Pauzé, and now his first cut was burning a hole in my inbox.

I turned off *SportsCenter* to give the opening a careful read. It was top-shelf. Sure, it could use six or eight coats of polish, but it was all there: the structure, the emotion, and of course the venomous digs at Bud's snaky tactics. I wondered, though, could Lundquist bring it to life? As written, I couldn't picture anyone but New York Pauzé delivering it. But this speech, my opening, had to come from my personal lawyer, "Minnesota nice" John Lundquist.

I had sensed that Lundquist was hesitant to go to the mat for me, and his pre-trial comment that he wanted to "work some humility" into my defense still stuck in my craw. In the crossfire of trial, I needed forceful advocates – not wafflers who were going to apologize to the jury on my behalf. For what? I was the guy in the courtroom who created 500 jobs, not the guys who were trying to destroy them. Sure, I have strict rules. And yes, I speak up when someone's not doing the right thing. There's a reason for that. We make medical devices that can save a patient's life or end it, and I'm not about to let employees' sensitivities endanger a patient. So no, I wasn't going to let Lundquist apologize for the way I ran my company or let him inject any "low energy" humility into Mike's high-octane script. In my mind, that was settled. Even if Lundquist didn't know it yet.

Later, over dinner, Beth and I had to work out a vital component of my remaining trial strategy: whether or not to bring in "The Big Gun." Hirschhorn wanted our side of the courtroom gallery packed during the trial's key moments so the jury could put real people behind the faceless facts. We pulled it off at the opening and planned to go just as big for closing, but when I took the stand to testify, it would only be Beth and some back-bench lawyers sprinkled throughout the gallery. That's where The Big Gun would come in.

It's standard for the defendant to have their well-dressed children in the front row, but Beth and I don't have kids. We do, however, have a catalog-cute 11-year-old niece named Grace who could easily pass as our daughter. And, as it happened, her spring break aligned squarely with the timing of her uncle's testimony in criminal court. It was almost too perfect.

I rightly dislike the strategy of using human props to "astroturf" a connection with the jury – especially when that prop would be a deeply bored child. But by now the prosecutors had made this trial dirty enough to justify it. So as long as it didn't take Gracie away from school, I wasn't opposed to subjecting my precocious young niece to a real world civics lesson. Why wasn't Lundquist coming up with this stuff, anyway? It was gold! Gracie's parents were on-board, too, but we decided to wait and see what happened in trial week three before mobilizing The Big Gun.

I told our lawyers many times: "If we win at trial and I come back to an empty building with Vascular Solutions' name on it, then we've lost." With that in mind, I pulled into work on Monday, ready to see and be seen by as many employees as possible. It was my only day in the office all month, and if I could come off as my usual confident, sarcastic self, it would go a long way toward soothing fears of the company's impending demise. But if I came off as worried or depressed or disengaged, word would spread quickly through the ranks, and business would grind to a halt. Instead of designing new medical devices, our engineers would be dusting off resumes and calling back headhunters.

This probably isn't something you'd expect to hear from the CEO of a publicly-traded company, but the timing of my criminal trial couldn't have been better. Our budget was squared away in December, our year-end financials were done in January, and most important, our GuideLiner product was continuing to push our sales over 100% of forecast. That would comfort Wall Street and institutional investors who had fallen in love with Vascular Solutions for under-promising and over-delivering. Missing our sales numbers now would be like stuffing a dead canary in the analysts' mail cubbies, inviting a stock tumble and speculation as to what exactly was happening in San Antonio. We needed to keep the trains on the tracks, and today was my chance to give the conductors a pep-talk.

My Monday schedule began with the quarter-to-nine ops meeting, a weekly rundown from a dozen department heads. During trial, I pushed this meeting back to 4 p.m. in order to participate by videoconference after court. But the picture always froze, making their boss look like Max Headroom on the massive conference room TV. Not exactly confidence inspiring. Today, though, I was live (and hopefully glitch-free).

"Everything in San Antonio is going as planned," I started. "Bud and Finley are even worse than I thought, and their witnesses are proving our case. As feared, the lawyers are taking longer than expected, so I think this trial won't be over until mid-March." I looked around. No surprised or skeptical faces. Good. I wrapped up my update with a smile and asked if anyone had questions. I knew every single one of them did, but their hands stayed down as silence took over. "Okay, well that's all I have. Carrie, what do you have in marketing?"

And with that, normalcy ostensibly prevailed. One by one, my team leaders shared their progress on projects I'd once poured my heart into, but which now seemed trivial at best. *New products for 2017 launch!* What did that matter when the company might be shuttered in a few weeks? *Improved training program for new sales reps!* I'd only be doing them a disservice, as my actual, bitter advice would be to get out of the industry altogether to avoid ending up where Glen Holden and I were. As we went around the room, I tried my best to project interest and attention, but I wondered if they could tell my mind was elsewhere.

The rest of the day moved like a slow-mo replay of the ops meeting. My schedule was jammed with one-on-ones with my direct reports, in which few details were spared and even fewer remembered (at least by me). The lowlight was a 200-slide, statistics-heavy quality systems review. In a brisk 45 minutes, our head of quality, Charmaine Sutton, gave an informative, to the point, and substantive presentation. It was, in essence, the perfect Vascular Solutions slide deck – but even I couldn't appreciate it today in my preoccupied state. When it mercifully ended, I went on a walk-through of our office and manufacturing buildings to show my face, then left an hour early because I had nothing left to do. For the first day in 19 years, I felt like an outsider at my own company. It was time to get back to San Antonio.

$$\dashv\!\!\sqrt{}\!\!\vdash$$

My flight that night arrived at 8:30, along with an unwanted text from Lundquist. "Howard, if you are not too tired, give me a call after you get settled in and we can chat a bit."

I hated these kinds of messages from lawyers. Something was happening. Something big. Something big enough that I needed to be told in person. I immediately regretted going home. The lawyers had stayed at Camp Springhill, continued putting in 16-hour days on the case, and now I was out of the loop. Who knows what rabbit hole they were scurrying down now.

I dropped my bags and headed straight for the War Room. There, Pauzé was squinting at a computer monitor in his weekend running outfit, while a young associate wrestled leftover Tex-Mex from a fridge precariously close to his head. Pauzé perked up as he saw me approach, and just then, Lundquist appeared at the doorway. They had me boxed in. Pauzé flashed a hotel keycard. "Let's go to one of the interview suites." I looked around at the War Room, teeming with computers and sleep-starved lawyers. It smelled like a locker room that regularly served Greek food.

Good idea.

$$-\!\!\sqrt{\Lambda}\!\!-$$

Room 116. We huddled in the parlor of a "luxurious" Camp Springhill mini-suite. We were using 116 as a witness interview room that doubled as a storage room, or maybe it was the other way around. Either way, the small table and large chairs made for a tight fit. Rob Hur leaned against the door as Pauzé, sitting next to Lundquist and across from Richter, looked me in the eyes.

"I want you to consider a new strategy," Pauzé began gingerly. "Judge Lamberth has gone beyond putting his thumb on the scales of justice. It's his whole fist now." *More like his whole fat ass,* I thought. Lamberth was letting the prosecutors ask whatever they wanted, show the jury whatever they wanted, and generally take a weedwacker to the rules of evidence. That would be fine, maybe, if there was turnabout. But when we tried to show the Basu memo, Lamberth blocked it on the grounds that it was an "internal" document, a made-up rule that never applied to our "internal" field trip reports. And when the Judge decided the prosecutors weren't doing a good enough job with a witness, he'd begun tagging in, waking up the jury, and grumbling some half-question that implied our guilt.

But, I thought, even with Lamberth's shadowboxing, we were still winning. So why were we even talking about this? "We're worried that Lamberth is going to exclude a lot of our witnesses," Pauzé explained. "Like Phil Phillips [our FDA expert]. We need him to testify about our filings and the mistakes FDA made, but Judge Lamberth might limit him to talking about the FDA approval process in general." That would be bad, but we already had Ogden's pivotal admission that perforators were covered by our indications, so we didn't really need our own FDA expert.

Pauzé wasn't done. "[Drs.] Vogelzang and Resnick, too. He's gonna cut them down to size." As he spoke, I followed Pauzé's eyes to Lundquist, Hur, and Richter. They all had that same look – one of patient bystanders who already knew the full story. I knew there was more.

"And then there's Dr. Lee," Pauzé said. I wasn't worried about Dr. Robert E. Lee, and still couldn't believe he actually went with the middle initial, but something about the John Goodman clone in a suit and sneakers spooked my lawyers. Even so, it didn't make sense. Just yesterday, Finley had sent us an email saying the government "does not intend to call Dr. Lee in [its] case-in-chief." So what was Pauzé worried about?

"They're holding him for their rebuttal case. And probably a couple of other witnesses as well," he added.

"Okay, fine," I responded. "But if we've seen what their starters have done, how much is their second string really gonna hurt us?" Pauzé disregarded my response as flip.

"They're going to wait until we rest," he said, "and then spring a whole new theory about how our design change triggered the need to file a new application with FDA. They'll bring in Dr. Lee to scare up the jury with how dangerous treating perforators is."

I had not considered this. "It's a classic sandbag strategy, and Lamberth will probably allow it," Pauzé said. Correctly sensing that I was still missing something, he dropped the criminal procedure hammer. "We won't be allowed to call any witnesses to counter it."

I could only shake my head. No respectable judge in America would let prosecutors get away with this, but a dug-in Lamberth probably would. Allowing a witness to slide down the government's witness list day after day, then fake illness, and then reemerge on rebuttal to push a new theory would be lunacy. It would be reversible error – our lawyers were sure – but a guilty verdict tossed on appeal, after the company was gone and I'd spent two years in prison, would be the cruelest joke of all in this protracted farce.

"So what's your plan?" I asked, unsure of what all this was building to.

"We think we should rest without calling any witnesses." I froze. Pauzé continued, "That way, they can't put on a rebuttal. There's no case of ours to rebut."

Lundquist looked away, undoubtedly afraid to see my reaction. I felt the anger steam inside me as I cataloged this methodical torture by déjà vu. *Speedy trial strategy* – great plan, ruined by Bill Michael's incompetence. *Better deal on the courtroom steps* – made sense, until it never happened. And now we spend two years lining up 20 great witnesses and my lawyers don't want to call a single one?

And then it registered. When Pauzé said "any witnesses," that included me. I knew this battle was coming, but I didn't expect the Trojan horse. I'd told my lawyers since the very beginning: *I will be testifying, period.* Three days of unsupervised attorney creativity, apparently, had eroded the clarity of that command.

This is my biggest issue with lawyers. They cling to inaction because they are never blamed for what *doesn't* happen. If a lawyer calls a witness and steps into a bear trap, everyone asks (aloud) why the lawyer called them in the first place. But if a great witness never testifies and a golden opportunity is missed – nobody sees it. As hockey god Wayne Gretzky famously said, "You miss 100% of the shots you don't take." I always liked that saying, but my lawyers evidently didn't. Because here we were, worried about what might go wrong, instead of trying to make things go right.

Something was telling me to storm out of Room 116 right then and there. *But wait.* What if they'd stumbled into the right decision for the wrong reason?

I've always believed that most people make decisions based on feelings, not facts. And I was worried that our well of emotional revulsion to the prosecutors' conduct was going to run dry once Carrie Powers left the stand at the end of the government's case. None of the witnesses we planned to call had even been interviewed by the prosecutors, meaning we'd have no more legal waterboarding stories to tell. With each extra day in court, the visceral response to hearing what Bud & Co. did to "poor piece of roadkill" Danny McIff would fade, along with the jury's attention to the tedious technical testimony we planned to offer.

That was important, but a different reason appealed to me even more, one that made the whole thing maybe worth it: the chaos of surprise. The prosecutors would never expect this strategy, and the trial calendar was lining up to make it impossible for them to react. Judge Lamberth had already canceled the upcoming Thursday and Friday to attend the funeral of his 101-year-old mother-in-law, and the short week meant the government's case likely would pour into Monday of the next week.

So while the prosecutors spent their four-day weekend piecing together outlines and prep binders for witnesses they'd expect us to call next week, our army of lawyers would be locked in on closing – mining the trial transcript for key quotes, cranking out polished visuals, and crafting a show-stopping argument. Pauzé assured me that in light of the mounting off-days, the judge wouldn't give the government extra time to prep after we unveiled our olé defense. Closing arguments would be scheduled for the next day, and if that's how it shook out, we'd get a tired and underprepared Bud against a fresh and practiced Pauzé. Plus Lundquist. I liked those odds … a lot.

"I want to sleep on it," I told the quartet of lawyers. "Let's talk tomorrow after court."

"Don't talk about this idea with anyone else on the team," Richter cautioned as I left. "Once people think we're headed down this path, they won't prepare like we need them to. So until you make the final call, we need to act like we're calling every single one of those defense witnesses." Great advice. What happened in Room 116 stayed in Room 116 – at least for another day.

$$\sim\!\!\bigwedge\!\!\sim$$

The finale of Shane Carlson's testimony would be the test. As Bud continued slogging through the regional manager's written admission on Tuesday, I watched the jurors to see if they were ready to vote. Alternate #1 Lisa kept up her trial-long head-shaking marathon at Bud, but she wouldn't get a say unless one of the 12 seated jurors dropped out. Of those, Necktie Stephen was definitely in our camp, judging from the sly scowl he kept directing Bud's way. Blue-Collar Steven and self-described Harry-Reid-hater (from the jury questionnaire) Debra also seemed to be leaning NOT GUILTY. Deanna, meanwhile, was NOT CONSCIOUS, having gone from zero-to-asleep in just 32 minutes, a new record for the 19-year-old. But the other eight jurors were difficult to read, responding with the courthouse poker face: a furrowed brow.

As Bud droned on, getting Shane to re-endorse the admission he'd signed after his second-interview-to-correct-that-first-interview, Richter was anxiously waiting to premiere a juicy episode of *VH1: Behind the Admission*. The second Bud ceded the witness, Richter hopped to his cowboy-booted feet with a smile.

> **RICHTER: Right off the bat in that second interview, [Bud] threatened you with prosecution for making false statements [in your first interview], right?**
>
> **SHANE: Yes, sir.**
>
> **RICHTER: And he told you what his personal views were about the case, right?**
>
> **SHANE: Yes.**
>
> **RICHTER: And he told you what other people had told him during the course of their investigation, right?**
>
> **SHANE: That is correct.**
>
> **RICHTER: And he told you that he wasn't trying to tell you what to say but, quote the *cat is out of the bag*, unquote. That's what he said, right?**
>
> **SHANE: Yes, sir.**
>
> **RICHTER: Right after he had threatened you for making false statements?**
>
> **SHANE: Yes, sir.**

Richter knew the answers, but he feigned incredulity to maximize the jury impact. Three weeks in and Richter – 20 years ago a hot-shot prosecutor and 10 years later a rusty bureaucrat – had recaptured his trial swagger. He was the one up there testifying; Shane was just an audiovisual aid.

> **RICHTER: And [Bud] told you there was another employee that they were going after for making false statements, right, to make clear that you understood their intentions?**

> **SHANE: That they meant business and were serious, yes.**

> **RICHTER: And you understood that that meant that if you didn't tell them what they wanted to hear they would come after you, right?**

> **SHANE: That is correct.**

Those were just words. What Richter really needed was an image. Something the jurors couldn't forget.

> **RICHTER: During your direct testimony, [Bud] used a really soft voice, didn't he?**

> **SHANE: He did.**

> **RICHTER: He didn't use a soft voice in that small conference room with you, did he?**

> **SHANE: No.**

> **RICHTER: He wasn't nice, like he has to be in front of all of us here today, was he?**

> **SHANE: No.**

> **RICHTER: He raised his voice with you?**

> **SHANE: I was definitely intimidated.**

Bud, who came off like a seersuckered pastor in court, was exposed. Something about his overdone genteelness almost made it easier to imagine the opposite, the real man. It underscored our most primitive theme – one we'd developed with every witness they threatened – *this is all a charade; look behind the curtain.*

Behind that curtain was Shane Carlson, a meek microbiology major who never imagined he'd find himself in trouble with the law, much less staring down a federal prosecutor's indictment barrel. Richter's voice turned softer – to near-Bud levels – as he invited out the ugly truth.

RICHTER: The way they came at you, you found threatening, right?

SHANE: Yes.

RICHTER: You have a family, right?

SHANE: I do.

RICHTER: Tell us about your family.

For Shane, that was all it took. He withdrew, lost in his own thoughts, and returned in tears and sniffles. The court reporter took his hands off the stenograph. The judge, jury, and gallery sat, beholding this everyman, broken by heavy-fisted prosecutors.

SHANE: I am sorry.

RICHTER: It's okay.

SHANE: I have a wife and two little girls.

RICHTER: And when the government was threatening you, it was them you were thinking about, right?

SHANE: Yes.

RICHTER: That's the leverage they had on you, Mr. Carlson, right?

SHANE: Yes, sir.

Seeing the enthralled 12 in the jury box was all I needed to make the final call on Operation Big Secret. Sure, we could call witnesses that would explain that our marketing clearance covered perforators, that the Short Kit was safe, and that it wouldn't make sense to risk the company over a meaningless product – but the jury had already heard as much from the government's witnesses. Putting on twenty of our own would only fade the jurors' memories of Shane Carlson and how this case really got here: through the coercion and distortion of prosecutors abusing God-like power. That feeling, I was convinced, would bring us the NOT GUILTY votes.

With three witnesses left after Shane and only one day before the extend-ed weekend, the government's case would now surely stretch into a fourth week, meaning Bud & Co. wouldn't learn of Operation Big Secret until after they'd blown their four-day break preparing to cross our ghost witnesses. And this weekend, I wasn't making the mistake of leaving San Antonio. I'd stick around to micromanage the entire process, from drafts to slides to practice sessions, plural. We were closing, people, and I was going to make sure we ran through the finish line.

Until Pauzé heard from Hirschhorn. *He doesn't like it.* Damn. I'd hired the nation's best jury consultant and then forgot to ask him about the most important jury call of trial. If Hirschhorn didn't like it, I needed to hear it directly from his mouth. We set up a call with the full legal team.

"I don't like it," Hirschhorn began, confirming Pauzé's report. "It's a sign of weakness to the jury. You promised them the world in the opening state-ment and now you're not delivering."

I got that, but Hirschhorn hadn't seen the big-drama moments we had delivered. He wasn't in the courtroom to hear Reuning and McIff and Carl-son, or how tone-deaf Bud & Co. were in their attempts to justify what they did. Plus, wouldn't the jury be grateful that we were saving two weeks of their lives and minimizing their exposure to Bud, Finley, and that asbestos-lined jury room?

"If you guys think it's the right call, then go with it," Hirschhorn de-ferred, "but it doesn't sit right with me. Howard, give me a call if you want to talk." I did. I was making a decision that could speed or prevent my incarcer-ation, destroy or save the company I'd worked so hard to build. So I needed to hear *everything* the slick-talking Hirschhorn had to say, without concern for my lawyers' feelings. I walked up to my room and called him back, this time alone.

Hirschhorn said he wanted to know where my head was at. For the first time, I was the guy *making* the argument to someone on our trial team, not listening to theirs. "The only important evidence we are giving up is my testimony, which is huge," I conceded. "But I love where we're at now, and I love even more what we'll be able to do with a surprise closing."

"What's Beth say?" Hirschhorn asked, still trying to pull me back. She was upset, I told him. In her mind, there was no way the jury would convict me if I testified – if they heard my voice, saw my concern for patient safety, and felt what this company meant to me. I assured Hirschhorn that I had considered this, what he said – all of it. I paused. Talking it out had only strengthened my resolve. "I think we have the jurors," I told him. "I think it's the right call."

"I just want you to get the right *verdict*," Hirschhorn said, and I believed him. "Call me if you want to talk." I thanked him, hung up, and marched down to the War Room. I gave Pauzé the nod, and the attorneys wiped our witness whiteboard clean. The Big Gun would stay in Minnesota; Operation Big Secret was a go.

CHAPTER 29

THE REVENGE
OF CARRIE POWERS

Trial Day 11

Everybody knew it – we'd only get through one witness on Trial Day 11. That witness was Carrie Powers, and if yesterday's 20-minute preview was any indication, it was going to be a cage match. Technically, Carrie was a cooperating government witness who'd repeatedly testified in the grand jury that VSI had engaged in illegal conduct. But she'd also declined to sign one of those written admissions the prosecutors cooked up, refused to meet with them before trial, and was irate about the way she'd been misled and mistreated. She would be, without a doubt, the prosecution's most hostile witness, which at this point was saying something.

I thought Carrie was going to be a star for us, but you never know how someone is going to hold up under the poorly-set fluorescent lights of the courtroom. If they could use her disastrous grand jury testimony as a net to drag her to the government's side, we'd be in trouble heading into closings. We might even have to reevaluate Operation Big Secret altogether.

In the previous day's 20-minute starter session, Finley immediately sought to undermine Carrie's credibility. The line of attack was that the former registered nurse was an unqualified, high-priced shill for the CEO.

FINLEY: Compared to other people, would you say that you rose quickly through the ranks of VSI to become Vice President of Marketing?

CARRIE: "Compared to other people?" I'm not certain, sir.

FINLEY: Do you have any prior marketing experience before you came to VSI?

CARRIE: No, I don't.

> **FINLEY: If people described you as the eyes and ears of Defendant Howard Root, would that be accurate?**
>
> **CARRIE: And who would be describing me like that, sir?**
>
> **FINLEY: Anybody. Just the important part of the question is, is it true? Would you say that's true?**
>
> **CARRIE: I don't know, sir.**
>
> **FINLEY: And your employer, the Defendant VSI, pays your salary?**
>
> **CARRIE: Correct, yes.**
>
> **FINLEY: What is your annual salary at VSI?**
>
> **CARRIE: In 2015 it was $665,000.**

She makes a lot of money, yes. Way more each year than the Short Kit made in seven years combined. I wondered if the jury was picking up on that type of stuff, but more likely their heads were melting at the idea of someone making nearly $2,000 a day. My job offer to Carrie 10 years ago was for $70,000 a year, and I told her that she wasn't worth any more than that because of the money I'd need to spend to train her. I was right then, but she'd advanced quickly, and today she was worth every penny of her much larger paycheck.

Carrie, you see, was special. She didn't just do what she was told. She had the vision to create a project, the discipline to think it through, and the energy to see it was finished the right way. It was one of the reasons that made her grand jury testimony so disheartening to read, but I knew that those qualities could yet make her a great witness, now that she had been prepared by a competent lawyer. Her early exchanges with Finley on the previous day, however, were over-the-top uncooperative.

> **FINLEY: You are aware that the Defendant Howard Root's personal financial success has been closely tied to the company's financial success over the years? Fair statement?**
>
> **CARRIE: I am not sure how he perceives his personal worth, sir.**
>
> **FINLEY: Okay. *Not quite the question.* The question is, "Is it true that over the years the financial success the Defendant Howard Root has realized has been linked to the financial success that the company**

has had?"

CARRIE: I believe Howard has worked for the company for 19 years, and I believe that he makes a very nice salary, but I don't know.

It was nice to know that the jury wouldn't hear about my million-plus compensation, but Carrie was picking fights we didn't need. The last thing we wanted was for her to look like she was totally in our pocket; that would play right into Finley's hand. He wanted to show that the only reason Carrie was backing away from her grand jury testimony, if she did, was because we'd gotten to her. And in the closing minutes of her first day on the stand, he went for it, mocking the testimony he expected her to give the next day.

FINLEY: At these ten hours' worth of meetings [with defense counsel over two days], did you talk about how you're not a regulatory expert?

CARRIE: I was asked if I have had any formal training in regulatory.

FINLEY: Did the subject of how you were not a reimbursement expert come up?

CARRIE: Again, I was asked if I had any formal training in reimbursement.

FINLEY: Did you talk about how the defendant, Howard Root, took compliance very seriously?

CARRIE: I can't recall if we talked about that or not.

FINLEY: Okay. Did you talk about how the Vari-Lase system and the Short Kit were approved for perforator use all along, despite what you thought at the time?

This was the warm-up for what promised to be an explosive main day of the Carrie-thon. The roles had been cast. Finley was going to punch, and Carrie (who has a heavy bag in her exercise room at home) was going to counterpunch. The next morning, as I drank my second glass of milk in the Camp Springhill lobby before heading over to the courthouse, I liked our chances. The previous day had shown the Carrie Powers I knew, not the "Ms. Powers" I'd seen run over in the grand jury.

Finley started Wednesday by leading Carrie from tab to tab in the hefty binder he plopped on the witness stand, a collection of his favorite documents.
And after each one, he asked if they showed illegal conduct, same as he did in
the grand jury. They were mainly documents that she had never sent, never
received, and which Judge Lamberth had no problem allowing into evidence.
But this time, Carrie wasn't going along for the ride.

> **FINLEY: That was inappropriate for [Kip Theno] to [email his region
> McIff's "Tips For Treating Perforators" PowerPoint]?**
>
> **CARRIE: Yes.**
>
> **FINLEY: And that's because use for perforators is not approved?**
>
> **CARRIE: I disagree with that.**

Finley was ready for this response and had Carrie's grand jury transcript in
hand, itching to use it like a leash to jerk her back.

> **FINLEY: Could you look at page 22 of your [grand jury] transcript?
> "Question: And this use for perforators is not approved, correct?"
> "Answer: Correct." Did I ask that question and did you give that an-
> swer?**
>
> **CARRIE: You did ask that question and I did give that answer.**

When he got to this point, as he frequently did that Wednesday, Finley liked
to ask one more question.

> **FINLEY: Did you tell the truth to the grand jury?**
>
> **CARRIE: For the knowledge I had at that time, yes, I believe I told
> the truth.**

On paper, you might say it was a stalemate. She'd agreed with it then, but
didn't now. But the sheer volume of documents in Finley's overstuffed binder,
which fell apart twice during her testimony, was turning the tide the government's way.

Many of the exhibits were, as I mentioned, of the ambush ilk, docs she would've had no reason to ever see. Transcripts from earnings calls, emails between two people not named Carrie Powers, the launch email for a product (the Short Kit) that she wasn't involved with at the time. But no matter what came at her, even Finley's signature syllogism of guilt, Carrie kept fighting.

> **FINLEY: So Step 1: Tell the sales force "Promote for short vein segments." Step 2: Teach the sales force that short vein segment includes perforator veins?**

> **CARRIE: I disagree. How do we do that? How are you saying that we did that? Can I see a document that states that?**

It was the CliffsNotes version of the case Finley had run through with nearly every witness in the grand jury, but this was the first time he'd used it at trial. He pointed Carrie to her grand jury answer – a "that's how it appears" response to the same question. Her backtracking on answers generally helped Finley, who could use a credibility boost with the jurors and had Carrie's prior testimony up his sleeve. But this time, Carrie added a little context.

> **CARRIE: ... I had much less information at that time, and I believe my answer was truthful. I completely disagree with my answer today.**

Carrie's tactic was starting to derail Finley, who more than once snapped with frustration as his planned waterfall of government exhibits was dammed to a trickle by her obstruction. But as Finley methodically reminded the jury of bad emails, he must also have forced them to ask themselves, *why is she being so uncooperative?*

Finley turned to a new document, one with two goals: To show that I, one, control everything at VSI and, two, am a jerk. An email from me to one of our product managers flashed onto the courtroom monitors.

> **"Liz, I'm not sure where you were going with this presentation, but it wasn't very good and it needs a lot of work ... Do not create new abbreviations for names, such as 'AD' for AngioDynamics. It is confusing and not helpful in any way. And don't just reword slides from the last presentation with the same content to make it look new. For many of these slides I needed to go back to the January presentation because what you did made them worse."**

I leaned back in my chair and tried not to groan audibly. *Wish I had that one back.* It wasn't that bad, but it definitely didn't make me look good. And it made me wonder what else Finley had.

With his last exhibit, Finley tried to send Carrie to the canvas. He pulled out an old bonus worksheet for an employee Carrie managed at the time – our traveling clinical vein expert, Tony Jakubowski. In 2010 she had approved a partial bonus for Jakubowski, giving credit to one section calling for him to "complete a minimum of 10 sales calls per quarter with documented results of increased sales or other significant benefits." Finley asked Carrie to read what Jakubowski wrote to support bonus credit for one of those sales calls:

CARRIE: "Perforator training resulting in kit sales."

FINLEY: Thank you. No further questions.

It was a rare moment of Finley-engineered drama that actually *helped* his case. I reminded myself this wasn't illegal, especially if the jury agreed we were allowed to market for perforators. And nothing about it was false or misleading. But still, *not good.*

—⋀⋏—

After more than four-and-a-half hours of direct, the longest of trial, Pauzé stepped up to cross-examine a weary-looking Carrie Powers. With only an hour left before the clock hit 3:30, Carrie would surely be coming back next week for her third day on the stand. Pauzé didn't have enough time to tear down what Finley had built, but he could at least loosen its foundation and punish Finley's rookie error of not running out the clock. As a bonus, whatever Pauzé could get off in the next hour would stay with the jurors over the last weekend of trial – a long one because of the funeral for Lamberth's mother-in-law.

PAUZÉ: As to a number of those trip reports, you testified [before the grand jury] that you thought that those were – and I'm paraphrasing here – examples of illegal conduct, did you not?

CARRIE: Correct. That's how I testified.

PAUZÉ: Okay. Now, you're certainly not a legal expert, right?

CARRIE: No.

PAUZÉ: Did Mr. Finley, before he asked you that question, let you know that providing truthful information to doctors about any uses of a device that's on the market is legal?

CARRIE: No, I was not aware of that.

But surely Bud did? Another chance to ask the same question.

PAUZÉ: Did Mr. Paulissen tell you before you testified that providing truthful information about a device that's on the market is legal?

CARRIE: I don't remember that, no.

What else did they leave out?

PAUZÉ: Perforator veins certainly can be varicose veins, right?

CARRIE: Yes.

PAUZÉ: Okay. Did the government walk you through this and ask you if perforator veins can be varicose veins?

CARRIE: I don't recall [that] we talked about the indications.

Of course not. The government desperately avoided showing witnesses the indications, either in the grand jury or at trial. We, on the other hand, trotted it out every chance we got. This wasn't some trivial document – it was the gatekeeper for the government's entire case. And it wasn't hard to find, either, it was printed on every brochure in every procedure kit we ever sold.

Carrie had transformed into a totally different witness on cross. Helpful, pleasant, and relaxed. That defiant look that received Finley's questions had vanished. And just before the day ended and the jury went away for their long weekend, they found out why.

PAUZÉ: After you testified [before the grand jury], was it communicated to you that the prosecutors indicated – and excuse my language – that your testimony was "pissing them off"?

CARRIE: Yes. That was communicated to me by my attorney.

PAUZÉ: Okay. That upset you, I imagine?

CARRIE: To say the least.

It was what windbag motivational speakers would call an *aha moment*. As the courtroom once again became transfixed by the injection of emotional controversy into the staid proceedings, something in the jurors' minds must have clicked. *There's more to this story.*

> **PAUZÉ: Before you testified here, did the prosecutors ask you to sit down and meet with them?**
>
> **CARRIE: Yes, they did.**
>
> **PAUZÉ: Did you choose to?**
>
> **CARRIE: No, I did not.**
>
> **PAUZÉ: Why not?**
>
> **CARRIE: Because the way in which I was treated between May 6th of 2014 and yesterday, when I came back here, I felt completely disrespected.**

I cheered her along in my head. As she kept going, the jurors' heads oscillated between Carrie and the disrespecting prosecutors like they were in the Wimbledon bleachers.

> **CARRIE: I felt that I did my duty by telling the truth to the grand jury … And one of them [said] I was not telling the truth and that I was being uncooperative. And that if I didn't start cooperating, they were going to recommend that I would lose my career.**

That is why she was fighting them. The jury had heard the threats before, but never before had they felt the impact of those threats. On Carrie's direct exam, it was obvious that something was up, and now the jury was seeing what that something was.

⎯⫩⎯

On Monday, after a weekend we spent prepping for closing and the government spent prepping for our never-coming witnesses,[24] the Carrie-thon entered its third and final leg.

---

[24]On Saturday we sent Bud & Co. 1,000 pages of background reading we said our experts might be covering, to satisfy discovery obligations as to our mirage expert witnesses.

Before the starting gun fired on the fourth week of trial, Finley lurched over to the defense table. This, I'd learned, was never a sign of civility. Finley asked Pauzé for an electronic copy of every document we intended to use in our defense case. Days prior, we had already produced these documents in hard copy form, exactly as the government had done. But it took a week and a half of begging before the government finally turned over the electronic copies of their exhibits, and Pauzé was more than happy to return the favor.

"We'll get it to you," Pauzé said flippantly, continuing to sketch notes as Finley hovered over his chair.

"When can we expect it? Today?" Pauzé put down his pen and looked up, although the look might also be described as sideways.

"How about exactly when you gave it to us? How about then?" The conversation abruptly interrupted by the *CLAP CLAP* of the bailiff, Finley walked off as Judge Lamberth walked in. The prosecutors immediately took their grievance to Daddy.

PLAYTON: We have requested electronic copies of the defense exhibits. We received – how many banker's boxes? Six? Five or six banker's boxes full of paper defense exhibits and it will be difficult for us to find them and use them during the course of these proceedings. Additionally, it will save time if we had an electronic copy. We provided the defense an electronic copy of all of our exhibits. The reason I was advised that we weren't going to get one is because it took us too long to get them ours, and so I am just asking for an electronic copy.

What a narc. For some reason, she still managed to be misleading even though it was unnecessary to get what she wanted. Pauzé said we'd get it to them, just not now. Which made this the second of three times I'd count Playton feeding the Court bad information.[25] And she didn't even speak that much.

Next, Playton requested that the government be excused from the very task we'd been forced to undertake throughout the government's entire case.

PLAYTON: And also, during the course of presentation, if we could just get handed to us the defense exhibits, so that we are not asking

---

[25] The first being Playton's distortion of their plans for Dr. Lee, including his reportedly-disqualifying sickness. Stay tuned for the last one.

anybody to wait for us to locate it in the six banker's boxes.

Whatever. It's not like we were putting on a case anyway. Pauzé graciously agreed under the judging eye of Lamberth, then picked up his cross-examination of Carrie.

Because of Operation Big Secret, we now needed Carrie to cover critical background on VSI. Our V.P. of corporate development, Phil Nalbone, was scheduled as a defense witness and had furiously reviewed every SEC filing and investor report, preparing to illustrate the insignificance of the Short Kit. Now that he wouldn't get a chance to testify, though, we'd have to work that into Carrie's testimony. But Carrie wouldn't know why we were asking her about this stuff, since she had no idea we'd decided not to call any of our witnesses. Hopefully she knew her stuff.

Pauzé asked Carrie to talk about when she was a nurse and her doctors used Vascular Solutions' products – how they had helped her patients. Then he moved to her work at the company, where she'd been part of a remarkable boom of innovation. VSI now sold over 100 different medical devices, she explained, with over 950 different models altogether. The Short Kit was just one of those 950 models, about 0.1% of our catalog (and sales), sold to the same doctors as those 949 others. Pauzé, in his final question in this line, zeroed in on why all this rendered the government's conspiracy theory debilitatingly near-sighted.

> **PAUZÉ: And if you lie about something that is 0.1% of your sales, you are going to jeopardize the other 99.9% of your sales; is that correct?**

> **CARRIE: If they are a physician that uses our other products, I would agree.**

After Pauzé finished, Lundquist tagged in, adding a Minnesota touch to the questioning as Carrie described what really happens day-to-day at VSI back home. She told the jury how VSI is the only company working with the U.S. Army to make freeze-dried blood plasma – a lifesaver for soldiers bleeding out on overseas battlefields, where traditional frozen plasma is unavailable. Just add water, and two minutes later you've got an injectable solution that replaces the wounded soldier's lost blood. I looked around at the faces in the jury box as Carrie described it, proud of the business I'd started and grown.

And on a more self-serving level that this trial had pulled me to, I hoped that somebody on the jury knew a soldier or two.

Carrie went on to talk about our GuideLiner catheter, the blockbuster medical device I'd invented that cardiologists loved for "making impossible cases possible." The points Carrie was making were simple but tangible. VSI makes great medical devices and employs 550 good people – don't kill us over one trivial product.

As Carrie charismatically testified, you could tell that Vascular Solutions meant something to her. She'd seen what having quality medical devices meant to a doctor performing life-saving heart procedures. For almost a decade, she'd been part of a team whose inventive and tireless work literally saved human lives, and you could feel how much she wanted that work to continue into the next decade. Next, Lundquist asked her a question I knew would draw an emotional response.

LUNDQUIST: What does that mean to you at VSI?

CARRIE: It means that through our dedicated work of bringing in product ideas, to developing them internally, to manufacturing them, to selling them, that we're committed in every way to provide good, quality products in an ethical way to the physicians in our space.

No one could have said it better. If the jurors didn't feel what was behind those words, then no one can beat the government. Carrie had connected and delivered. Her cross-examination was over. It was time to turn her over to Finley again.

$$-\sqrt{}\!\!\!\!\!\!\sqrt{}-$$

You're about to experience the worst re-direct of this trial. Somewhere along the line, and it appears this happened at the outset, a tactical decision was made by the prosecutors. *Every time they accuse us of misconduct, we're going to set the record straight. Don't just let it go, because that will look like an admission – bring it back up and try to knock it down.*

It is with this as background that I share the beginning of Finley's re-direct of Carrie Powers.

FINLEY: Good morning.

CARRIE: Good morning.

FINLEY: I wanted to go back to what you told Mr. Pauzé and Mr. Lundquist about hearing from your lawyers after your grand jury testimony that your testimony was "pissing them off," referring to the prosecutors. Do you remember that?

CARRIE: I do.

FINLEY: Did Mr. Paulissen or I say that to you *directly*?

CARRIE: No. But my understanding is you're not allowed to talk to me directly, only through my attorney.

Here, Finley has asked witness Carrie Powers a simple question. A question he's planned; a question he knows the answer to. *Did we say to you what you said we said?* Her answer – "no" – only confirms Finley's assumptions, and, it seems, he is just one question away from having the offending testimony stricken from the record as hearsay.

FINLEY: Did you witness that statement with your own eyes and hear it with your own ears?

CARRIE: I heard it with my own ears.

Boom! All of a sudden, not only will the offending testimony not be stricken, Finley has unwittingly given it a major credibility boost. The courtroom is left in disbelief, laboring to work out the apparent contradition. Judge Lamberth jumps in, begging for an understanding.

JUDGE LAMBERTH: From your attorney?

CARRIE: No, Your Honor. I was standing out in the hallway when they were talking.

There it was, the answer. Finley looks punch-drunk, coming to the sobering realization that the contradiction has turned on his own superfluous use of the word "directly." Lamberth continues to play the role of *Whodunit*.

JUDGE LAMBERTH: So you heard the prosecutor say it?

CARRIE: I did, sir.

Stunned disbelief sets in about the courtroom. The court clerk's eyelids peel back from her ordinarily-bored face. Juror Deanna remains awake. Now here's where you might think, "Maybe don't step in that beehive again." And here's where Finley couldn't help himself, seeming just as curious about as he was shocked by the beehive he found his foot in.

> FINLEY: Which one of us said it; Mr. Paulissen or me?

> CARRIE: Mr. Paulissen.

> FINLEY: You heard … Was Mr. Paulissen aware that you were listening?

> CARRIE: I'm not certain. It was out in the rotunda.

Lost in whimpers of unfairness, Finley accidentally steps in it again.

> FINLEY: So whatever you said, we shouldn't question, we shouldn't ask follow-up questions; we should simply believe?

> CARRIE: I don't have an issue, sir, with you asking a follow-up question. But being emotional about it and getting angry and pointing fingers, I do think that's disrespectful.

> FINLEY: Okay. When did somebody get angry and emotional and point fingers?

> CARRIE: I remember towards the end of my testimony, right before we broke for lunch, I was asked to go home and do some research. And at that point, Mr. Paulissen got extremely angry and was pointing fingers at me.

… and again …

> FINLEY: And raising his voice?

> CARRIE: Yes.

> FINLEY: Shouting?

> CARRIE: Raising his voice.

> FINLEY: Pretty loud?

> CARRIE: Yes.

This was a little repetitive, but it was damn entertaining. Somehow, the pressure in the room kept rising, and rising, just waiting for Finley to put one final bow on the package.

FINLEY: Uh-huh. So if somebody was disrespectful towards you and used a raised voice with you and gestured at you in a disrespectful manner, that would have been something that would have been witnessed by about 16 to 20 grand jurors?

CARRIE: Some of them are sleeping, but yes.

FINLEY: Okay. So the anger and disrespect that was shown towards you, according to you, during your grand jury session, apparently was not sufficient to keep some of the members awake?

CARRIE: I don't know, sir. I don't know if they were awake during the times you were yelling at me or not. I was there for two hours.

FINLEY: *I* was yelling at you now?

CARRIE: You were speaking very disrespectfully to me, yes –

FINLEY: Uh-huh …

CARRIE: – in a loud voice.

Searching for a way to make up for his self-inflicted wound, Finley directed Carrie to her grand jury transcript. Specifically, the 12 minutes – exactly 12 minutes, for some reason – before the lunch break. He pointed Carrie to the corresponding pages and said something to the effect of, *"See, lady, nobody harassed you during these 12 minutes."* Of course, you only needed to go back another two minutes to see where Bud scolded "It's really not a joke" and exclaimed "No, but they were used!" But this was re-direct, so the government would get the last, unanswered word on the exchange.

Eventually, Finley returned to the substantive issues in the case. Like *was there a vast conspiracy to promote the Short Kit against the law?* By now, though, he was dealing with a supremely confident witness, one who was way quicker on her feet than he was.

CARRIE: Sir, I was the V.P. of marketing. And apparently in the beginning of my testimony, someone has described me as the eyes and ears of Howard. I don't describe myself that way; however, if that's

how people feel, you would think I would know if there's some corporate plan in place.

Carrie was credible there, and credible a moment later when asked why she'd retracted so much of her grand jury testimony.

FINLEY: So when you testified in the grand jury that it was against the law to sell devices for unapproved use, was it because somebody took a tone with you that you didn't like?

CARRIE: I would say that you were making statements and then saying "correct?" And I will also say that, because you're the U.S. government, I believed everything that you were saying during that, and it's an extremely intimidating process, sir.

FINLEY: So when you testified in grand jury that it was against the law to sell devices for unapproved use, you didn't really think that?

CARRIE: I probably *did* think that because I was being told that.

It was the truth of this whole experience, and by now the jury must've been catching on. The prosecutors were able to get unknowing witnesses to say anything they wanted, because most people assume wisdom and honesty from those representing the government. Everyone involved on our side of this case, from our employees to our lawyers to our customers, now questioned that assumption. And because of this case, I'll spend the rest of my life assuming the exact opposite.

After 75 minutes – a full half-hour longer than the next longest re-direct of trial – we hit the lunch break, at which point Finley remarkably announced he still had more to cover. So after returning from the break, Carrie perched herself on the stand once more, digging in for another exchange of body blows. What she didn't know was that apparently someone behind the scenes on the government's side had already (mercifully) thrown in the towel on Finley's last crack at a VSI employee.

JUDGE LAMBERTH: All right. You may be seated, ladies and gentlemen. All right, Counsel, you may proceed.

FINLEY: Ms. Powers, Mr. Lundquist showed you a picture of a series of kits. And at the tail end of that picture was a little, tiny, 5-centimeter kit [smaller than the Short Kit]. Do you remember that?

CARRIE: I do.

FINLEY: What year did that kit come out?

CARRIE: I don't know.

FINLEY: No further questions. Thank you.

Finley had asked one feeble, meaningless question just to avoid the embarrassment of returning from break empty-handed. Carrie's brow once again furrowed, but this time in amused confusion. She'd just knocked out Tim Finley.

CHAPTER 30

SCAVDIS' LAST STAND

Trial Day 13

In the dead of winter, they hunkered down in San Antonio, a land foreign to them in both geography and local tongue. Some questioned their reasons for being there in the first place – surely there were more logical locations. But their hard-headed commander assured the rag-tag troupe of volunteers (and the enlisted hot-shots sent in to take over the operation) that being in Texas, on the front line, was critical. And over time, he mentally prepared each and every one of them to defend the principle of liberty and fight to the death, if attacked. Their very presence in San Antonio all but assured they would be.

Forces from the native land arrived before spring did. Although their capacity for destruction was as limitless as their resources, the federal troops were inexperienced, poorly trained, and in many cases conscripted into their slow march toward battle.

Their long-awaited arrival was announced with the flutter of a blood-red flag. It was an unmistakable signal – no prisoners would be taken. Last minute overtures at a reasonable negotiated resolution failed, prompting the small force of settlers to fire a cannon shot at the behemoth stalking their gates. *Come and take it.*

In the early days of the siege, the settlers held up. They scratched and clawed as the federal forces made their initial advances, collecting small victories that boosted morale in the shabby quarters they struggled to keep sanitary. But external forces conspired to swing the pendulum of battle. The settlers' resources were thinning, just as illness and increasing sleeplessness were taking their toll.

The settlers awaited the arrival of a powerful man whose reinforcement, they believed, would transform the dialectic of the skirmish. But with each passing day, it became increasingly clear that this man would not arrive. The settlers would have to make do with what they had at hand, and nothing else, if they were to have any chance at survival.

On the 13th day of the siege, General Santa Anna launched his final assault on the Alamo.

On the 13th day of trial, Tim Finley called his final witness to the stand – FDA *Special Agent* George Scavdis. He was by now known to the jury as "that intense guy with chronic stubble who sits at the prosecution table but never talks." I can't say we knew much more about him. He was the author of most of the hundred-plus interview memos the government turned over in discovery, but no one on our team had ever heard him say a word. His Internet footprint was ghoulishly small – no Facebook and an eerily-blank LinkedIn profile with zero connections.

The little we did know about Scavdis had been gleaned from the Abbott & Costello act he and Finley put on to get the grand jury indictments. Finley would walk his partner through the findings underlying the draft indictment, ask a few conclusory questions about the charges (*e.g.* "Was it your conclusion from the investigation that Defendants Root and VSI [conspired to introduce misbranded medical devices into interstate commerce]?"), get a "yes" from Scavdis, release the grand jury for lunch, and when they returned, *voila* – indictment.

From the transcripts, we gleaned that Scavdis was a lawyer turned Secret Service agent turned public corruption investigator turned FDA *Special*

Agent. What would lead somebody down that career path, I wondered. It apparently wasn't enough for George Antonios Scavdis to join his father Antonios Scavdis and brother Antonios Scavdis Jr. at their family law firm outside of Akron, Ohio, to transform Scavdis & Scavdis into Scavdis & Scavdis & Scavdis. Young George, it seemed, wanted something bigger – to protect the president, to expose crooked politicians, and now, to lock up those medical device misbranders keeping the public up at night.

Scavdis sashayed to the stand, beard freshly outlined, looking confident in the grey suit that was clearly the best in his arsenal. No bowling shoes today, and no more weird self-talk – Scavdis was on the big stage now. This was the moment he'd waited for ever since he started "working up" the case in July 2011. The moment where the clever *Special Agent* steps up as the last witness and connects the dots so clearly, so succinctly, and with such irreproachable credibility that the jury resolves then and there to convict both defendants on all counts.

As expected, Finley would ask the questions, capitalizing on the chemistry they'd built over their grand jury dry runs. Pauzé originally planned to cross-examine Scavdis, but we wanted him focused on closings. And Richter had already cross-examined Mark Valls (our former director of U.S. sales) that day – a forgettable event except for Richter finding a way to ask Valls if he knew that I was an Eagle Scout, piquing the attention of Necktie Stephen and locking in the Scout's honor connection. So with Pauzé and Richter out, Rob Hur was once again summoned on short notice to handle cross and objections.

Finley started his exam by practically begging for objections, asking Scavdis what he looks for in a corporate criminal.

FINLEY: When you're investigating possible corporate crimes, do you try to figure out if the conduct is an isolated incident versus widespread?

HUR: Objection. [Irrelevant.]

JUDGE LAMBERTH: Overruled.

SCAVDIS: Absolutely. That's one of the first things that we look for in my squad. We're a small squad and the cases that we want to invest our time and resources in are cases in which the conduct is top down

and wide ranging.

As Scavdis talked about his "squad," the words came in passionate, aggressive spurts. I had never before considered that Scavdis was the guy behind the prosecution, but his emotion on the stand revealed a man on a mission. Somebody had to do the grunt work to get this big ball of bunk rolling, and that guy was Scavdis. I'd always wondered, of all the companies and all the whistleblower suits, why the government picked my small medical device company in the suburbs of Minneapolis. As Scavdis continued, the reason was revealed.

> **SCAVDIS: We're looking for instances where the conduct is either known about by management or directed from management and pervades down through the organization to the sales rep level.**

I now realized my mistake. This was *never* about the company – it was always about me. That's why it didn't matter if the company had a spotless compliance record and never received so much as a warning letter from the FDA. Or that the Short Kit made up 0.1% of our sales and never harmed a single patient. Because they had me. The founder, the CEO, the micromanager with his fingers in everything. DOJ wanted a CEO, and Scavdis found them one. That easy feeling of being targeted only intensified when Scavdis described the cases he *wasn't* looking for.

> **SCAVDIS: What we don't want are cases where we're talking about a rogue rep or rogue region, [where] the company has strict compliance, but there's a rep or a district manager somewhere in Florida that's creating their own materials and promoting this off-label –**

I wanted to shout "McIff and Theno!" in open court. How could Scavdis say this stuff when the rogue rep and rogue manager had already taken the stand? Because he can, I guess. Rob Hur rose to his feet in annoyance and asked to approach the bench.

> **HUR: Your Honor, this witness is using that one question to launch into a multi-minute disquisition of the types of crimes he is looking for. And we think that it is not the proper kind of characterization of this particular matter. We're not here for a lecture on what he looks for in his job.**

Finley offered to rephrase. Lamberth said "alright," and then continued to let Scavdis editorialize about his approach to the case until he was blue in the face. Finley, it was clear, had prepped him to do just that. It didn't matter that the *witnesses* in the trial hadn't agreed with the prosecutors' theories – here was a *Special Agent* who did.

Next in the Finley & Scavdis variety hour was a highlight reel of purported misdeeds – an effort to prove the big charge, the conspiracy. There were so many ways the company tried to evade law enforcement, Scavdis said, and thus so many ways they could make their felony conspiracy case. There was the "sham" investigation into the whistleblower letter,[26] Shane Carlson's "lie,"[27] Glen Holden's "lies,"[28] and using the code words "short vein segment" in trip reports to evade law enforcement. The idea was to have Scavdis fill in some of these disparate theories, which they'd only sporadically floated throughout trial, and pray one stuck. Finley was trying, even if he was unable to pose a proper question.

> **FINLEY: Now, in reality nobody was fooled by [Mr. Carlson's] statements? [Objection Sustained]**
>
> **FINLEY: Did anybody who was at that interview believe Mr. Carlson? [Objection Sustained]**
>
> **FINLEY: Did Mr. Holden have any reason to not tell the truth about these matters when he's in the grand jury? Any personal reasons, any financial reasons? [Objection Sustained]**

After stumbling through Scavdis' endorsement of the conspiracy charges, all that was left for Finley to do was to sum it all up, his whole case. But how? Onto the courtroom monitors Finley beamed a timeline, nothing more than a skeleton with a few key dates in the case. And then, with one click, Finley

---

[26]The claim here was that I "knew" about the plan to promote for perforators, so when I assigned our general counsel to investigate the five claims in the Bui whistleblower letter without disclosing our illegal perforator plot, I ordered a sham investigation.

[27]Recall that Shane, wearing a polo shirt, said he told McIff to stop promoting for perforators multiple times but later admitted that wasn't true. Before trial, Finley actually told Shane that he didn't think this was a lie, but Bud took the opposite position once Shane took the stand.

[28]Holden was charged with perjury for making nine allegedly-false statements, including the one about whether his goal in selling Short Kits was to "help the patient population" or increase his sales. He was indicted and stripped of every "weapon" in his house, including his antique bow and arrow which hung over his fireplace, pending trial.

put meat on the bones. The events Scavdis testified about appeared in the suddenly-packed graphic, along with a menacing red bar highlighting everything that happened after VSI received that withdrawal form letter from FDA.

There was something theatrical about Finley's red ink, but I still couldn't believe this would be the end of their case. Surely they had a few sucker punches waiting for us on re-direct. A document we hadn't seen, maybe, or a clever new theme to connect everything together. But before we could find out, we'd have to cross-examine Scavdis.

$$-\bigwedge\!\!\!\bigwedge-$$

After his heroic cross of McIff and a more pedestrian outing against Dr. Asbjornsen, future Supreme Court Justice Rob Hur was back at the lectern to lock horns with Scavdis. Perhaps he thought Operation Big Secret meant he wouldn't get a crack at another witness, but here he was in a crunch-time showdown. And this time, unlike with the shape-shifting quasi-expert Dr. Asbjornsen, Rob had a stationary target.

> **HUR: You testified yourself in the grand jury that the FDA cleared indication for the Vari-Lase product included varicose veins; is that right?**
>
> **SCAVDIS: I'm not sure. Can you point me to –**
>
> **HUR: Sure. Take a look at tab A, Page 8, line 6. "What was the Vari-Lase system approved for?" That was the question Mr. Finley asked you, right?**
>
> **SCAVDIS: Correct.**
>
> **HUR: Okay. And the answer says: "It was approved for the treatment of varicose veins, for the greater saphenous vein, and for superficial veins."**
>
> **SCAVDIS: Correct.**

Yes, that was the FDA *Special Agent* reciting our clearest evidence of innocence, while simultaneously ignoring it, as he tried to get us indicted. As Scavdis pointed out in that first grand jury session, the indications should be read as three clauses. And since there's no reasonable argument for why the treatment of perforator veins wouldn't be encompassed by the first, that bit of testimony was a problem for the prosecution team. So when Scavdis returned to the grand jury to coax out the do-over indictment, they "fixed" it. The second time around, Scavdis falsely said that the indications only covered superficial veins and, later, that it excluded perforators. But in a breakneck Rob Hur cross, where the jury's focus was a cherished commodity, there was no time for all that cute stuff. So Rob booked Scavdis' initial admission that varicose veins were covered and moved on to a different credibility attack that would ring familiar to the jurors.

It wasn't just Shane Carlson whom Scavdis, Finley, and Paulissen brought in for a second interview to "fix" prior statements or face perjury charges. In fact, on the same day they did the same thing with another witness, Beth Matthews. The three-hour "interviews" Matthews and Carlson sat for that day were identical. I use "interviews" loosely, because they each began with a two-hour presentation from Bud and Tim about what they believed the facts to be. Those briefings infamously featured the improper disclosure of secret grand jury testimony, with each witness receiving the same premeditated leak. And each ended with the government force-feeding the witness a prosecutor-authored admission to sign.

Rob would get to all that stuff, but first he had some questions about another, curious commonality: Scavdis didn't take any notes during those first couple hours. Luckily, the employees' lawyer (and my good buddy) Jon Hopeman did, and we had them.

HUR: You didn't write down that Mr. Finley actually read excerpts of grand jury testimony from other witnesses to Ms. Matthews, right?

SCAVDIS: That's correct.

HUR: Now, your understanding is that these grand jury transcripts are supposed to be secret; isn't that right?

SCAVDIS: That's correct.

HUR: I see. So in context of these negotiations to persuade the person to cooperate, one of the things that you all thought it was proper to do was to take transcripts of secret grand jury testimony of other people and trot those out and read those excerpts to Ms. Matthews when you were meeting with her?

SCAVDIS: That is correct. The intention was to provide the witness, in this case Ms. Matthews, with some confidence that people in the company were already admitting that this conduct was occurring.

To give them confidence. Threatening a witness with perjury because they didn't like what the witness had to say ... then telling the witness exactly what to say ... all to *give them confidence.* More like conformance. As sickening as the practice was, what mattered now was that Rob had his theme. Watch him run with it.

HUR: I see. Okay. Well, let's talk a little bit more about *giving a witness confidence.* Do you recall the prosecutors telling Ms. Matthews that if she didn't fix her testimony, that they would charge her with perjury?

SCAVDIS: I don't recall those statements being linked so closely together. What I recall –

HUR: It's not in [the interview memo you wrote], right? Do you recall them being made?

JUDGE LAMBERTH: Let him finish his answer.

Judge Lamberth had waded in to stop Rob from jumping down Scavdis' throat, but this turned out to be only a temporary fix.

SCAVDIS: What I recall is that Mr. Finley informed Ms. Matthews that we believed that she had given misleading testimony in the grand jury and that we were going to give her an opportunity to fix her testimony. And what he then did was lay out for her warnings about what she was potentially facing if her misleading grand jury testimony stood uncorrected, and he told her that he would recommend to VSI that she not be employed there anymore.

That is just laying your cards on the table. It's saying, "Hey, this is where you stand in the investigation. This is the evidence we have that says that you're involved in this." And in my experience, in 15 years of law enforcement –

HUR: Agent Scavdis, you need to answer my question. I'm not asking about your experience.

Rob now had Scavdis on the ropes, wobbly. It was time to pull it all together and wind up for the haymaker.

> **HUR: So you talked about perjury to get her confidence bolstered. You talked about exclusion to get her confidence bolstered.** *Oh, yeah.* **Do you remember Mr. Finley bringing up the subject of Ms. Matthews' kids during this upfront part of the conversation?**

> **SCAVDIS: I don't recall that.**

> **HUR: But, again, that would have been made in the up-front part of the interview when you weren't actually writing down what the attorneys said to her, right?**

> **SCAVDIS: I would imagine.**

> **HUR: But that would be in the notes taken by the attorney who was writing down that part of the conversation, right?**

> **SCAVDIS: If it was said during that part of the conversation and it was in the notes of the attorney, then it was said.**

Oh shit. That wasn't in Hopeman's notes. Maybe it was in his partner Marnie's notes, but we didn't have those right now. The story had come from my wife, Beth, who heard Matthews say "they actually threatened my firstborn son" during a managers' social event at our house. Later I learned more, with Matthews reporting to me that in her interview the prosecutors told her "if you don't deliver us the answers we want to hear today, it should be made known that we have the power to withhold rights and privileges provided to your natural born son." That freaked Matthews out, as it would any mother. I'd told this story to our lawyers many times, but in his fire-drill prep Rob must have assumed it was from the attorneys' notes. *Not good.*

It was telling, though, that Scavdis didn't deny the threat, instead saying something to the effect of, "I don't remember, but it sounds like something we might have said." Rob recovered well by hitting that very point, getting Scavdis to admit that the prosecutors *had* brought up witnesses' children before, pointing to Shane Carlson and Danny McIff's interviews, where the same tactic was employed. Rob then tried to move on, but Judge Lamberth wasn't so ready – he wanted those lawyer notes.

HUR: There's no way that I can access them immediately, Your Honor.

JUDGE LAMBERTH: Well, you want to recess for the day? Access them now.

HUR: Well, Your Honor, an additional issue that we're going to have to take up is it implicates the joint defense agreement between Mr. Hopeman and VSI.

JUDGE LAMBERTH: I don't care. I told you to produce them.

HUR: All right. We'll do our best to pull them together as quickly as we can, Your Honor.

Rob was now in a race against time to finish his cross before Lamberth angrily shut down court for the day. Hopeman and Marnie had both skipped town once Carrie, their last client, left the stand. While our paralegals scrambled to find the notes among what we had and our attorneys scrambled to call Marnie, Rob changed direction to outrun the shit-storm Lamberth was about to unleash over those lawyers' notes.

Rob returned to the FDA elephant in the room: Our indications permitted us to do the very thing the government alleged was illegal.

HUR: In this meeting with Ms. Matthews, did you actually take out the indication that was cleared by the FDA for the Vari-Lase product, and did you actually put it in front of her and walk her through it?

SCAVDIS: No.

HUR: You didn't do that?

SCAVDIS: No.

HUR: Okay. You didn't think it was important to actually put in front of her the words of what the FDA has actually cleared and walk through her understanding?

SCAVDIS: She works for the company. She has access to that information. And when I'm interviewing these people, I'm not there to make the defense's arguments for them.

Scavdis had just given up the game! This was never about finding the truth; this was about finding a conviction. Scavdis' words sounded so casual, so obvious … and then I looked at his face. He knew he'd just blown it. Rob circled his limping prey for a few minutes and then swooped in for the kill.

> HUR: I think I remember you saying, "I'm not supposed to make the defense's argument for them." You remember saying that?

> SCAVDIS: Yeah. I think I said "I'm not there to make the defense's argument."

> HUR: Okay. So your job was to make the prosecution's argument; is that right?

> SCAVDIS: No. My job is to find out facts from the witness and to gain what their understanding was at the time.

> HUR: And you're doing that through documents, and questions, and 2-plus-hour presentations of threats by Mr. Finley and Mr. Paulissen. That's how you're accomplishing [that]?

> SCAVDIS: I don't characterize them as threats. I characterize them as warnings, as sort of laying out what their exposure was. But the rest of that statement is accurate.

> HUR: Agent Scavdis, you're a federal law enforcement officer – isn't that right?

> SCAVDIS: I am.

Rob softened his voice.

> HUR: Your job is to find the truth and the whole truth, is it not?

> SCAVDIS: I'm a fact finder.

> HUR: [Disgusted voice] That's all I have.

Scavdis, a federal government investigator, refused to agree that his job was to find the truth. Instead, he said, it was to find the facts. And I knew exactly which facts he was trying to find, and which ones he ignored, even when they were right in front of his specially-trained, *Special Agent* eyes.

After decapitating Scavdis with it, Rob fell on his sword in front of Judge Lamberth. He said that he overpromised; the attorney notes weren't coming. He offered to settle the matter with a negotiated statement to the jury saying that the attorney notes did not reference any threats to Matthews' children. The government agreed, more than happy to catch us over-reaching on a misconduct allegation. *All of these "misconduct" allegations were bogus* was the tone they'd strike in closing, pointing always to the "Mr. Hur" example. But they couldn't undo the damage done by Scavdis. For Rob Hur, it was still a victory – he'd tucked away another potent soundbite heading into closings. One that practically *made the defense's arguments for them.*

As expected, Finley reached into his bag of defective tricks on re-direct. But first, he and Scavdis had to counterproductively address that pesky FDA indications.

> **SCAVDIS: The reason why I didn't walk [witnesses] through the indications statement and say, "It says varicose veins; a perforator is varicose; isn't it covered?" [is because] all of that is irrelevant to my investigation.**

I'd think determining whether a crime had been committed would be a pretty important part of his investigation, but I guess I don't have *15 years of experience in law enforcement.* There was more to Scavdis' scripted answer, though, a lead-in to a new theory Bud & Co. were itching to advance.

> **SCAVDIS: Because once VSI filed an application for perforators with the FDA, FDA flagged a safety issue. Once that happens, that triggers a legal requirement for them to file [an application with FDA].**

It was the exact argument Pauzé had predicted in Room 116, during that cramped meeting to discuss Operation Big Secret. But it had arrived sooner than expected. Pauzé said it would come in later, during the government's rebuttal case, when we wouldn't have a chance to answer it. Wait a minute ... did they know we weren't going to put on a case?

Finley didn't explore this new legal argument any further, though. Instead, Scavdis stepped down and the jury was sent out on break. But before Judge Lamberth called the jury back to tell them the government's case was over, Pauzé tripped an alarm that something was up.

> **JUDGE LAMBERTH: All right. Bring the jury.**

PAUZÉ: Your Honor, may I talk to the Court *ex parte* about scheduling?

JUDGE LAMBERTH: Yes. But after I let the jury go. Let's not waste any more of their time.

PAUZÉ: I need to do it now, Your Honor.

The prosecutors looked like they'd eaten bad tuna, exchanging narrowed glances and disturbed faces. Judge Lamberth took Pauzé's extra-low-volume-concern at the bench, as the prosecutors tried not to be seen eavesdropping (while trying to eavesdrop). When it was over, the judge brought the jury back into the courtroom.

"With that, the government has rested," he told the jurors. They'd done so without calling anyone from Austin Heart (where the only four Vari-Lase products mentioned in the criminal charges were sold), without calling Dr. Lee, and without calling DeSalle Bui. Amazing.

$$\mathord{-}\mkern-2mu\Lambda\mkern-6mu\Lambda\mkern-2mu\mathord{-}$$

The jury departed, but there was still an important procedural matter to attend to this afternoon before letting the government in on Operation Big Secret. What followed was 90 minutes of tedium in which Richter listed the ways in which the government failed to prove its case. If he prevailed with this "Rule 29" motion, we could get one of the charges – or even the whole case – tossed right then and there, on the grounds that no reasonable jury could find us guilty. This was, in theory, the justice system's safety mechanism to prevent wrongful convictions.

In practice, though, it was a slow-motion confirmation of my decision to have Pauzé do the closing. When Richter finally reached his last word in a much-too-long argument and motioned the Court to dismiss the charges, something incredible happened. Oh wait, it didn't. As expected, Lamberth reflexively rejected our motion.

And with that, it was surprise time.

JUDGE LAMBERTH: All right. The Defendants' motions are denied. Defendants want to talk about where we are now?

PAUZÉ: Yes, sir.

As Pauzé stepped to the podium, my eyes were trained on the prosecutors, waiting to capture their reactions.

PAUZÉ: Your Honor, tomorrow morning, when the jury comes back, we intend to rest.

I scanned the faces at the prosecution table. Not a one of them looked panicked. *What the hell!?* Scavdis looked pleasantly amused, and even turned back to wink at Bud, who smirked calmly like an old chess master who'd just snatched his opponent's queen. And Christina Playton – Christina Playton looked ecstatic, smiling from cheekbone to cheekbone. Finley stepped in to make sure this wasn't too good to be true.

FINLEY: Sorry to belabor it. I just want to be perfectly clear. I heard counsel say VSI's going to rest. Is that also the case with –

LUNDQUIST: Oh, I'm sorry. Yes.

JUDGE LAMBERTH: Yes.

LUNDQUIST: Both defendants.

FINLEY: Okay. That's what I thought. I just wanted to be clear.

I felt nauseous. Maybe this wasn't a stroke of genius after all. Maybe they were ready for their closing, and I'd just blown my only chance to testify and prove my innocence. If they showed up tomorrow prepared, Operation Big Secret was going to go down as the biggest mistake of my life.

CHAPTER 31

BAMBOOZLED

Trial Day 14

JUDGE LAMBERTH: The government having rested, at this time the defendants will have the opportunity to call witnesses. The defendants are not required to testify or call any witnesses, but they have the opportunity to do so if they choose to do so. First, I will call Vascular Solutions, Incorporated.

PAUZÉ: Thank you, Your Honor. Vascular Solutions rests, Your Honor.

JUDGE LAMBERTH: All right. The Defendant Root?

LUNDQUIST: As does Mr. Root. Thank you.

JUDGE LAMBERTH: All right. A nice surprise.

JUROR: Wow.

I'd never seen a juror quoted in a trial transcript. I didn't know which juror made the comment, and I also didn't know whether that "wow" was good or bad for us. But I saw the jurors trading confused grins after our surprise announcement, and I knew they'd be happy about getting the next two weeks of their life back.

Less than five minutes after they'd arrived on Wednesday, the jurors were herded out of the courtroom so the lawyers could argue over which party's legal instructions – submitted months ago – they would actually see. For some reason, this is done after all the evidence is heard. A little like deciding where the holes are in golf after the round's been played. Each side argues which putts should have gone in, while tournament referee Royce C. Lamberth weighs in, one stroke at a time.

There was only one instruction I really cared about: the one on truthful speech. If the jury was told they had to find our speech to doctors untruthful to convict, I figured, my chances of an acquittal would skyrocket. Judge Lamberth had told the jury exactly that at the beginning of trial, but that wouldn't matter much unless it was on the written instructions that went back to the jury room for deliberations.

As we kicked off one last session of attorney jousting with the judge, I prayed that I wasn't about to witness another Judge Lamberth ambush.

> **LAMBUSH: All right. Does the government want to start? I did note in your proposal you did not have the line in that you have in [your First Amendment motion response] – [where] the government had conceded it was willing to have as a jury instruction: "If you find that VSI's promotional speech to doctors was solely truthful and non-misleading, then you must find the defendants not guilty of the misbranding offenses."**
>
> **Where did you think would be an appropriate place to add that?**

Wait – Lamberth just ambushed *the government!* His condescending barb at the end left Finley squirming in his baggy suit.

> **FINLEY: Your Honor, I confess, I can't remember conceding that.**
>
> **JUDGE LAMBERTH: I have it in front of me. I will hand it down to you.**
>
> **FINLEY: Okay. [Handed document.] Thank you. Oh, this is in response to the [defendants'] Motion in Limine [to Set First Amendment Ground Rules]?**

Finley's question would've been more aptly phrased as, "Oh, so this is what's going to screw us?" The brief Lamberth handed down was the government's response to one of many motions our Bucholtz Brigade dumped on Bud & Co. in the weeks leading to trial. Another that Lamberth disappointed us by brushing aside, calling this one "largely meritless or not legally cognizable." But forcing the government to respond to our adjudicated-as-meritless motion smoked out a sentence that caught the eye of the judge. When he came onto the case, Lamberth promised that he'd read "every page" the parties filed, and it was now clear that he'd at least read page two of docket entry 178:

> **If – and only if – the Court decides that the charges treat speech itself as the crime ... the jury could address that issue with a simple**

instruction, such as: "**If you find that VSI's promotional speech to doctors was solely truthful and not misleading, then you must find the Defendants not guilty of the misbranding offenses.**"

Finley tried to walk it back, arguing that the instruction should only be given if the Court found that the government was seeking to punish speech, whereas this case concerned *conduct*.

JUDGE LAMBERTH: I found it does not [punish speech] in my motion, in the ruling on the motion in limine.

FINLEY: I believe you are right, Your Honor, you did.

It looked like Finley had righted the ship. But Judge Lamberth, it turned out, was just toying with him.

JUDGE LAMBERTH: I will let [the defense] address that.

PAUZÉ: Your Honor, I would submit that now that we have heard the evidence, so there is no more speculation about what the case is going to be about, and it truly was all about speech. I do think, Your Honor, we need to instruct the jury that before they can consider speech to doctors, they need to find beyond a reasonable doubt that it is not truthful or misleading.

JUDGE LAMBERTH: Well … I think on page 31, I will simply add [the instruction].

The sleepy-eyed prosecution table erupted in hushed confusion and paper shuffling. It was, as I'd learned over the last four weeks of watching lawyers in court, the telltale symptom of panic. Meanwhile, Pauzé looked well-rested and calm, watching on with amusement as Finley made a final, desperate swipe at the Court.

FINLEY: Your Honor, you ruled against the argument that was just made in your [prior opinion].

JUDGE LAMBERTH: I understand.

"Okay," was all Finley could mumble like a sad child. Lamberth knew exactly what he was doing. Judges hate seeing their rulings overturned on appeal, especially in jury trials. And at no stage was Lamberth more vulnerable to getting overturned than on the jury instructions. He could get away with swinging all the ticky-tacky in-trial rulings the government's way, because those decisions could only be overturned if the higher courts found that he had "abused his discretion." But the jury instructions were a different, toothier beast. To get a verdict overturned on jury instructions, the appellate court would simply need to find that one instruction was wrong, period. No deference would be given to Lamberth's decision.

Maybe, just maybe, this was Lamberth's plan all along. Put a few obstacles in our way to make it a race, knowing he'd trip up the government at the finish line. I barely had time to wrap my head around the judge we'd written off coming to our rescue before he did it again. This time he selected our verdict form – the simple scorecard that could mean the difference between my bed in Minnesota and a prison bunk.

Once again, sleep-deprived Finley was unprepared. His form asked jurors to "circle one" instead of Lamberth's preferred check-box method. Rookie mistake. Far worse, it had language that said, "We, the jury, unanimously find beyond a reasonable doubt that the defendant is – not guilty or guilty." Required to be found *not guilty* beyond a reasonable doubt? Preposterous! For the first time, I was blissful at the prosecutors' overreaching. With the instructions and verdict forms locked in, Judge Lamberth called the jury back for the highest art of trial practice – closing arguments.

—⋀⌄⋀—

THE COURT: The way we'll go about this is the government argues first because they have the burden of proof, then each defendant gets to argue in turn. And then the government has an opportunity to speak to you last in rebuttal.

Judge Lamberth asked the government to proceed, but "Bud," Walter L. Paulissen, did not move from his chair. In fact, he was at one of those chairs behind the attorney tables that was mostly reserved for paralegals. After his poorly-received opening statement, this chair – the back bench – would be Bud's vantage point for closings. Christina Playton stepped up instead.

It was undoubtedly the biggest speech of her life – a world away from those thankless immigration cases she cut her teeth on trying in bunches. Her support group of similarly-professional-looking-friends gathered in the government's half of the gallery, amidst a scattering of DOJ employees and, for some reason, the still-sneakered Dr. Robert E. Lee. Our side, cinematically, was crammed to capacity with Vascular Solutions' employees, friends, and board members. Beth was in the front row, close enough that she was a legitimate risk to jump the gate and snatch the mic from Playton at any moment. With nine days to prepare, I could say without hesitation that we were ready. The question was, *could the government say the same?*

After throwing a nervous nod to Finley – the other lawyer at the prosecution table and now a shoo-in to give the rebuttal argument – Christina Playton began the government's closing. I'm not going to spend much time on the substance of it, because it was largely unremarkable. I will say that, like Richter, Playton's odd skill with witnesses didn't translate to stand-up oratory. Playton plodded on for over an hour at a frequency that was easily tuned out. Her script, meanwhile, tracked the indictment charge-by-charge, making it disjointed, repetitive, and anti-climactic. There were no slick slides to grab the jury's attention or recount trial highlights, and the force of her argument wasn't keyed to specific untruthful or misleading statements – surely the result of having little time to prepare. I got the impression that she stayed up late into the night writing, got to 3 a.m., and said "good enough." *It wasn't.*

Some of what Playton said was just strange – like when she suggested that the jury didn't really have to look at the evidence. They, too, could settle for "good enough."

> **PLAYTON: You do have a duty to deliberate. But ladies and gentlemen, if the evidence is overwhelming, you don't need to look through all of the documents. You don't need to read it all. If … you know really what happened and you can make a decision, no one is going to be offended if you don't read [all these exhibits] again.**

And some of it was just plain wrong – like when she told the jury they could convict me of conspiracy even if I didn't know about the conspiracy, as long as they found that I was in charge of a company that engaged in a conspiracy.

> **PLAYTON: The defendant knew and participated in this conspiracy. We do not have to prove that he knew.**

Uh, yeah you do. That's what a conspiracy is: An *agreement* between two people to do something illegal. Before she could even finish her mis-instruction, Lundquist objected, Lamberth overruled, and we had our clearest example of reversible error to date. Finley, in damage control mode, would later try to correct this butchery, but for now, Playton continued her fallacious lecture in criminal law.

> **PLAYTON: I submit to you that he knew. He knew. But even if you're not sure, it doesn't matter.**

It was telling. Four weeks and 18 witnesses since trial started, and the government still hadn't done anything to prove that "I knew" employees were violating our overly-cautious policy prohibiting perforator promotion. Playton having "to submit" (legalese for *to claim without evidence*) that "I knew" was as forceful an impeachment of their case as I could imagine. Of course, they were still trying to convict me, and Playton's last words of trial aimed squarely at the CEO chair.

> **You have heard from a lot of lawyers. You've heard us speak, and you have listened attentively. But with your verdict, now it's your turn to speak. I submit to you, ladies and gentlemen, it is time for the defendant, Howard Root, to be held responsible for his conduct. It is time for VSI to be held responsible. I ask you to return a verdict of guilty because the defendant is guilty and *he* needs to be held responsible. Thank you.**

Like I said, *unremarkable.* She sat down.

Next up was the guy I'd handpicked, VSI's fourth different lead lawyer and the only human on Earth I trusted to save my company today. There was something about Pauzé I identified with. Maybe it was his brash, combative style. Or maybe it was just the balding thing. Whatever it was, he was about to deliver the most important speech of my life. It was well-written and extensively rehearsed, but could he deliver it with precision under pressure? And more important, could he connect with those 12 jurors in a box 10 feet away?

Presented now, without comment, is the (lightly edited) closing argument of Vascular Solutions, Inc., by Mike Pauzé.

Ladies and gentlemen, during the more than three weeks that we've been together, you've heard testimony from 18 witnesses. You've seen more than 200 exhibits. And when I made my opening statement to you those weeks ago, I figured that we would prove our case through our witnesses. I had no idea that we would prove our case through the government's witnesses.

I told you in my opening statement that we would call an FDA expert to talk about the FDA clearance, but we didn't have to. Because the government called Neil Ogden – who's been at the FDA for 20 years – and Neil Ogden admitted that the FDA clearance could cover the treatment of perforator veins. Folks, this testimony is absolutely devastating to the government's case. Because Vari-Lase is cleared to treat perforator veins, as Neil Ogden admitted to you, Vari-Lase is not misbranded.

I told you that we would call expert doctors to testify about the safety and effectiveness of Vari-Lase. But we didn't have to because the government called Dr. Duncan Belcher, who told you that for 11 years he's used Vari-Lase to treat perforator veins, and after 11 years, he's had nothing but good outcomes.

When this trial began, Mr. Paulissen stood before you and said that "When you hear the evidence, you'll know it's about the money." And you heard that again today from Ms. Playton. Now you've heard the evidence. You've heard it from 18 witnesses, and not a single one said it's all about the money. In fact, you learned that the Short Kit made up about 0.1% of the company's sales. Every single witness told you it would make no sense for them to mislead doctors to sell the Short Kit. So after three weeks, the only person who came into this courtroom and told you that it was all about the money was the prosecutor, Mr. Paulissen.

John DeVito made about $47 a year selling the Short Kit. Bob Lehoullier made about $100 a year selling the Short Kit. Does it make sense that these folks would commit federal crimes for $47 a year?

What was the goal? To double those sales to $200 a year? Does it make sense that a company's going to commit federal crimes for 0.1% of its sales? What was the company trying to do? Double those sales to 0.2% or triple them to 0.3%?

The charges boil down to misbranding and conspiracy. Those misbranding charges apply to four sales of Vari-Lase products to a group of doctors at Austin Heart. Four sales. And in a federal criminal trial about four medical devices sold to Austin Heart Hospital, you'd expect to hear some witnesses from Austin Heart. But you heard none. The main doctor at Austin Heart, Dr. Matthew Selmon, is just an hour and a half up the road. But the government didn't have him come down here and testify.

The government says that the clearance didn't cover perforators. And, folks, this is the key point that you're going to deliberate on, you're going to talk about, and you're going to vote on. This is the crux of the government's case.

But far from proving this beyond a reasonable doubt, the government's own evidence proved the opposite. The evidence proved that the indication covered the treatment of varicose veins, and varicose veins include perforator veins.

And you know this, because the government's hand-picked witness, Neil Ogden, he admitted it! We asked him:

> Q: The indications for use statement that was cleared, it refers to varicose veins, correct?
>
> A: Yes.
>
> Q: And varicose veins can include perforator veins, correct?
>
> A: It could, yes.

Folks, he admitted it. Neil Ogden admitted the truth. The government's hand-picked FDA witness testified that the indication covers perforator veins. And this was one of those moments in the trial when I just wanted to stop and walk up to you and say, "Did you hear what he just said? He admitted it!"

After five years of investigation, the government didn't have to go any further than its own backyard to learn that the FDA clearance covers perforator veins. The company didn't need to file another [application] under the law, because the clearance covers perforator veins. *There is no misbranding.* And because there's no misbranding, *there is no conspiracy.*

Now, it's interesting. Over the last three weeks, and again today, see if you can recall a single time, just once, when one of these four prosecutors showed a witness the actual cleared indication statement. You didn't hear Ms. Playton talk about that. In a case about the FDA clearance, ask yourselves, "Why wouldn't the government walk through that clearance with every single witness?" It's by far the most important thing in this case.

But the government didn't ask anybody about it. Why? Well, Agent Scavdis told you why he didn't show anybody the actual FDA clearance. He said because it wasn't *his job* to make the defense's arguments for it. *And here I thought the job of a federal law enforcement officer was to search for the truth.*

If Howard Root wanted to skirt the law, he would have said, "Look, if there is any argument that it's already covered, don't file the [application]." Right? "Just market. Sell. Just make money because it's all about the money." But that's not what happened. The highest regulatory person at the company thought it was covered, she told you that. She wrote that in 2007. But guess what they did? They filed anyway. And what does that tell you about Howard Root and this company?

VSI adopted a policy to stick to the words that are specifically on the label. "Don't market for perforators until the word is specifically on the label." And this policy, folks, was stricter than what the law required. And you saw that again and again. You heard salesperson after salesperson testify that they got the message: They weren't supposed to market for perforators.

Now, did every single sales representative follow the company's policy? I think you saw more than 65 field trip reports during this trial. That's out of about 35,000 trip reports that were prepared over this seven-year period. Many of those trip reports had salespeople talking to doctors about perforators or responding to questions about perforators, all of which is perfectly legal. And not just legal, folks, it's in the best interest of the patient.

Assume – just assume all of those violated the company's policy. That's less than 1% of all of the field trip reports during this entire seven-year period. That means this company had a policy in place that salespeople followed 99% of the time. And they call that *a federal crime.*

Let's talk about this hiding. What VSI and Howard Root did, it wasn't hiding. It was the opposite of hiding. The government's conspiracy theory says that Howard Root and VSI started to hide this plan to market for perforators in May of 2007. But the very next month, the first thing that they did was to notify FDA that they had a plan to market for perforators. That's not hiding. *That's the opposite of hiding.*

When Howard Root learned that Daniel McIff had deleted computer files, what did he do? He hired a computer forensics expert to retrieve those deleted computer files so he could give them to the prosecutors. That's not hiding. *That's the opposite of hiding.*

Talk about hiding. How about the government not telling witnesses that truthful speech to doctors about any use is legal? How about the government not showing witnesses the actual FDA clearance?

Folks, arguing that this device is unsafe, like you've heard during this trial, is truly the worst kind of fear mongering. How "this device might hurt one of us," you heard from Ms. Playton. All you've heard is that this device has helped many and harmed none. That's fear mongering. "Profit before safety" … "The American public as test subjects." This is fear mongering, ladies and gentlemen. And don't take my word for it. Take Dr. Belcher's word for it. He's been using Vari-Lase to treat perforator veins for 11 years. He's never seen a single DVT.

Now, we've talked about the charges, but step back for a minute and think about what's happening here. The government's brought federal criminal charges against a man and a company that's got a spotless compliance record over the last 20 years, since Howard Root founded the company. It's a company that makes and sells 100 different medical devices that help the lives of patients throughout the world.

The government spent five years doing this investigation, threatening federal criminal charges, threatening to deprive employees of their livelihoods, all over a product that the government's own witnesses say was safe, over a product that made up 0.1% of the company's sales. Over a product that the sales representatives were making a few hundred dollars, at most, a year from selling. Over a product that treated a vein that was literally a quarter of an inch away from another vein that even the government agrees *was* specifically cleared.

The government's theory, it doesn't make sense. And supporting a theory that doesn't make sense takes some doing. The government had to work hard to get these sales representatives to admit to doing something that wouldn't make sense. So the government gave many of these witnesses immunity from prosecution. *You've got immunity. Can't be prosecuted.* They could have taken the stand and admitted to intentionally engaging in a conspiracy with VSI or Howard Root. They wouldn't get in any trouble.

But witness after witness testified that they didn't think they were doing anything wrong. Daniel McIff had a deal with the government. He told you he didn't think he did anything wrong. Kip Theno had a deal with the government. He didn't think he did anything wrong. Five years of investigation, the government's got the power to offer immunity to witnesses across the country, yet not a single one came in here and testified that they were trying to hide anything from FDA.

And when that wasn't enough, these prosecutors resorted to threats of criminal prosecution, of federal prison, and of exclusion from the healthcare industry. The government's first witness, Fred Reuning, told you he didn't think he did anything wrong until the prosecutors sent him a draft federal indictment with his name on it. Daniel McIff, he told you he didn't think he did anything wrong until the prosecutors threatened to charge him not just with conspiracy but with obstructing justice – which carries a potential sentence of 20 years in federal prison – for deleting documents the prosecutors already had.

Now, ladies and gentlemen, during this trial you heard these four prosecutors invoke the name of the United States of America time and again. And for sure, they are acting on behalf of the federal government. But the United States of America means something much more.

The United States of America means that people can work hard, and they can make a living, and companies can make a profit. The United States of America means that when four prosecutors tell you that they want to meet with you before trial, you can politely say "No thank you."

The United States of America means that when federal government charges you with criminal offenses, the prosecutors don't get to decide. They have to come into this courtroom and prove their case beyond a reasonable doubt to the satisfaction of each and every one of you.

And I ask you, folks, I ask each and every one of you to consider the evidence in this case. And unlike the government, I ask you to look at all of the evidence, look at every shred of the evidence. Deliberate about that evidence. And, ladies and gentlemen, I ask you to come back into this courtroom and return the only true and just verdict in this case: A verdict of not guilty.

The intensity lingered in Courtroom 2 even after it emptied for a 10-minute break. I watched a juror wipe away tears as Pauzé's "America" closing hit its steely climax, visual confirmation that it had landed. The day had already been a whirlwind for the jury, and I wished we could fast-forward and send them back for deliberations right now.

But first Lundquist and Finley would each get a crack at playing hero. To be my hero, I just needed Lundquist to splash the jury with his wholesome accent and deliver the speech we'd written and edited together over the long weekend. Nothing fancy. If he stuck to the script and avoided any extended improv, I was convinced it'd be a helpful – albeit less fiery – supplement to Pauzé's closing.

But before he could even begin, Lundquist was already pulled off script. Over the break, Bud tip-toed over to the defense table. "Say, what do you have here?" Bud asked, gesturing at the six-foot stack of paper against the wall, hidden beneath a black sheet.

"It's a replica of the Washington Monument," Lundquist said.

Bud chuckled through his teeth, then snapped, in a darker tone, "What is it?" Lundquist said he'd have to wait and see. But he never got a chance, because as soon as Judge Lamberth returned to his seat again, Bud went back to Daddy.

BUD: Judge, Mr. Lundquist has some sort of demonstrative device. He won't even tell me what it is, and he says he plans to use it this afternoon. I get to find out at that point, as we have no idea what it is.

JUDGE LAMBERTH: What is it?

LUNDQUIST: I told Mr. Paulissen it was a little monument, an image of the Washington Monument. I must admit I was pulling his leg. It's a stack of field trip reports for one year.

JUDGE LAMBERTH: All right.

BUD: I wonder who, Judge – I wonder who's going to testify that it's a stack of field trip reports for one year, other than Mr. Lundquist.

LUNDQUIST: It's just a demonstrative, Your Honor. It's not going to the jury.

BUD: No foundation.

JUDGE LAMBERTH: Well, that objection may be valid. Okay. I'll sustain that objection.

BUD: Thank you, your Honor.

Losing my Tower of Trip Reports wasn't a big deal by itself, but I was worried that an overdose of Lundquist without any visual aids would put the jury out cold. During trial, they'd only experienced Lundquist in short doses, asking a few questions after Pauzé or Richter finished, and usually sprinkling in a joke or two. This was going to be a full hour of unadulterated Lundquist. And there weren't even any jokes.

Still, I didn't anticipate just how painful it would be. For the first 80 minutes – already 20 over the entire budget and still not close to finished – Lundquist strolled from one topic Pauzé had already addressed to another he'd already addressed. It was like watching a bootleg version of a movie you'd just seen. Our employees in the gallery writhed in agony on the unforgiving maple church pews, always a bad sign.

I'd sat through four weeks of the government calling me a criminal and suggesting that I'm a heinous asshole, but it was only my own lawyer's closing that I found unbearable. Knowing what he was supposed to be saying made it worse. Lundquist was completely off-script, improvising undeveloped legal theories – at one point raising his arms over his head while calling the government's DVT argument a "big boogieman" designed to scare them. That last one was actually kind of funny. But each time he shifted to a new topic without moving back to the script, I felt a sharp pain in my side. *Why was he doing this to me?* The rehearsal the night before had gone fine. *Why not do that?*

I knew that my clenched jaw and red face wasn't the look I was trying to project to the jury. I tried to cool down, but I couldn't. And then, after the longest hour-twenty of the trial, Lundquist mercifully returned to the script for his final 10 minutes, closing with a catchy piece I'd scribbled from the defense table earlier in trial.

> **Please remember, in spite of what the prosecutors have called him during this trial, his name isn't "The Defendant, Howard Root." It's Howard Root.**
>
> **He's a man with a family who has the same hopes, the same fears that all of us do. He's a man who had the courage to start a business 20 years ago from scratch, literally from nothing, without any guarantees of success. None. And through his hard work and many coworkers, some of whom you've met on the witness stand, some of whom you can see in the Court's gallery …**

I could almost feel it hit the jurors. *That's who those people are.* Finally, the company had a face.

> **He's created a good company, with good employees, who make good**

products, who get good salaries, and whose products benefit millions of patients. So please do not punish Howard Root for his good deed in creating Vascular Solutions. Do not convict him of any of these serious federal criminal charges because he is innocent of them.

And with that, he finished. As the jury departed for a much-deserved recess, Lundquist whispered to me, "How long was that?"

"Too long," I whispered back. After the jury and judge had left, I felt the need to unload my anger on Lundquist. "I have rules, you know that – and they apply to everyone. One of those rules is that we do what we agree to do."

"I'm sorry," came his polite response. I stormed off, cooled down, and we never spoke of it again. I genuinely respected Lundquist as a lawyer and man – but *man*, that was too much.

I set off on my ritual climb up the stairs to use the fourth floor bathroom, hoping it would diffuse the venom I'd built up. In a few minutes the jury would get their last look at me, and a red-faced snarl wasn't the look I'd want them to remember during deliberations.

$$-\!\!\bigwedge\!\!-$$

I arrived back in my seat, the tall one. My face had cooled down, but my blood pressure was still up, either from running the stairs or knowing that whatever the prosecutors had left in the tank for rebuttal – be it new arguments or insults or chicanery – was coming at me. Throughout trial, they'd used the rebuttal round to sneak in their most damaging material, knowing we'd have no chance to respond. But now it was heightened; this time, the government truly had the last word.

As suspected, it would be DOJ Trial Attorney Timothy Taesong Finley, the prosecutor who had been with the case the longest, who would get the last word. Finally, after five years, he was here. *One speech away from putting Howard Root in prison.* I wonder if he had it memorized, what zingers he'd tucked away, and how well he'd adjust on the fly to counter Pauzé's points (and Lundquist's boogieman impersonation). I'd seen Finley frenetically jotting notes as the defense lawyers spoke; final tweaks, I assumed, to whatever draft he'd written the night before.

As Finley side-stepped around Pauzé's personal podium to get to the government's, I braced for the worst. Finley gripped the lectern edges and, after tumbling another cough drop in his mouth, panned his eyes up to the jury. He held there for a moment, and then rocket-launched into wacko world.

Without speaking, he jerked his head back down and hurriedly flipped through his papers. For *way* too long. When he finally found the one he wanted, he peeled from it three Post-its and pressed them, one at a time, to the top of the podium. Now, finally ready to begin, Finley leaned forward, stared at the jury like a man possessed, and unloaded the single most bizarre speech I've heard. In any setting. Ever.

> **Members of the jury, it's so complicated, so confusing. The defendants need you to be confused. Do you remember being confused when they were talking? Do you remember the defendants telling all the witnesses how you need to be an expert to understand what's going on here?**

> **You're not an expert, are you? You're not an expert in medicine. You're not an expert in reimbursement. You're not a regulatory expert.**

> **What did they use to confuse you? *Words! So many words.* The thing that's going to help you cut through the confusion is the evidence and the judge's instructions.**

> **The case is not complicated. This is a case about a CEO and a corporation who deliberately broke the law that keeps us safe. Why? You know why. For money.**

> **And when they got caught, they covered it up and they lied.**

After his slam poetry opening,[29] Finley cycled to his next sheet of paper. From it, too, he peeled Post-its, adding them to his podium like notches on the handle of a gunslinger's six-shooter. Then, he raised a (wrinkled) photo of planned defense witness Dr. Daniel Pepper, stepped out from behind the podium, took a few steps forward, and thrust it at the jury.

---

[29]You might think I edited that. Not a word.

You remember this man's face? You don't remember this man's face because he never came here. And the Defendant said in their opening statement, "We invite the government to call him. And if they don't, we will."

And they talked about a lot of other people who were going to come. Experts that were going to come. And I want to be clear about something. The defendants don't have to put on any evidence. They have that right. But the defendants' promises about what these people, whose pictures they showed you, were going to say, that's not evidence. That's just words. It counts for nothing if it's not backed up with evidence. So, please, don't be confused by words that have not been backed up by evidence.

Dr. Daniel Pepper – *Oh*, and they said, "Sorry we didn't call these people, but, you know, we're just so blown away by how well we did when questioning the government's witnesses, we didn't need to call them." If that's true, then why were they talking and making promises about what their experts were going to say right up 'til the last witness? Right up till the last witness. "You're not an expert. You need be an expert to talk about this." *Not evidence.*

Oh, he was going to say – by the way, he was going to say those DVTs, completely meaningless. *Nothing to worry about.*

This was really happening. A federal prosecutor who'd nit-picked every word in our sales reps' trip reports was trying to put me away with free-association speaking. That it was happening in a closely-watched case that could incapacitate the Department of Justice's multi-billion-dollar off-label enforcement regime made it all the more surreal. He wasn't even making arguments. He was basically just heckling ours. And then somehow it got even odder.

And, by the way, this "words are not evidence" – I want to be clear about something. I probably used some words that there was no evidence about. I think I said this guy [a vascular surgeon hired to analyze the RELIEVE study] made $250 an hour. There was no evidence about how much he was paid. So forget about that. Disregard that. I was expecting him to get called and I would have asked him. But forget about that. That's not evidence. That counts for me too. What I say is not evidence. It needs to be backed up.

Finley raised his hands like a basketball player protesting a foul call. We prob-ably could have objected to his transparent attempt to slip non-evidence into evidence, but it's not like it was helping his cause. *Just let him go ...*

> **This is a case about a company that at every turn has avoided respon-sibility at all costs and in all the different ways that corporations try to avoid responsibility. They've used excuses – excuse, after excuse, after excuse. Have you ever heard so many excuses?**

> **They pointed the finger of blame. There was nobody that they wouldn't point the finger of blame at, in order to – as Mr. Playton, sorry – as *Ms. Playton* said, "Take everybody's eye off the ball. Don't look at the conduct. Look over here."**

> ***Excuses.* Here's one you heard: "We had a policy that said don't do this." How easy is that? To say "See, we had a policy"? A policy, again – just words. Just words. What counts is what you do in the field. What counts is your actions.**

Finley tried to display a document on the courtroom projector, but on this day, he couldn't even do that smoothly. After some tense tinkering, he threw his hands skyward in frustration and retreated back to the podium. Sensing a full meltdown, Playton gallantly abandoned her seat and pressed the projec-tor's "on" button.

> **Ms. Playton is helping me with the [projector]. She didn't need my help when she did her argument, but you may have noticed by now she's a little more squared away than I am.**

The jurors laughed. *Too much.* Finley's joke – was it even a joke? – killed. It did better than any joke during trial, and some of Lundquist's one-liners were decent. I looked at the jury box to make sense of it. Half the jurors had their arms crossed, and most wore faces sour with confusion. That was awkward laughter – good. Projector now running, Finley rolled out a series of bumbled comebacks to our best points ... and in the process reminded everyone about our best points.

> ***Such a small amount of money.* Can't be guilty because it was just a little bit of money. That's like saying, "I didn't really mean to steal that wallet because when I opened it up, there was a dollar in it, so I couldn't have meant to do that."**

Pointing the finger. You heard [about] DeSalle Bui. His problem was he was breaking his non-compete. So forget about that evidence that he had and that he gave to the company. He was breaking his non-compete. That's not the right thing for DeSalle Bui to do.

Shane Carlson: *The government put words in your mouth.* They bamboozled you. That threatened you. It was so bad that you, effectively, you lied. The government forced you to lie.

Remember Randolph Copeland, who was at the FDA? He got attacked. He was – the mistakes – all the mistakes that the FDA made, remember those in the opening? The first mistake, you'll remember this. The first mistake was that the FDA hired this man named Randolph Copeland, and Randolph Copeland used to be a manager at a McDonald's, and that was a mistake for them to hire him. You didn't hear any evidence about Randolph Copeland working at a McDonald's. But somebody who used to work at a McDonald's cannot tell Howard Root what to do. Somebody who used to work at a McDonald's cannot tell him that he needs to produce safety and effectiveness evidence before selling this kit to people.

This is interesting: *We had permission from the beginning so we were allowed to do this.* But anyway, it was the sales force's fault. That's like saying my dog didn't bite you and I don't have a dog. Which is it? That's what an excuse sounds like.

Actually, that's what the 81st minute of *The Pink Panther Strikes Again* sounds like.[30] Not sure if our youngest jurors, 19-year-old Deanna and 22-year-old Valentin, caught Inspector Finley's reference, though. I wondered if this sounded good in last night's dry run.

Next up was the boogieman section of the program:

Where is the injured person? That was another excuse. Nobody died. Nobody got hospitalized. Nobody had a pulmonary embolism. We are not trying to wait here until somebody dies. If we wait for that to happen, then we're not doing our job. When somebody dies, you don't get that person back. The defendants don't get it. It's about safety.

---

[30]Inspector Clouseau: "Does your dog bite?" A: "No." … Clouseau: "Nice doggie" [Bends down to pet dog, gets bitten] … Clouseau: "I thought you said your dog did not bite." … A: "That is not my dog."

Did they have adequate instructions for use? Well, they don't even say perforator in there. And every piece of evidence you've seen says you can't do a perforator the same way.

And you know that from the sales force. When the sales force was trying to get doctors to do this, they'd ask each other, "Hey, bro. You have some instructions for me on how to do this?"

At this point Finley became possessed by a ghost who snowboarded in the '90s, throwing up a barrage of awkward hand gestures and assuming a second voice.

"Well, I've seen somebody do this a couple of times. Yeah. Here you go. *Here's a little email.*"

Let me remind you that this man is a federal prosecutor. Finally, somehow, Finley made it to his last sheet of paper. Evidently, it said, "Close with random, undeveloped theme."

This is a case about accountability. When does this conspiracy end? It ends when you run out of excuses. It ends when you run out of lies. It ends when you run out of people to point the finger at. It ends when you run out of employees to throw under the bus. It ends when you finish deliberating and speak your verdict, and we will ask you to hold these defendants accountable. Hold them accountable at long last for their crimes. Thank you.

—⌁—

Sit through a day like that – and a speech like Finley's – and you need a drink. After politely stifling our laughter on the way out of the courthouse, we convened at a Tex-Mex joint on San Antonio's Riverwalk. There, our 20-deep trial team had their first chance to collectively unwind. I don't know if it was the super-sized margaritas or the afterglow of Tim Finley's performance art, but a giddy wave of elation seemed to have washed over them.

Their jobs were done. It was the end of four weeks of high-stress, low-sleep work, capping off months (and for some, years) of prep. There were no more witness outlines to edit or over-tabbed binders to assemble. This was it.

But while the lawyers' work was done, I was still on the hook for federal crimes. As I scanned the joyful, booze-reddened faces around the table, I remembered that 12 other faces – each completely unknown to me just one month ago – would soon decide whether to destroy my life's work and put me in prison. And it could all happen as soon as tomorrow. I finished my drink.

CHAPTER 32

THE WAIT

Day 1 of Deliberations

I woke up the next morning with nothing to do but wait, so sitting bored in the courtroom while Judge Lamberth read 15 pages of instructions to the jury was at least something. At the end, he cautioned the jurors not to talk with *Nightline* if they called, as "they're just looking for an angle for a story." There hadn't been one TV camera outside the courtroom the entire trial, and I hoped Lamberth's exaggerated warning hadn't made the jurors think a conviction would be their chance to get on national news. Then came his final instruction.

> **JUDGE LAMBERTH: It's all up to you, your pace of deliberations, to reach a fair and impartial verdict. With that, we'll stand in recess.**

On Thursday, February 25, 2016, the jurors filed out at 9:30 a.m. to begin their deliberations, and the shadow deliberations kicked off in my head.

I got back to Camp Springhill and plotted how to kill time. The lawyers were either talking or packing, and I didn't have much patience for the nervous energy of either. I could catch up on my day job, but I didn't know if I'd even have it after today, and I wasn't in the mood anyway. I could go out and do some San Antonio sightseeing with Beth, but we'd already seen the Alamo.

I turned my attention to this book. I'd kept diaries in the months leading up to trial, thinking I'd one day be able to share the madness around me with the eight to 10 people I could persuade to read it. It was an idea I'd begun floating in casual conversation, mostly because people kept telling me "you should write a book" when they heard my story. None of them gave any indication they'd actually want to read it, though, and I suspected "write a book" was a polite alternative to "I don't really care about what you're saying right now, but you seem to think it's important."

In any event, all that talk had turned tangible in my mind, and a convenient distraction now. *Would the book be better if I'm acquitted or go to jail,* I wondered. I couldn't write that part yet, so I opened up my computer and started what I could. "It all began with ice cream" – words to start the great American CEO memoir, I was sure. As I entered what us "writers" call "the zone," I forgot where I was and what could be coming later that day.

Then I got a text. I stopped typing as my vision narrowed and the nausea returned … but it was only a "wish you well" text from a friend. I turned back and read what I'd written: three paragraphs, none good.

There were two schools of thought on verdict timing. The first one – held by every attorney in the War Room – was that a snap verdict (as Playton called for) meant a conviction. The competing, more uplifting theory (mine) reasoned that a quick verdict meant a full acquittal. Under my construct, a sizable chunk of the jury is foaming at the mouth after seeing example after example of Bud & Co. abusing our innocent employees. One of them wrestles control of the foreman post and polls the question that ends all others: Did the indications cover perforators? Unarmed with even a shred of evidence to answer "no," any initial holdouts begrudgingly flip. Verdict.

The hours passed. No verdict. Lunch was delivered to the Alamo Room in those massive tin catering trays. While picking at a plate of Tex-Mex, I went on a tour of half-hearted small talk, alternating between Richter's team in the War Room, Lundquist's team in a side room, and Beth in our room. We never strayed far from our favorite topic: these unhinged prosecutors. No one dared talk to me about the actual verdict, much less offer predictions on the outcome. That wasn't surprising, and I was too afraid or too superstitious or who knows what to discuss mine.

Then, after three hours of quiet, Pauzé's cell phone rang. Someone pressed mute on the War Room chatter and all attention turned to the Bat Phone. "Okay," Pauzé said into it, and hung up. "The jury's got a question," he announced. The lawyers in suits funneled out of the room quickly, implicitly knowing the protocol. I'd been waiting around in my best Hickey Freeman suit in case the fire alarm went off, but being summoned for a question was like knowing it was just a drill. It was nonetheless intriguing. *Were they confused? Deadlocked? Did somebody botch their lunch order?*

Question: "What is the difference between clearance and approval?"

A little drier than I was expecting. The answer is that "approval" is the tedious process that brand new and totally novel medical devices must go through before FDA lets them on the U.S. market. These are medical devices that FDA is worried about, so they ask lots of questions and usually require clinical trials. Clearance, on the other hand, is what a company applies for when they have a near-copy of an existing medical device. Vari-Lase only ever needed clearance, and we first got it way back in 2003. We attempted to use this same clearance mechanism in 2007 when we wanted to add the word "perforator" to the indictions, but you know how that went.

This case, therefore, was about whether Vari-Lase was cleared for perforators. Somehow Bud & Co. never seemed to grasp the distinction. They frequently used the terms approval and clearance interchangeably – including, most erroneously, in the indictment. And since the jury instructions tracked the language of the indictment, they said that "[t]he defendants are charged with … conspiring to defraud the United States by concealing their distribution of medical devices for *unapproved* use on perforator veins" (emphasis added).

The answer Lamberth gave to the jury question was easy: this case is about clearance, not approval. But what did it mean that they were asking this question? Had they skipped over the on-label-so-acquit argument and were now closing in on a guilty verdict? Were they about to let us off because Bud & Co. didn't even know which law they should be prosecuting? I compared the whimsical handwriting of the jury question to the jury questionnaires and found a perfect match for Deanna, the 19-year-old with trial-induced narcolepsy. Did that mean she was the foreperson? *How could that happen?*

Running various permutations of those questions in my head, I shuffled back to Camp Springhill to begin waiting anew. There was no call back, no knee-jerk verdict after Judge Lamberth's answer. When 3:30 finally struck, we knew there'd be no verdict that day.

Beth was disappointed. To her, my acquittal was a six-inch putt the jury should've knocked in the moment Lamberth pulled the pin. But increasingly, I wasn't so sure. I began questioning our decision not to call our score of witnesses, especially me. On the other hand, the surprise element of Operation

Big Secret that attracted me most had paid off. And who knew how our witnesses would've held up under a cranky, meddling judge. I didn't know what to think now, and now I had another night to do nothing but.

I did know one thing. I wasn't getting on that neon-lit party bus that just pulled up to Camp Springhill, waiting to take the trial team out to a steak dinner. A loud, quasi-celebratory dinner wasn't what Beth and I had in mind, to say nothing of the unsavory transportation. I looked past the portable monstrosity.

And there lurched a monstrosity of a different sort: San Antonio's 750-foot tall knock-off Space Needle. Beth's friend Jackie had dined atop it while she was here to play courtroom gallery extra, gave it good marks, and from a distance I couldn't see any neon lights. "Let's go there," I suggested, to Beth's agreement. But then I pictured the discomfort of a meal where so much would be said with so few words. "Let's bring Greg Smock," I suggested, knowing our patent lawyer's prowess at forcibly plowing conversation through awkwardness.

"Yeah," Beth said knowingly. "Good idea."

As I finished the shrimp cocktail, I felt my place in the world, along with the room, slowly spinning.

How'd I get here? No, not this restaurant serving seafood in the sky. How did I get to the point where I was one night, one verdict, one word away from seeing my life's work demolished and my wrists in handcuffs?

All it would take was that one word – GUILTY – from a dozen people who'd never so much as heard my voice. With it, the $500 million company I'd built ground-up over the last 20 years would vanish. The 100 medical devices we'd invented would be auctioned off to our rivals, and my 550 employees would only be around long enough for the garage sale. Two loyal colleagues would be axed immediately, and three others would be "disciplined" by vengeful federal prosecutors finally getting the chance to pick apart their elusive corporate prey.

Beth and I had spent many nights venting over this snowballing threat, with Beth usually taking the government's jackbooted tactics even more personally than I did. But tonight, neither of us was up for feisty indignance, and that's why we brought along Greg. I had pulled him off his job writing our patents to come to San Antonio to serve as witness coordinator, but that role evaporated when we decided not to call our witnesses. Instead, Greg's role tonight would be to carry the conversation as I poked my cedar plank salmon and sipped a pink Cosmopolitan. I know … I just like the drink. Focus.

I couldn't focus, though. Over and over, I replayed the trial in my head. Just the negative stuff – the attacks that stung, the witnesses we never called, the judge's sweetheart rulings for the prosecution. *A lot of those.* And as the wheels in my mind slowly spun away from the dinner table, so too did the view. The Chart House's carousel floor does a full revolution every 60 minutes, just slow enough to forget about that shriveled-mushroom of a courthouse beneath us. Until it reappeared, triggering another jolt of adrenaline.

When you're waiting for a verdict, your verdict, every distraction is a good distraction. The rotating scenery. Greg's chipper banter. The waiter botching the dessert order and bringing out the soufflé instead of the chocolate lava cake – all good. But the biggest distraction of all was imagining those two little words: NOT GUILTY. They were what I ordered when trial started, but the long wait left me doubting whether they'd ever make it to my table. Tomorrow – the fourth Friday of trial, the second day of deliberations – a 10-count verdict would almost certainly emerge from the jury room, cooked up by a dozen of my peers. I hoped they wouldn't bring the soufflé.

Whichever verdict they served me, I knew it would change my life forever. By this time tomorrow, I'd either be the outspoken CEO who beat false criminal charges, or an unemployed white-collar convict staring down three years of federal time in an orange jumpsuit. My Cosmo was long gone by now, but out of the corner of my eye I saw that grim courthouse swing back into view. Tomorrow, I'd wake up and return there ... to judgment day.

If I could get any sleep, that is. As trial went on, I was finding it harder and harder to sleep. Drifting off was never the problem; it was staying asleep. My body kept telling me I was missing my wake-up call. I started waking up at five, then four – and today, the big day – at 3:30 a.m. I tried to read without waking Beth, and then write without waking Beth, but my attention was shot from the weight of what was waiting for me. When the sun caught up to my schedule, I put on a baseball cap and went for a run, the only surefire way I knew to re-capture a mind gone AWOL.

Three miles later, I returned sweaty but at peace as the breakfast spread went out at Camp Springhill. I'd eaten the same thing for the last month – scrambled "eggs," yogurt, two milks, and some fruit. But today I switched things up, doing the one thing I'd been warned not to by the Camp Springhill foot soldiers.

I tried the turkey sausage. It appeared normal, especially next to the "eggs," which seemed to offset its color in a comforting way. But this was no turkey sausage. It tasted like an antacid dipped in bacon grease. It was not pleasant, and looking back I can't really say it was an accomplishment, but I finished it. I was ready for the day, wherever it took me.

After a shower, I popped into the War Room, where Richter and the associates had already moved onto their next case. That felt a little weird, but

I was at least glad I wouldn't see billing entries for "Wait to see if client is convicted." I retreated to the eerily-hollow Alamo Room to read my hometown PowerLine blog and hold court with whoever wandered in. After chatting politics with my affable local counsel, Johnny Sutton, Lundquist walked in at 11:02 a.m. with a severe look on his face. "Howard, there's another question."

Another drill; another orderly march to the courthouse. But this time, the prosecutors were already waiting for us, hunkered down at the prosecution table, poring over the jury note.

Question: "Who put together [the] questions on the verdict form?"

This curious question signaled one thing – the jury was looking at the verdict sheet, which meant they were getting close. And it appeared they were still stuck on the anomaly they'd spotted in their previous question. Lamberth said the case was about clearance, not approval, but the verdict form – mimicking the indictment and jury instructions – asked whether the company and I had "defraud[ed] FDA by concealing the sale of medical devices for *unapproved use* on perforator veins" (emphasis added).

If the verdict form asked about the wrong legal issue, and the prosecution wrote the verdict form, then the jury would be left with no choice but to acquit, at least for the felony. But if some backroom procedure allowed the defense to write the verdict form, and those fancy D.C. attorneys had slipped in this clearance/approval business, maybe they had more to think about.

Judge Lamberth appeared from his chambers and gruffed, "This one's easy."

But as he asked the parties to weigh in on a response, Bud launched into a last-ditch effort to complicate it. "Your Honor, I think we should tell them the truth," he said without a glimmer of irony at his newfound regard for veracity. "The defense wrote this jury verdict form, so that's what the answer should say."

Pauzé responded with a dismissive calm. "There is, I think, only one answer to this question. That's that this is the Court's verdict form. And I think the answer is as simple as that." Lamberth pondered, agreed, and then sent back the jury the answer to its final question.

Answer: "I did, after consulting with counsel."

With a verdict seemingly on the horizon, we thought about hanging around the courthouse to wait. That'd be excruciating, I thought – plus it was 11:20 and paralegal Sara had ordered Greek food. So back we went to our entrenchments at Camp Springhill, past the phalanx of prosecutors who had nowhere to go except the taco hut behind the courthouse.

On the way back, I worried about Daphne, the juror who throughout trial continued her *voir dire* habit of vacillating between puzzled and troubled looks, the faces sometimes indistinguishable. She had been the one juror I was unsure of during selection, and she had signed this last question as the "Presiding Juror" (*i.e.* foreperson). *Uh-oh.*

As I nibbled at some hyper-spiced stick-meat with Beth at my side, I searched for my next round of distractions. We figured the jury would want to enjoy their last lunch as a group before turning in their verdict, so we had at least an hour before the bomb dropped. With that in mind, the Minnesota State High School All Hockey Hair Team videos on YouTube were a perfect Minnesota-themed diversion to show my D.C. legal team. Here's a taste:

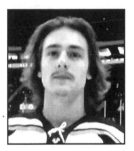

It harkened back to my own old-school flow, seen here in 1981:

I wondered what *that guy* would think if he saw himself 35 years later, eating shawarma in a hotel conference room, waiting to see if he'd be convicted of a felony and go to prison. Would he be happy he ever made it this far, or would he have taken a different path to avoid the coordinates at which he now found himself?

I mindlessly clicked to another year's hockey hair video, but before we met our first mullet, the Bat Phone rang. I hit pause. The Alamo Room's eyes focused on Pauzé. "It's the court," he said before answering the phone. He listened, saying only two words: "Yes. Okay." He hung up.

"We have a verdict." The baklava was abandoned.

CHAPTER 33

THE VERDICT

The call to Pauzé went off like a grenade, scrambling the lunchtime occupants of the Alamo Room. Distrusting of Camp Springhill's spasmodic elevator, I ran up the stairs to retrieve my passport, which I'd need to surrender if I caught a guilty verdict. Beth lingered by the spanakopita as Pauzé paced, shaking his head at the door. "Fuck," he sighed, before realizing the defendant's wife was next to him.

"Mike," Beth responded, "we won." This prediction from the woman who had line-edited the Texas national motto for my trial ...

By the time I made it to the lobby, those previously unsuited had gone full metal jacket, and those already in court attire continued to linger nervously. Richter looked like he was headed to a funeral, and Pauzé resembled the corpse. With my arrival, the group was ready to depart.

"Wait," Richter asked, "is Beth coming?" She had gone up to our room, and wasn't. I told the group she was going to watch the real-time transcript on her phone. That drew a few sideways looks from the lawyers, but with Beth and me it's always been about substance, not appearance. I just hoped the next time we saw each other, I wouldn't be in an orange jumpsuit. Either way, we had to go. Destiny was waiting.

Richter, Pauzé, and I made the plank-walk to the courthouse, flanked by 20 lawyers and paralegals. At the edge of the Camp Springhill parking lot, I turned to Pauzé and said, "There's no use speculating anymore, we'll know it all in about 15 minutes." He acknowledged, but didn't respond to, my obvious assessment. I turned back, looked down, and didn't say another word as I took the 800 steps to the courthouse for the last time.

For the first time in San Antonio, I was feeling helpless. The jury's decision would be all or nothing. There were five charges against me and five against the company, but just one would do the trick. Any personal conviction would mean losing my job and going to prison. A corporate felony conviction would automatically shutter the company as a criminal enterprise, while a misdemeanor would foist a death penalty decision at the feet of the Department of Health and Human Services – whose medical leader, Julie Taitsman, had publicly-announced they intended to make an example out of us.

At least there was a verdict. That meant that a hung jury, forcing trial to start over, a sentence of death by a thousand cuts, was off the table. But that wouldn't be much consolation if the jurors negotiated a partial conviction to break the stalemate. I knew the government hadn't made their case, but that's what scared me – a "compromise verdict" where we won nine counts but the government still got a "guilty" box checked out of pity or let's-get-this-over-with expediency. It would be a haunting disaster of a magnitude the jury couldn't grasp, because we weren't allowed to explain it to them.

The other pieces of the courtroom were in place, waiting, when we arrived 45 minutes past noon – the bailiff, the court reporter, and of course Bud & Co. We took our places to an overpowering silence that ruled the room until Judge Lamberth filled his chair. I used each of those four painful minutes to survey the prosecutors. Playton looked the most nervous by far, leaning forward in her chair as her calf bounced her knee into a frenzy. Finley – the only other attorney at the big kids' table – looked calm, but ill. Bud was on the back bench, physically bracing himself, palms flat against his knees. The judge walked in.

"We have a verdict," Judge Lamberth announced from the bench. I kept staring ahead, catching Richter and Pauzé out of the corner of my eye. Someone dropping in on trial for the first time would have a tough time telling the lawyers from the accused; we all had the same blank, worried expression. There was no going back now, no last-minute settlement, no more time to take my pre-trial case worker's advice and flee the country. The jury was summoned.

Through the thin, makeshift walls of the old Confluence Theater, we could hear the jury falling into line before the bailiff opened the courtroom door. *Wait – was that laughter?* I shot an inquisitive glance at Pauzé, who pinched his eyes as if to ask the same question. The laugher was accompanied by louder, more booming voices. Pauzé looked over and whispered, "That's good. That's really good."

It made sense: a happy jury is not a convicting jury. Either that or it was a ruthless jury who delighted in the suffering of others. But I didn't think so. All I needed was to see their smiling faces march into the courtroom, and I'd know we had a wholesale acquittal.

CLAP CLAP. The door swung open, and the jurors entered according to their seating assignment, just as they had all trial. The first trio – Daphne, Valentin and Christine – marched in without so much as a glance at me, much less an assuring smile. That's fine, I guess; none of them showed much emotion throughout trial. I waited for Necktie Stephen, my fellow Eagle Scout. *He'd be the bellwether.* But he entered with his head down, expressionless, never once looking up as he found his seat in the box. My breathing shallowed. *I didn't like this at all.* I searched desperately for a look – any look – that would set my mind at ease, but there was none to be found. My scan turned to panic, wishing I could slow down the car crash developing before my eyes.

My pupils darted around Courtroom 2 as Foreperson Daphne passed the verdict sheet to Judge Lamberth. He quickly skimmed it, nodded solemnly, and dropped it down to the waiting clerk of court. At 12:53 p.m. on February 26, 2016, the clerk read the verdict into the record. I wish I could say I was thinking of Beth and the employees back in Minnesota watching the real-time transcript, but I wasn't. I was thinking about me.

Which is to say, I was thinking about the first charge: conspiracy against my company. There was only one conspiracy charge against four misbranding charges. If the jury was going to give us only one conviction, this was the one – the conspiracy charge against the company. But what the jurors didn't know (and under the court rules could not be told) was that although the *selling* of a misbranded medical device was only a misdemeanor, *planning* to do the same was a felony that would automatically kill the business I'd created. Unfortunately, the most damaging charge was also the most attractive compromise. And I'd be held responsible for it.

I held my breath.

In Count One, Conspiracy, the jury finds the Defendant, Vascular Solutions …

NOT GUILTY

I closed my eyes and mouthed to myself one word: "*Yes.*" The clerk didn't wait for my internal celebration to end, and before I knew it, she was reading off count two, the conspiracy charge against me. I figured I couldn't be guilty if the company was innocent, but there's no requirement that a jury's verdict be internally logical. And if it wasn't, it could cost me years in prison.

In Count Two, Conspiracy, the jury finds the Defendant, Howard Root …

NOT GUILTY

I pushed out the deep breath I was holding. Even though there were eight more counts to go, it would all swing on the next one, count three. The misbranding charges were identical – the same allegation on each of four Vari-Lase units sold to Austin Heart, multiplied by two defendants. If the company went free on count three, we both would be in the clear on all the rest.

But the danger on this one was real. Count three was a strict liability crime. The jury didn't have to find that anyone intended to misbrand, just that it happened. It was the charge Bud said he had "more than enough evidence to convict" us on as far back as 2013. And as the clerk started to read the verdict on count three, my mind went back to Danny McIff's coerced plea to this same charge.

In Count Three, Misbranding, the jury finds the Defendant, Vascular Solutions ...

NOT GUILTY

I finally allowed myself to believe it was all over. That freed my eyes from their thousand-yard stare, and their first stop was Finley.

NOT GUILTY

He remained expressionless. Like he knew it was coming. A check he wrote that he knew would one day bounce.

NOT GUILTY

Playton played the sad role, her sunken eyes giving away the crush of defeat. She recoiled slightly each time the clerk read off another ...

NOT GUILTY

Scavdis looked bored, lips pushed forward as he waited for the next ...

NOT GUILTY

I stopped to look at the jury one last time. Sure enough, Necktie Stephen cracked a slight, proud smile, looking right at me.

NOT GUILTY

And then there was Bud, whose full body obscured Biro like a Russian nesting doll. Bud cycled through extended blinks, seemingly opening his eyes just enough each time to be reminded that this wasn't a nightmare.

NOT GUILTY

I'd lost track of where we were in the verdict form, but a slight pause from the clerk served as a bookmark. It was the last charge. And for the first time, I welcomed it.

In Count Ten, Misbranding, the jury finds the Defendant, Howard Root ...

NOT GUILTY

We the Jury so find.

It was over. Somehow, after a five-year marathon, I'd made it to the finish line on my feet. The endorphins kicked in. Judge Lamberth asked the government if they wanted to poll each juror to confirm the verdict, but Christina Playton declined, an official wave of the white flag. The jury was thanked for their service and excused.

Once the jurors cleared the box for the last time, the judge was left alone with us, presumably so he could offer congratulations to each side on a well-argued case, or maybe an apology to me for suffering through this abusive legal process. Nope. None of that. Lamberth rose out of his chair without saying a word. And with the Bailiff's last "All rise," the Honorable Royce C. Lamberth exited both his borrowed courtroom and my life, hopefully forever.

The emotional seal had burst. Our side of the court erupted in hugs, smiles, and tears – including from my New York bulldog Mike Pauzé. I stood with a drunk smile, still trying to take it in, suddenly in a judge-less, jury-less courtroom.

Our team funneled the celebration outside, with me being the last to leave (after covertly snapping this photo with my iPhone).

As I pushed through the saloon doors, the plastic clasps of my briefcase clipped the oak paneling, making a noise loud enough that Playton looked back over her shoulder. She saw me, and I looked in her eyes, but she immediately turned away, back toward the grieving circle of prosecutors. I took a long last look at the quintet that tried to destroy my life. Their power over me was gone.

We exited the courthouse just as the last jurors were abandoning their basement quarters. But instead of heading toward the automatic sliding doors like the rest of them, Necktie Stephen made a line straight for me. With a bright smile and loosened half-Windsor, he stuck out his hand to shake mine. "It's nice to meet a fellow Eagle Scout," he said. After four weeks of trial, 18 witnesses and 65 hours of testimony, that's what he remembered – one throwaway Richter question. It meant more than that, though. It was a placeholder for doing things the right way, I thought, standing in bright contrast to those who didn't. *He knew.*

Outside, I was surprised to see Beth, standing there, chatting up a big group of jurors. Evidently she'd come up with a secret plan to trail behind our group to the courthouse, read the real-time transcript on the courthouse steps, and then meet the jury as they trickled out. She had executed her plan quite well, grabbing all 12 for a debriefing, with nine of them still there. In retrospect, I shudder to think of the verbal hell she would've given them if the verdict had come back GUILTY.

But that wasn't today. Today was a sunny day, down to the weather. Like a middle school dance, all the lawyers stood off to one side, while Beth held court with the jurors on the other. Slowly the two groups converged in a cathartic revisiting of the last month's happenings. For almost half an hour, we stood around taking pictures, chatting about Finley's rebuttal (after which Blue-Collar Steven went home and told his fiancée "make it a double") and Richter's boots (described as "so awesome!").

After the jurors wandered off, we took a trophy shot of me and our legal team. And in it, one last triumphant message for these profane prosecutors, from me, entered over my co-counsel Dulce Foster's physical objection.

Pictured (*from left to right*): Rob Hur, John Richter, Mike Pauzé, Dulce Foster, Howard Root, John Lundquist, Kevin Riach, Stephen Saltarelli, Ed Power

And then reality crept back in. I pulled out my iPhone to check VSI's stock price. In the last 15 minutes it had jumped 7% on heavy volume. *Shit.* Some investor had been watching the real-time transcript, not just Beth and a few employees in our conference room. The last thing I needed was a shareholder lawsuit dragging me right back into court.

I called Phil Nalbone, who manages our investor relations, pulling him out of the conference room celebration underway back at the home office. I buzz-killed into the phone, "Email me our current draft of the press release and I'll run back to the hotel and proof it. We need to issue it in the next 10 minutes." I'd probably revised this thing more than 100 times over the last five years, and now, thankfully, the world would get a chance to read it. The best part was that no (other) lawyer was going to change a single word. I hustled back to the hotel, proofed it one last time, and gave Phil the green light to put it on the wires. Here you go, world:

VASCULAR SOLUTIONS AND HOWARD ROOT FOUND NOT GUILTY ON ALL CHARGES IN SHORT KIT LITIGATION

The company and I are vindicated by today's verdict, but outraged by the obscene legal process we were forced to endure.

We are appalled by the malicious behavior and lack of substantive oversight of the government officials who pursued this matter – in particular Assistant U.S. Attorneys Bud Paulissen and Christina Playton of the Western District of Texas, Consumer Protection Branch Trial Attorneys Timothy Finley and Charles Biro, and FDA Special Agent George Scavdis.

We greatly appreciate the jury's complete rejection of the government's false allegations. But to get to this result, we were subjected to five years of attacks which forced us to hire 10 separate law firms at a cost of over $25 million to defend against a criminal prosecution that clearly was never warranted by the facts.

While this matter is now over for Vascular Solutions and me, an upcoming criminal trial remains scheduled for one of the company's sales representatives on obstruction of justice charges because he refused to change his grand jury testimony to match what these prosecutors wanted to hear. It should now be obvious that our sales rep's indictment was merely a malicious retribution by misguided prosecutors, an action that needs to be corrected immediately. And after his indictment is dismissed, if the U.S. Attorney in San Antonio still wants to prosecute someone for obstruction of justice in this case, in my opinion he wouldn't even have to leave his own office to find the most suitable person to indict.

Gratuitous public allegations are easy for the Department of Justice to make when a lawsuit starts and the accused is unable to respond. But now that the trial is over and the jury has rejected all of the government's accusations, Vascular Solutions demands a prompt and complete corrective press release.[31]

Next, from my hotel press room I sent an email to all Vascular Solutions' employees, announcing that "today we were vindicated" and attaching the press release. I closed by reminding them that "there are many people who've suffered in this outrageous prosecution by unethical prosecutors. But today we won. Enjoy our victory, I know I will."

And with that, I shut my laptop and joined the lawyers for champagne in the Alamo Room. When I arrived, "We Are The Champions" was obligatorily blaring from the outmatched mini-speaker. But this was my victory, not the Mighty Ducks'. So I changed it to my favorite party band, the BoDeans and their celebration-appropriate "Good Things" as someone handed me a paper cup of bubbly. I read the lawyers my press release for the first time, and they howled with laughter, as there was nothing else anyone could do about the already-issued statement. As we toasted to a rugged and smartly-fought victory, for once there was no question that my attorneys and I were on the same page.

---

[31] This, of course, never came, allowing DOJ's libelous allegations against me and my company to live forever on the Internet.

As the party rolled on, I pulled Pauzé aside and thanked him for fighting for me. I've had problems with plenty of lawyers over the years who ignored my comments or instructions, but never with Mike. He always listened to me, even when I was wrong, telling me what he thought with more tact than I'd ever been able to muster myself. I told him that to win a case like this, I needed a lawyer who would personally shoulder the stakes and injustice, and that he'd done so with tireless grace.

And then I found Richter. I recounted my initial fear about elevating Pauzé to first chair, especially after I'd seen Bill Michael and RJ Zayed let their egos take precedence over results. But John didn't let it affect his work in any way. He continued to grind on with the same dedication in the second chair as in the first. I told him it was the most professional response I had seen in a lawyer, ever. And for someone as accomplished and decorated as him to react that way, it was as impressive as it was appreciated. His eyes welled as he thanked me for my trust in him and his team, sharing a brief window into what this case had meant to him personally.

Just before I left to pack my clothes to catch the 6:30 p.m. flight back to Minneapolis, I thanked John Lundquist, the genteel architect of my individual defense. A lawyer with more ego than the unassuming Lundquist would've bristled at taking the backseat to a micromanaging client and a bombastic D.C. duo. It would've jammed up our entire defense. But Lundquist's steady stewardship allowed me to stay aligned with the company, and dare I say, even added a little levity to my defense. Take as long as you want with that victory speech, John.

As I left Camp Springhill for the final time, I felt instantly nostalgic for an experience that had been at times frightening, elating, and physically draining. It already felt like a dream. A few Dixie cups of champagne didn't quite feel like closure to me, but I guess this would be a process. The fight – masterminded from our small War Room – would live eternal in the minds of those who took up arms. Remember the Alamo (Room).

The next morning I woke to a sight more beautiful than the Lake Minnetonka dawn – the Minneapolis Star Tribune.

 Front page, above the fold. It was early, and I was mildly hungover from an impromptu celebration with the Vascular Solutions team at Carrie Powers' house once we landed. Still, after I read the article online, I drove over to our neighborhood Holiday Stationstore, a Midwest gas chain with a name worthy of the occasion. I cleared out the newspaper rack.

I grabbed nine copies – one for framing, two for the office, five for the D.C. lawyers, and one for Bud, just in case I had the guts to send it to him (I didn't). As I checked out, I asked the sleepy clerk, "You want to see something unusual?"

"Sure," he replied, as I worried I was setting him up for disappointment. I held up the newspaper photo to my face. He looked at the picture, looked at me, and looked at the headline saying "acquitted."

"Wow," he said, in a tone that made it unclear whether he was impressed or just trying to get rid of me with the fewest words possible at 7 a.m.

As I walked off with those nine self-centered papers under my arm, I realized how little my story mattered. Whether one small Minnesota company went out of business or whether one CEO spent a few years in prison was of significance to few. But everyone is at risk of catching a disease that has penetrated America's criminal justice system – trophy-hunting prosecutors with nearly-unlimited power, operating in a system that's ill-equipped to act as a check on that power. You might say my victory is proof of the opposite – but going through all I went through made me understand just how fortunate I was and just how stacked the deck is against every defendant.

For me, it was all over. But for the cause, into which I'd been unwittingly thrust, my journey was just beginning.

REACTIONS

R eactions are a funny thing. Often sweeping in their conclusions, they're usually based on very little. Robbed of the ability (or desire) to gather more facts, we latch onto a small bit of information, fumble to fit it into our existing beliefs, and ignore the rest. In the months following my acquittal, I heard reactions from strangers and judges and investors and inmates and senators. They ranged from appalled to apathetic, with few landing in the middle. People's beliefs on American criminal justice, I found, are as set as they are polarized.

Here's one from the appalled side, an email I received less than two hours after the verdict, from Alternate Juror #1, Lisa:

> **Mr. Root – I could hardly sleep last night as the NOT GUILTY should have come back 10 minutes after the jury headed into deliberations (I'm sure you've had many sleepless nights over the last month, not to mention 5+ years) …**
>
> **I turned 52 years old yesterday and in all my life I have never feared the government. As a law abiding, tax contributing citizen one should not have to fear our federal government. Unfortunately, I will never feel that way again. What the federal government did to you, your company and your employees is nothing short of criminal.**

Lisa's reaction was a holistic one. She'd seen both of Bud's faces up close, heard the threats Danny McIff had been subjected to, and felt the prosecutors' disregard for truth and decency through witnesses like Carrie Powers. From Lisa's jury questionnaire, we knew she was skeptical of the federal government all along, and it was only because her juror number was a spot too high that she wasn't included in the jury's deliberations. But what she saw during those four weeks in court took her distrust to new depths. Lisa's reaction resonated with me because I had followed the same path over the last five years, watching as my worst fears about our government were confirmed, one employee threat and ethics violation at a time.

I'm certain my fears are shared by every innocent defendant in America, from small businessmen to inner-city youth, many of whom have suffered far worse than me at the hands of our prosecutorial system. Only a fortunate financial situation separated me from them, my result from theirs. *That's not a justice system* was the message I tried to capture in an op-ed for the Star Tribune a week after the verdict. I explained that "when prosecutors can use false criminal charges to destroy everyone except the few wealthy and unbroken defendants like me, then virtually everyone is in danger – even if you've done nothing wrong." Changes need to be made, I warned, "so that what happened to me doesn't happen to you."

But even to my populist call for betterment, some reactions stayed tethered to existing prejudices. "Poor little rich guy. Nice crocodile tears," read one of the online comments. A few days later, an anonymous letter came in the mail: a cut-out of my op-ed, scratched over in red ink with the words "Rich Man's <u>Bullshit</u>." There were supporters, to be sure, but many Minnesotans attacked me for who I was – in their eyes an evil CEO – and ignored my message. With home-state love like this, maybe I was better off with a San Antonio jury after all …

I figured I'd get a more receptive response from the medical device community. Surely those standing in my shoes would hear my story and appreciate that they too are potential targets of trumped-up regulatory "crimes." Some did, but as I spoke at industry conferences, I consistently found half of the audience unmoved. *I was leaving out the part where I did something wrong*, they must have thought. *Prosecutors wouldn't go so far over nothing*, they apparently knew, based on their experience watching *Law & Order*. Subconsciously, they were living in denial. *I don't want to believe this could happen to me, so Howard must have brought it on himself … nothing for me to worry about.*

At one of those industry conferences, though, I did get some support, and it came from a very surprising source. As the featured speaker at a May 2016 healthcare law conference in Washington, D.C., The Honorable Judge Royce C. Lamberth addressed my case at length. Shockingly, he called my acquittal "expected." "It was very difficult," Judge Lamberth said, "for the government [to] get a guilty conviction after their high level FDA employee – along with many others, I should add – testified that the device's previously approved indications could be interpreted to include perforator veins."

If that was the case, an attendee asked during the ensuing Q&A, why did the judge allow the decision to reach the jury in the first place? Why not grant our motion that the government had failed to meet its burden and toss the thing before closings? "I did think about whether the motion should be granted," Judge Lamberth said, but "it seemed to me, after a trial like that, it was better to let the jury make the first cut at that and I could always do something if I needed to."

Wait a minute. The "Rule 29" motion is supposed to be a gatekeeper to protect defendants and the system against unsupported jury verdicts. Waiting until *after* the jury decides defeats its purpose. Lamberth waived our protection because *maybe* the jury would get it right and *maybe* if they failed he would still toss the verdict? Would he have done so if the jury reached a single-charge compromise verdict that still would have destroyed our company? Or if a hung jury required us to do it all over again? Scary stuff to hear from a man charged to protect justice.

Even though Judge Lamberth's actions didn't provide much comfort, I still appreciated his words – hearing him say that Bud and Finley didn't have a legitimate case. And for the first time, it seemed that someone in the U.S. Department of Justice shared that opinion. A little over a month after the verdict, Bud(!) asked the judge to dismiss all charges against Glen Holden, our Connecticut sales rep accused of committing perjury during his grand jury testimony, writing:

> **Because it appears that issues resolved by the jury's verdict in [*U.S. v. Vascular Solutions and Howard Root*] may preclude issues in the pending action, the United States has concluded that in the interest of justice it will not go forward with this prosecution.**

You think? A jury's decision that no crime occurred *may* preclude the perjury prosecution of a witness for saying no crime occurred? As obvious as that should be, five days before filing his request to dismiss, Bud – evidently still holding the reins – reportedly told Glen's lawyers that his trial was going forward as planned. In the intervening five days, though, it appeared somebody in DOJ finally kicked Bud off his high horse.

So after spending $1.4 million on legal fees defending Glen, I could finally call him to talk about his case. To thank him for standing up to the prosecutors' bullying, despite great personal risk. Circumstances had seen Glen arrive at Vascular Solutions 15 years ago, talent and hard work had led him to become a top-ranked sales rep, truthfulness had gotten him indicted, and now perseverance had us both standing tall after the dust settled. And now, Glen could even get back his antique bow and arrow, a "weapon" that had been confiscated by his pre-probation officer. I congratulated him and said he should have a drink and take tomorrow off. But Glen said he'd rather spend the day helping his physicians get a feel for our new Turnpike catheter. All about the money? *Yeah right.*

Glen was now cleared, but what about Danny McIff? Unlike Glen, the author of "TREATING PERFORATOR VEINS!!!" had admitted that he was guilty of a crime. But he wasn't, and after his testimony at trial, everybody knew that Danny only made his false misbranding confession to avoid a possible 20-year prison sentence for obstruction. But he'd still signed the plea agreement. All the prosecutors needed to do was enter it with the court and they'd have one "body" to put into their empty bag.

Weeks and months went by – still no news out of Utah. Danny was stuck in limbo. But with May came the final white flag from the Department of Justice and their first true act of mercy. "We're walking away from McIff," Charles Biro said on a call with Danny's lawyer, reportedly citing Main Justice's desire to wash their hands of the entire case. There'd be no misdemeanor misbranding conviction, no probation, no criminal record, and no ban from the healthcare industry. Danny was the prosecutors' puppet no longer.

So after three indicted defendants, countless witness perjury threats, one signed plea deal, five signed written admissions, a non-prosecution agreement, 16 immunized witnesses, and five years … the government got nothing. They succeeded only in running up the taxpayer bill and transferring over $25 million of our shareholders' money to over 100 lawyers.

Finally, though, people were starting to ask questions.

First, The Wall Street Journal. In an opinion piece titled "No Justice For Business," the editorial board railed against the lack of any legal remedy for us to recover the $25 million we spent fighting a fabricated case. The 1997 Hyde Amendment was intended to reimburse attorneys' fees for victims of lawsuits brought by "the United States [that are] vexatious, frivolous, or in bad faith." You only needed to prove one, and we had all three! Buried in the fine print of the law, though, is a provision excluding recoveries for businesses worth over $7 million, which, ironically, are the only businesses that could afford to fight such a prosecution. The WSJ went on to explain that "the real villain here is the Justice Department." Bud and Finley were called out by name – their shakedown tactics exposed to the paper's two-million-plus readership. Something very wrong was happening inside DOJ, the editorial board concluded, urging "Congress and DOJ [to use] the occasion to institute reforms to ensure accountability for prosecutions that never should have happened."

Taking up the WSJ's call for inquiry were two members of the Senate Judiciary Committee – Senators Chuck Grassley of Iowa and Mike Lee of Utah. In a five-question letter to Deputy Attorney General Sally Yates, they described numerous misconduct allegations lodged in our case, then methodically asked whether the prosecutors' actions violated DOJ policy and what if anything was being done to discipline the individuals responsible. Even though the call for answers wasn't coming from Senator Klobuchar who represented my 500 Minnesota employees, but instead came from senators in states where we had a combined two employees, I didn't care. I just cared that somebody cared. Okay, I also cared about DOJ's response.

That response came 20 days late, replete with the characteristic arrogance I'd seen from DOJ throughout this matter. The disappointing, one-page reply was from the desk of Peter Kadzik, a man to whom it was not addressed. This DOJ stand-in for Yates, who apparently was too busy to even sign her name to a Senate Judiciary Committee response, explained, "As you know, the District Court [for the Western District of Texas] considered [these] facts carefully, and ... rejected each one as unfounded. Indeed, based on all of the evidence, the Court found that *'attorneys for the government did not commit prosecutorial misconduct'*" (italics added).

There it was again, the exact language from Bud's proposed order on prosecutorial misconduct. It had worked exactly as planned, wrapping Bud and Finley in a security blanket that Judge Biery tucked in gently by affixing to it his signature, without inquiry or hearing. Kadzik did offer a boilerplate concession that DOJ's Office of Professional Responsibility (OPR) "is conducting a preliminary inquiry related to this matter," but something told me that inquiry was going to start and stop with that same Biery order.

To see that it wouldn't, Pauzé shot off a 17-page letter to OPR describing conduct that occurred after Judge Biery's order. In it, he cited Biro's "gimme that" email as evidence that "the prosecutors knowingly advanced arguments to the trial jury that they knew to be false" and suggested that they ask Dr. Lee whether he was, in fact, too sick to testify as scheduled. Hopefully this new information would prevent DOJ from hiding behind Biery's skirt and convince them to launch a full investigation, but you can't control other people's reactions.

But sometimes, I was learning, you can respond to them. The verdict gave me a rush of vindication, allowing me to respond to a few local naysayers, host a big victory party, and do a couple local talk radio appearances to blast DOJ and Senator Klobuchar for their lack of oversight. And then I needed to get back to business.

As I prepared to conduct my first Monday ops meeting after the verdict, I needed a way to recapture the focus that had made our company so successful. During the last year, too many things had drifted. Some of our officers were engaged in dangerous legal gossip, some were worried about how to unload their stock, and talk was taking precedence over results. During the past year, with trial looming and the lawyers not wanting me to make any changes, I couldn't address any of these issues when they came up. But now I could, and I didn't like either option I had to fix them.

On one hand, I could do the feel-good post-verdict Monday Morning ops meeting, bring in some donuts, and everyone would have a happy morning. But then how many more meetings would I wait before correcting what I'd had to overlook for the last year? On the other hand, I could be the ultimate buzz kill and raise the issues before the celebration had even died down. I picked the latter, because as my board member Dick Nigon often reminded me, "Bad news isn't wine. It doesn't get better with time."

I sat down that Monday morning with 12 smiling faces around a conference table. After going around the room with our customary updates, I announced I had one more item we needed to discuss. I ran through a list of changes we needed to make, starting today: *If you're not a lawyer, don't speculate about legal issues … If you're looking to sell stock as soon as you can, don't expect any more stock … If your attitude says you're not happy here, then either change your attitude or change your job.* I looked around. The smiles had turned to looks of disbelief and concern.

I adjourned the meeting and silently went back to my office. *I don't want to do this anymore*, I thought as I sat there, alone. *Nobody should.* But being inches away from prison made me never want to get put in that position again. I needed to make sure no one stepped out of line, because I would always be held responsible.

One officer immediately submitted her resignation, while another agreed to change his attitude. The message had been received, but I knew I'd have to do more than just send a message. I'd need to reestablish direct reporting from regulatory, sales, marketing and quality – with me having the final review and sign-off on everything that the law was going to make me accountable for. In essence, I – who already led the industry in micromanagement – would have to become a nanomanager.

That realization confirmed what I'd been thinking for some time – *I hate this job.* I could't even celebrate the biggest victory of my life, because I was worried that someone out there was creating the next unauthorized Power-Point that could land me in prison. I was sick of being the jerk, but that was the man the prosecutors were forcing me to be. I didn't want the unrelenting responsibility, the uncertainty, the risk of another criminal indictment. I didn't start Vascular Solutions for the money, and the money wasn't going to keep me here.

I called each member of our board over the next month and told them that, while I wasn't going to take any rash actions, we should start planning my exit. They understood. They knew what I'd gone through. And they agreed that we would start planning the company's next chapter – a Vascular Solutions without Howard Root.

My improbable CEO journey was going to end. And even though they lost, the prosecutors would get what they wanted – I would leave the company I built and the medical device industry I love.

THE CRIMINALIZATION
OF AMERICA

I wish I could say my story was a lightning strike in the perfect storm – a few unscrupulous prosecutors conned by desperate whistleblowers. But I can't. Because prosecutions like mine are exploding today across the United States of America, an inevitable byproduct of ever-expanding regulations and a foul prosecutorial climate. And whether you know it or not, the criminalization of America affects every one of us.

Vascular Solutions is hardly the only medical device company to find itself in DOJ's talons. In the last five years alone, half of the public medical device companies in the U.S. have disclosed at least one federal criminal investigation, by my count. From the giants (Medtronic,[32] Boston Scientific,[33] and Abbott Labs[34]), all the way down to little 150-employee DFINE, Inc.[35]

And I'm not the only CEO to be charged. Former Acclarent, Inc., CEO Bill Facteau was indicted on off-label promotion charges similar to mine, handcuffed, and made to sit on his front lawn for 30 minutes while his neighbors gawked. Facteau stood trial in the summer of 2016, beat 14 felony counts of fraud, but was still convicted on six strict liability misdemeanors by virtue of his position as the "responsible corporate officer." Think about that – Facteau was convicted of a crime because of who he was, not because of anything he did. I suspect he will win on appeal, but for now at least, his career and his freedom remain in limbo.

---

[32]Four-year investigation into off-label uses of Infuse bone graft.

[33]Investigation into substandard resin used in vaginal mesh implants, grand jury reportedly convened in 2016.

[34]Whistleblower lawsuit alleged paid speaking engagements to prominent physicians were kickbacks to induce their purchase of vascular devices, settled in 2013 for $5.5 million.

[35]Paid survey alleged to be kickback to physicians, settled in 2011 for $2.3 million.

This isn't the medical device industry being singled out, either. Prosecutions are piling up in all major sectors of American business. Healthcare,[36] banking,[37] energy,[38] shipping,[39] and even guitars[40] have been the target of recent criminal sweeps using tactics eerily similar to ones I saw from Bud & Co.

The prosecutorial maxim used to dismantle the Mafia and street gangs is now being deployed against middle managers and their bosses. *Use vague crimes to apply big pressure, get what you want.* It works. Federal prosecutions have a 91% conviction rate against less than half a percent jury acquittal rate, according to 2012 statistics from the Bureau of Justice Statistics, and 97% of those convictions occur without a trial.[41] The leverage over the street criminal is the threat of prison – excessive, soul-crushing time. The leverage over the corporation used to be damage to its reputation, but that has proven so financially lucrative, so easy, that its goals have expanded, post-Yates-Memo, to get the money *and* the scalps.

Standing up to the DOJ threat machine requires guts and money – lots of both. Even if you're innocent, it will cost you millions to pay the lawyers to organize the facts, write the briefs, and prove it at trial. And during the years it takes to get there, your life will be turned upside down. To avoid that, or without the money to fight, defendants do something every day in this country that is truly incredible. They plead guilty to crimes they did not commit.

If you're saying that doesn't happen or wouldn't happen to you, I'm here to call *bullshit*.[42] With an offer that guaranteed VSI would stay in business

---

[36]In 2015, the U.S. Attorney for the District of New Jersey boasted about having recently convicted more than 60 physicians of health care fraud.

[37]New York's tiny Abacus Federal Savings Bank was indicted in 2012 on 184 counts of fraud based on $123,000 in servicing fees on loans, even though no one lost money on any of the loans.

[38]In 2013, Weatherford agreed to pay $252 million to settle allegations that it violated a federal anti-bribery statute, after reporting the conduct to DOJ and SEC and spending over $125 million in legal fees to investigate it.

[39]In June 2016, DOJ took FedEx to trial over criminal allegations that the company shipped packages from illegal online pharmacies, but four days into trial DOJ abruptly dropped all charges. FedEx said in a statement that the government made a "tremendously poor decision to file these charges," noting that "[m]any companies would not have had the courage or the resources to defend themselves against false charges."

[40]In 2009, Gibson Guitar was raided by armed FBI agents and temporarily shut down because Gibson imported wood from India allegedly in violation of a trade protection law in India.

[41]Federal Justice Statistics, 2012 – Statistical Tables, DOJ Bureau of Justice Statistics, Table 4.2 (January 2015).

[42]Estimates put the number of innocent people who plead guilty to felonies they didn't commit at between 2% and 8% of confessions. Jed Rokoff, "Why Innocent People Plead Guilty," New York Review of Books, November 20, 2014.

without handing over any of its employees for sacrifice, I am certain my board of directors would've taken the guilty plea. No question – the mandate to maximize shareholder value would've virtually required it. And to avoid prison time as the leader of an admitted-guilty company, I might have done the same. It's an agonizing and powerless thought-hole to find yourself in, even when you're one of the lucky few who can afford million-dollar legal defense shovels.

Let me pause to save the obvious straw man from being savaged. There are criminals in business and there are criminals on the streets. All criminals need to be punished – period. Bernie Madoff hurt people, and I wish prosecutors had taken him down sooner. When I warn here against the criminalization of America, I am not suggesting that we move to a "lawless" free enterprise wild west or bring back the robber barons. To the contrary, I want the Department of Justice to aggressively prosecute each and every business and each and every businessperson that commits a crime.

But the operative word there is "crime."

In 1790, there were just four federal crimes – treason, counterfeiting, piracy, and murder on federal land. Under that system, every businessperson in America could be certain they hadn't committed a federal crime when they came home from work each day, provided "home" wasn't the Jolly Roger.

But today, no one who manages employees can be so sure. Estimates put the number of federal criminal laws at 4,500. And that's just the tip of the iceberg. Regulations are what truly fatten the Federal Register – a record 81,000 pages in 2015 alone, spread over 3,378 new rules. Now consider that prosecutors regularly use a few of the broadest laws – principally conspiracy and wire fraud – to alchemize a violation of a regulation into a felony. Rather than pick one law and scour the country for violators, prosecutors now draw their lines backward: find the target, then find the crime, usually by pairing a conspiracy with some nebulous regulation. Like, say, *misbranding*.

That's the game, and junior prosecutors learn it quickly. Just as they learn that their path to advancement is paved with convictions. Not declinations, not cases rethought on the courthouse steps, not exonerations correcting some other prosecutor's blunder. Convictions. In 2015, the Department of Justice handed out 279 employee service awards for court victories and major settlements, and not one for dropping an unwarranted investigation. It's a different type of greed – not for money, but for recognition of individual contribution to organizational "success." And at DOJ, "success" is measured in jail cots and dollar signs, celebrated annually with a big press release. In 2015, it was $4.7 billion in "recoveries" and a precisely-calculated 610% ROI for each dollar "invested" in fighting the vague "Healthcare Fraud" beast. This stat-ification of justice is perverse, unjust, and begets unseemly outcomes. Like when Bud explained he'd "invested his blood, sweat, and tears" into chasing us, and therefore "need[ed] a body" in return. Not exactly the blind scales we expect from Justice.

There's no way to escape what I'm about to say. The American justice system is corrupt. Not in the "bag of cash under the table" way, but in the more mundane, institutionalized, more-defendable-but-equally-pernicious way. And that's arguably worse. The guy taking the bag of cash knows he's corrupt, but the young line prosecutor hunting a promotion by chasing a bank CEO can always convince himself he's doing *good* – holding the feet of money-motivated executives to the indictment fire.

I believe there are *good* people in the Department of Justice. Absolutely. Some of them probably even touched my case at some point. I don't believe the institution is doomed to failure and corruption, nor can America afford for it to be. But it imbues relatively low-level employees almost unthinkable power, then drops them into an environment that incentivizes rule-breaking, and compounds that problem by protecting those who do.

That's a taxpayer-funded powder keg. But I think I know how we can start to disarm it.

1. **Eliminate strict liability crimes.** American criminal law is built around the idea that an act should be punished only if the defendant knows (or should have reason to know) he is committing the illegal act. That might seem like common sense, but there are a handful of "strict liability" crimes that permit conviction regardless of the defendant's knowledge or even negligence. That's wrong: laws that make so-called "responsible corporate officers" *criminally* responsible for unauthorized acts of their employees are unconstitutional and should be abolished, either by the courts or Congress. If they aren't, then I would like to see a "responsible government officer" law enact-

ed to hold the Attorney General criminally responsible for each and every rule violation by each of his or her prosecutors.

2. **Measure twice, indict once.** Proving guilt beyond a reasonable doubt is a high burden. DOJ should recognize this and assign an independent lawyer from an independent unit to make sure that each case meets this standard before assailing a defendant's reputation with an indictment. Criminal indictments should only be pursued for the clearest and worst offenses. The existing systems of administrative fines and civil penalties can handle the rest.

3. **Prohibit all DOJ publicity before a conviction.** If an indictment is merely an accusation, then the Department of Justice should treat it as such and save the grandstanding for later. The standard DOJ indictment press release rages on about the defendant's guilt in a transparent attempt to bloody up the defendant before trial. There is no legitimate purpose for this practice, and it should be abolished. Any fair notion of justice requires that "innocent until proven guilty" apply in the court of public opinion as well as in the court of law.

4. **Punish prosecutorial misconduct through the Office of Inspector General.** Currently, allegations of prosecutorial misconduct are investigated by DOJ's Office of Professional Responsibility, which reports exclusively to the Attorney General. That's the fox guarding the hen house. DOJ's Office of the Inspector General, which is designed to be independent and reports to Congress, is the more appropriate investigative body. The Senate Judiciary Committee should take an active role in calling for investigations of DOJ misconduct through OIG, and post detailed findings online to identify bad apples and deter future misconduct by others.

5. **Remove the limits in the Hyde Amendment.** If DOJ brings a malicious, frivolous, or vexatious criminal prosecution against you and you win, you should be able to recover your legal expenses, no matter what your net worth. The current $7 million cap on the Hyde Amendment shields DOJ from answering to the only corporations that can fight a malicious prosecution. And while we're at it, let's remove the immunity protection for prosecutors. If they engage in fraud, they should be subject to the same penalties a lawyer in private practice would face for doing the same.

6. **Reform the whistleblower cash-grab.** It's true that many legitimate whistleblowers come forward to expose their employers' misdeeds. That's great. But a $100 million payout to a whistleblower is absurd; Congress should cap it at $1 million. And to discourage a whistleblower (and his lawyer) from selling the government a bill of goods, the accused should be given a chance to answer the factual allegations before the government decides to intervene and dig in its heels. Finally, if the whistleblower is found to have filed factually-incorrect or grossly exaggerated claims, they should forfeit their right to recovery. A little more balance in the whistleblower system would result in a lot more truth.

The criminalization of America will not stop or slow down on its own. We can choose to turn a blind eye if we want. We can pretend that stories like mine are curious one-offs, not the predictable outcome of a broken system. But there's a price for that blindness, one that everyone will pay: the demise of innovation.

Over the five years Vascular Solutions fought the government, we grew slower, invested less in R&D, hired fewer employees, and were robbed of $25 million we would have otherwise spent on productive medical activities. The interventional catheter I didn't invent because I was sitting in a San Antonio courtroom will never be seen by anyone, and when you need it, you won't even know it's not there. Multiply that by all the medical device and pharmaceutical companies that have come under criminal investigation, and imagine how many medical breakthroughs you'll never see. Then multiply that by each industry that is currently being squeezed by DOJ, and ask yourself, is there any wonder why productivity of American business is in the midst of its biggest ongoing slide since 1979? Criminalization, and its little brother over-regulation, is stunting the growth of the American economy.

You say that doesn't bother you? Then consider where this is headed. As the criminalization explosion continues and we continue to see American job numbers *unexpectedly* flat-line while businesses *unexpectedly* contract and the birth-rate of new businesses *unexpectedly* declines, remember the words of science fiction writer Robert Heinlein.

> Throughout history, poverty is the normal condition of man. Advances which permit this norm to be exceeded – here and there, now and then – are the work of an extremely small minority, frequently despised, often condemned, and almost always opposed by all right-thinking people. Whenever this tiny minority is kept from creating, or (as sometimes happens) is driven out of a society, the people then slip back into abject poverty. This is known as "bad luck."

I won my battle, yes, but my brush with "bad luck" – spending five years on the Feds' hit-list – was enough to drive me from the medical device industry. That doesn't mean I'm giving up, or that I will stop fighting to prevent my "bad luck" from becoming America's. But it means that this isn't my case anymore, it is my cause, and I hope you will join me in this call to reform the American criminal justice system. And with that, I wish all of you, except the profane prosecutors who make this fight necessary, "good luck."

ACKNOWLEDGMENTS

With much appreciation to: my co-writer Steve Saltarelli who took my drafts and thoughts and turned them into a book; my colleague Carrie Powers who stood tall and survived to tell her story; my pro bono editors Phil Nalbone and Barb Danson who helped guide the narrative; my professional editors John Oslund and Adam O'Brien who smoothed out the rough edges; my graphic designer Thomas Ashby who made it all look pleasing to the eye; my co-defendant Glen Holden who persevered in the face of great personal risk; my wife, Beth, and my family and friends who supported me during this ordeal; and most of all my co-workers, board members and shareholders at Vascular Solutions who refused to let the federal government destroy our wonderful medical device company.